ELSEVIER'S
DICTIONARY OF
FOOD SCIENCE AND TECHNOLOGY

ELSEVIER'S
DICTIONARY OF
FOOD SCIENCE AND TECHNOLOGY

IN FOUR LANGUAGES
ENGLISH-FRENCH-SPANISH-GERMAN
with an index of Latin names

compiled by

IAN DOUGLAS MORTON

Professor of Food Science
University of London

and

CHLOE MORTON

ELSEVIER
AMSTERDAM - OXFORD - NEW YORK - TOKYO

ELSEVIER SCIENCE PUBLISHERS B.V.
Sara Burgerhartstraat 25
P.O. Box 211, 1000 AE Amsterdam, The Netherlands

Distributors for the United States and Canada:
ELSEVIER SCIENCE PUBLISHING COMPANY, INC.
655 Avenue of the Americas
New York, N.Y. 10010, U.S.A.

First edition 1977
Second impression 1979
Third impression 1990

Library of Congress Cataloging in Publication Data
Morton, Ian Douglas.
Elsevier's dictionary of food science and technology.
1. Food–Dictionaries–Polyglot. 2. Food industry and trade–Dictionaries–Polyglot.
3. Dictionaries, Polyglot. I. Morton, Chloe, joint author. II. Title.
III. Title: Dictionary of food science and technology.
TX349.M64 664'.003 77-10907
ISBN: 0-444-41559-9

© ELSEVIER SCIENCE PUBLISHERS B.V., 1977

Electronic data processing:
Dipl.-Kfm. Karlheinz Wenzel KG
and
ADV-Service Wilfried Meyer GmbH,
Hanau, W. Germany

Printed in The Netherlands

PREFACE

Food Science and Technology is an applied science dealing with the production, processing, preservation and preparation of food on both the technological and domestic scale. It is based on a sound knowledge of the pure sciences including Chemisrty, Physics, Biology and Mathematics. Although the majority of scientific papers are now published in English, for research work it has been essential to read scientific papers in languages other than English. Multilingual dictionaries have already been published dealing with Dairying and with Cereal Products. We have not been able to locate a dictionary covering the field of Food Science and Technology. We have attempted to fill this gap with the following volume and express our thanks to our colleagues for their advice, freely given, on the inclusion of terms. We also would like to thank colleagues at meetings of IUFoST for their help in suggestions and criticisms of terms. We have tried to make this volume as up to date with current usage as possible.

One difficulty is that some English terms may have a number of quite separate technical meanings. We have endeavoured in these cases to include a definition of each of the meanings of the English term and given the equivalent words in other languages. We also hope that this dictionary will be of help to non-English food scientists and technologists. We particularly thank Dr. Alfredo Rosas Romero for his work on the Spanish terms. We alone must accept responsibility and would be grateful if errors and omissions were brought to our notice.

London, June 1977.

BASIC TABLE

3 acetoglyceride

A

1 abalone; ormer; sea ear
Haliotis sp.
f ormeau m
e oreja f marina
d Seeohr n

2 abattoir; slaughter house
f abattoir m
e matadero m
d Schlachthaus n

* absinth oil → 2067

3 absolute temperature
f température f absolue
e temperatura f absoluta
d absolute Temperatur f

4 absorption
f absorption f
e absorción f
d Absorption f

5 absorption tower
f tour f d'absorption; colonne f
d'absorption
e torre f de absorción
d Absorptionsturm m

6 acaricide
f acaricide m
e acaricida m
d Akarizid n

7 accelerated filtration
f filtration f accélérée
e filtración f acelerada
d beschleunigte Filtrierung f

8 accelerator
f accélérateur m
e acelerante m; acelerador m
d Beschleuniger m

9 acetal
f acétal m
e acetal m
d Acetal n

10 acetaldehyde
f acétaldéhyde m
e acetaldehido m
d Acetaldehyd m

11 acetate
f acétate m
e acetato m
d Acetat n

12 acetic acid
f acide m acétique
e ácido m acético
d Essigsäure f

13 acetic anhydride
f anhydride m acétique
e anhídrido m acético
d Essigsäureanhydrid n

14 acetic bacteria; acetobacter
Bacterium acetii.
f acétobacter m; bactéries fpl
acétiques
e bacterias fpl acéticas
d Acetobakterien fpl

15 acetic ether; ethyl acetate
f acétate m d'éthyle; éther m
acétique
e acetato m de etilo; éter m acético
d Äthylacetat n; Essigäther m

16 acetic fermentation
f fermentation f acétique
e fermentación f acética
d Essigsäuregärung f

17 acetifier
f acétifiant m
e acetificante m
d Schnellsäurer m

18 acetin; glyceryl monoacetate
f acétine f
e acetina f
d Acetin n

* acetobacter → 14

19 acetoglyceride; fatty acid glyceride
f acétoglycéride f
e acetoglicérido m
d Acetoglyzerid n

20 **acetone**
 f acétone *f*
 e acetona *f*
 d Aceton *n*

21 **acetoxyl group**
 f groupe *m* acétoxyle
 e grupo *m* acetoxilo
 d Acetoxylgruppe *f*

22 **acetylation**
 f acétylation *f*
 e acetilación *f*
 d Acetylierung *f*

23 **acetylbenzoyl peroxide**
 f peroxyde *m* d'acétylbenzoyle
 e peróxido *m* de acetilbenzoilo
 d Acetylbenzoylperoxyd *n*

24 **acetyl group**
 f groupe *m* acétyle
 e grupo *m* acetilo
 d Acetylgruppe *f*

25 **acetyl value**
 f indice *m* d'acétyle
 e índice *m* de acetilo
 d Acetylzahl *f*

26 **acid**
 f acide *m*
 e ácido *m*
 d Säure *f*

27 **acid amide**
 f amide *m* d'acide
 e amida *f* de ácido
 d Säureamid *n*

28 **acid chloride**
 f chlorure *m* d'acide
 e cloruro *m* de ácido
 d Säurechlorid *n*

29 **acid ester**
 f ester *m* acide
 e éster *m* ácido
 d saurer Ester *m*

30 **acidify** *v*; **acidulate** *v*
 f acidifier; aciduler
 e acidificar; acidular
 d ansäuern

31 **acidimeter**
 f acidimètre *m*
 e acidímetro *m*; pesa-ácidos *m*
 d Säuremesser *m*

32 **acidimetry**
 f acidimétrie *f*
 e acidimetría *f*
 d Acidimetrie *f*

33 **acidolysis**
 f acidolyse *f*
 e acidólisis *f*
 d Acidolyse *f*

34 **acid radical**
 f radical *m* acide
 e radical *m* ácido
 d Säureradikal *n*

35 **acid salt**
 f sel *m* acide
 e sal *f* ácida
 d saures Salz *n*

36 **acid solution**
 f solution *f* acide
 e solución *f* ácida
 d Säurelösung *f*

* **acidulate** *v* → 30

37 **acid value**
 f indice *m* d'acide; valeur *f* de l'acidité
 e índice *m* de acidez
 d Säurezahl *f*

38 **aconitine**
 From *Aconitum napellus.*
 f aconitine *f*
 e aconitina *f*
 d Akonitin *n*

39 **actin**
 f actine *f*
 e actina *f*
 d Aktin *n*

40 **activated alumina**
 f alumine *f* activée
 e alúmina *f* activada
 d aktivierte Tonerde *f*

* **activated carbon** → 42

* activated charcoal → 42

41 activated sludge process
f traitement m des boues activées
e tratamiento m de fangos
d Belebtschlammprozess m

42 active carbon; activated carbon;
activated charcoal
f charbon m actif; charbon m activé
e carbón m activado
d Aktivkohle f; aktivierter Kohlenstoff m

43 activity
f activité f
e actividad f
d Aktivität f

44 activity coefficient
f coefficient m d'activité
e coeficiente m de actividad
d Aktivitätskoeffizient m

45 actomyosin
f actomyosine f
e actomiosina f
d Aktomyosin n

46 additive
f produit m d'addition; adjonction f;
ajoût m
e aditivo m
d Zusatzmittel n; Additiv n; Zusatzstoff m

47 adenine
f adénine f
e adenina f
d Adenin n

48 adenosine triphosphate; A.T.P.
f triphosphate m d'adénosine
e trifosfato m de adenosina
d Adenosintriphosphat n

* adermin → 2012

49 adsorbent
f agent m adsorbant
e adsorbente m
d Adsorptionsmittel n

50 adsorption
f adsorption f
e adsorción f
d Adsorption f

51 adulterated flour
f farine f falsifiée
e harina f adulterada
d verfälschtes Mehl n

52 adulteration
f fraude f; falsification f
e adulteración f
d Fälschung f

53 aerate v
f aerer; ventiler; battre à mousse
e ventilar; batir a espuma
d belüften; Schaum schlagen

54 aerobe
f aérobie m
e aerobio m
d Aerobe f; Aerobier m

55 aerobic fermentation
f fermentation f aérobie
e fermentación f aeróbica
d aerobe Gärung f

56 aerosol
f aérosol m
e aerosol m
d Aerosol n

57 aflatoxins
From *Aspergillus flavus,*
Penicillium puberulum.
f aflatoxines fpl
e aflatoxinas fpl
d Aflatoxine npl

58 agar-agar
f agar-agar m
e agar-agar m
d Agar-agar n

59 agar slant
f gélose f inclinée
e agar m inclinado
d Agarschrägfläche f

60 ageing; aging
Improvement of quality of freshly

milled flour by storage.
  f maturation f
  e maduración f
  d Nachreife f

61 ageing; aging
  Change in physical properties of a
  substance with the passage of time.
  f vieillissement m
  e envejecimiento m
  d Älterung f

* agene → 1289

62 agglutination
  f agglutination f
  e aglutinación f
  d Agglutination f

63 agglutinin
  f agglutinine f
  e aglutinina f
  d Agglutinin n

* aging → 60, 61

64 agitator
  f agitateur m
  e agitador m
  d Rührwerk n

65 air bleed valve
  f soupape f d'évacuation d'air
  e válvula f de escape del aire
  d Entlüftungsventil n

66 air classification; air separation
  f séparation f par air; classification f
    par air; turbo-séparation f
  e separación f de partículas en
    corriente de aire
  d Windsichtung f

67 air conditioning
  f conditionnement m de l'air
  e acondicionamiento m del aire
  d Klimatisierung f

68 air pump
  f pompe f à air
  e bomba f de aire
  d Luftpumpe f

* air separation → 66

* albumen → 658

69 albumin
  f albumine f
  e albúmina f
  d Albumin n

70 albuminate
  f albuminate m
  e albuminado m
  d Albuminat n

71 albuminoid; scleroprotein
  f albuminoïde m
  e albuminoide m
  d Albuminoid n

72 albumose
  f albumose f
  e albumosa f
  d Albumose f

73 alcohol
  f alcool m
  e alcohol m
  d Alkohol m

74 alcoholic fermentation
  f fermentation f alcoolique
  e fermentación f alcohólica
  d Alkoholgärung f

75 aldehyde
  f aldéhyde m
  e aldehido m
  d Aldehyd m

76 aldehyde acid
  f acide-aldéhyde m
  e ácido m aldehídico
  d Aldehydsäure f

77 aldohexose
  f aldohexose m
  e aldohexosa f
  d Aldohexose f

78 aldol
  f aldol m
  e aldol m
  d Aldol n

79 aldose
  f aldose m

e aldosa *f*
d Aldose *f*

80 aldosterone
f aldostérone *f*
e aldosterona *f*
d Aldosteron *n*

81 aldrin
f aldrine *f*
e aldrina *f*
d Aldrin *n*

82 ale
Beer flavoured with hops.
f ale *m*
e ale *m*
d Ale *n*

83 aleurone layer
f couche *f* d'aleurone
e capa *f* de aleurona
d Aleuronschicht *f*

84 alga
f algue *f*
e alga *f*
d Alge *f*

85 alginate
f alginate *m*
e alginato *m*
d Alginat *n*

86 alginic acid
f acide *m* alginique
e ácido *m* algínico
d Alginsäure *f*

87 alicyclic
f alicyclique
e alicíclico
d alizyklisch

88 alimentary pastes; pasta
f pâtes *fpl* alimentaires
e pastas *fpl* alimenticias
d Teigwaren *fpl*

89 aliphatic
f aliphatique
e alifático
d aliphatisch

90 alkali
f álcali *m*
e álcali *m*
d Alkali *n*

91 alkali metal
f métal *m* alcalin
e metal *m* alcalino
d Alkalimetall *n*

92 alkalimeter
f alcalimètre *m*
e alcalímetro *m*
d Alkalimeter *n*; Laugenmesser *m*

93 alkaloid
f alcaloïde *m*
e alcaloide *m*
d Alkaloid *n*

94 allantoin
f allantoïne *f*
e alantoína *f*
d Allantoin *n*

95 allethrin
f alléthrine *f*
e aletrina *f*
d Allethrin *n*

* **alligator pear** → 181

96 allomeric
f allomérique
e alomérico
d allomerisch

97 allose
f allose *m*
e alosa *f*
d Allose *f*

98 allspice
Fruit of *Pimenta officinalis.*
f toute-épice *f*; piment *m*
e fruta *f* del pimiento de Jamaica
d Nelkenpfeffer *m*; Gewürz-Myrte *f*

99 allyl caproate
f caproate *m* d'allyle
e caproato *m* de alilo
d Allylkaproat *n*

100 allyl isothiocyanate
 f iso-thiocyanate *m* d'allyle
 e isotiocianato *m* de alilo
 d Allyl-isothiocyanat *n*

101 almond
 Nut of *Prunus amygdalus.*
 f amande *f*
 e almendra *f*
 d Mandel *f*

102 alpha-amylase
 f alpha-amylase *f*
 e alfa-amilasa *f*
 d Alpha-Amylase *f*

103 altrose
 f altrose *m*
 e altrosa *f*
 d Altrose *f*

104 alumina
 f alumine *f*
 e alúmina *f*
 d Tonerde *f*

105 alveograph
 f alvéographe *m*
 e alveógrafo *m*
 d Alveograph *m*

106 ambergris
 Secretion of *Physeter catodon* or
 Physeter macrocephalus.
 f ambre *m* gris
 e ámbar *m* gris
 d grauer Amber *m*

107 amide
 f amide *m*
 e amida *f*
 d Amid *n*

108 amine
 f amine *f*
 e amina *f*
 d Amin *n*

109 amino acid
 f amino-acide *m*; acide *m* aminé
 e aminoácido *m*
 d Aminosäure *f*

110 ammonia
 f ammoniac *m*; gaz *m* ammoniac
 e amoníaco *m*; amonia *m*
 d Ammoniak *n*

111 ammonium
 f ammonium *m*
 e amonio *m*
 d Ammonium *n*

112 ammonium persulphate
 f persulphate *m* d'ammoniaque
 e persulfato *m* amónico
 d Ammoniumperchlorat *n*

113 ampholyte
 f ampholyte *m*
 e anfólito *m*
 d Ampholyte *m*

114 amphoteric
 f amphotère
 e anfótero
 d amphoter

115 amyl acetate
 f acétate *m* d'amyle
 e acetato *m* de amilo
 d Amylacetat *n*

116 amyl alcohol
 f alcool *m* amylique
 e alcohol *m* amílico
 d Amylalkohol *m*

117 amylase
 f amylase *f*
 e amilasa *f*
 d Amylase *f*

118 amylo fermentation
 f fermentation *f* amylique
 e fermentación *f* amílica
 d Amylalkoholgärung *f*

119 amylograph
 f amylographe *m*
 e amilógrafo *m*
 d Amylograph *m*

120 amyloid
 f amyloïde *m*
 e amiloide *m*
 d Amyloid *n*

121 **amylopectin**
f amylopectine f
e amilopectina f
d Amylopektin n

122 **amylopsin**
f amylopsine f
e amilopsina f
d Amylopsin n

123 **amylose**
f amylose f
e amilosa f
d Amylose f

124 **amyl propionate**
f propionate m d'amyle
e propionato m de amilo
d Amylpropionat n

125 **anaerobe**
f anaérobie m
e microorganismo m anaeróbico
d Anaerobe f

126 **anaethole**
f anéthole m
e anetol f
d Anethol n

127 **anchovy**
Engraulis encrasicholus.
f anchois m
e anchoa f
d Sardelle f; Anchovis f

128 **androgen**
f androgène m
e andrógeno m
d Androgen n

* **aneurin** → 2010

* **angel fish** → 1247

129 **Angström unit**
f unité f Angström
e Angström m
d Angströmeinheit f

130 **anhydrite; calcium sulphate
(anhydrous)**
f anhydrite m
e anhídrita f; sulfato m de cálcio

anhidro
d Anhydrit m; wasserfreier Gips m;
Karstenit m

131 **anhydrous**
f anhydre
e anhidro
d wasserfrei

132 **animal charcoal**
f noir m animal; charbon m d'os
e carbón m animal
d Knochenkohle f; Beinschwarz n

133 **animal protein factor**
f protéine f animale spécifique
e factor m protéico animal
d tierischer Eiweissfaktor m; Tierproteinfaktor m

134 **anion**
f anion m
e anión m
d Anion n

135 **aniseed**
Seed of Pimpinella anisum.
f anis m
e anís m
d Anis m

136 **anise oil**
f essence f d'anis
e aceite m de anís
d Anisöl n

137 **anisole**
f anisol m
e anisol m
d Anisol n

138 **annatto**
f annatto m
e anato m; achiote m
d Annatto-Farbstoff m

139 **anode**
f anode f
e ánodo m
d Anode f

140 **anti-albumose**
f anti-albumose f
e antialbumosa f
d Antialbumose f

141 antibiosis
f antibiose f
e antibiosis f
d Antibiose f

142 antibiotic
f antibiotique m
e antibiótico m
d Antibiotikum n

143 anti-caking agent
f agent m anti-mottant
e antiglutinante m
d Zusammenbacken verhütendes
Mittel n

144 anti-catalyst
f anticatalyseur m
e anticatalizador m
d Antikatalysator m

145 anti-enzyme
f antienzyme f
e antienzima f
d Antienzym n

146 antihistamine
f antihistamine f
e antihistamina f
d Antihistaminstoff m

147 antioxidant
f antioxydant m
e antioxidante m
d Antioxydant m; Antioxydationsmittel n

148 antiseptic
f antiseptique m
e antiséptico m
d Antiseptikum n

149 anti-spattering agent
f agent m anti-éclaboussant
e agente m antisalpicador
d Mittel n gegen das Spritzen

150 anti-staling agent
f agent m qui retarde le
rassissement
e preservativo m
d Mittel n gegen Altbackenwerden

151 apple
Fruit of *Malus*.
f pomme f
e manzana f
d Apfel m

152 apricot
Fruit of *Prunus armeniaca*.
f abricot m
e albaricoque m
d Aprikose f

153 arabinose
f arabinose m
e arabinosa f
d Arabinose f

154 arachidonic acid
f acide m arachidonique
e ácido m araquidónico
d Arachidonsäure f

* **arachis oil → 1376**

155 arginine
f arginine f
e arginina f
d Arginin n

156 aroma
f arôme m; bouquet m
e aroma f; fragancia f
d Aroma f; Duft m; Würze f

157 aromatic compound
f composé m aromatique
e compuesto m aromático
d aromatische Verbindung f

158 arsenic
f arsenic m
e arsénico m
d Arsen n

159 artichoke
Flower head of *Cynara scolymus*.
f artichaut m
e alcachofa f; arcacil m
d Artischocke f

* **ascorbic acid → 2014**

160 aseptic
f aseptique

e aséptico
d aseptisch

161 aseptic filling
f remplissage m aseptique
e envasado m aséptico
d aseptisches Abfüllen n

162 ash content
f taux m de cendres; teneur f en
cendres
e contenido m en cenizas
d Aschengehalt m

163 ashless filter paper
f papier-filtre m sans cendres
e papel m de filtro sin cenizas
d aschfreies Filterpapier n

164 asparagus
Young shoots of *Asparagus
officinalis*.
f asperge f
e espárrago m
d Spargel m

165 aspartic acid
f acide m aspartique
e ácido m aspártico
d Asparaginsäure f

166 aspic
f aspic m
e espliego m
d Aspik m

167 asymmetric carbon atom
f atome m de carbone asymétrique
e átomo m de carbono asimétrico
d asymmetrisches Kohlenstoffatom n

168 atmosphere
f atmosphère f
e atmósfera f
d Atmosphäre f

169 atom
f atome m
e átomo m
d Atom n

170 atomic weight
f poids m atomique
e peso m atómico
d Atomgewicht n

171 atomizing nozzle
f buse f d'atomisation
e nariz f atomizadora
d Zerstäubungsdüse f

* A.T.P. → 48

172 Atwater factors
f facteurs mpl de Atwater
e factores mpl de Atwater
d Atwaterfaktoren mpl

173 aubergine; egg plant
Solanum melongena.
f aubergine f
e berenjena f
d Aubergine f

174 autocatalysis
f autocatalyse f
e autocatálisis f
d Autokatalyse f

175 autoclave
f autoclave m
e autoclave m
d Autoklav m

* autoclave → 1458

176 autolysis
f autolyse f
e autólisis f
d Autolyse f

177 automation
f automatisation f; automation f
e automatización f
d Automation f; Automatisierung f

178 autoxidation
f autoxydation f
e autoxidación f
d Autoxydation f

179 avidin
f avidine f
e avidina f
d Avidin f

180 avitaminosis
f avitaminose f
e avitaminosis f
d Avitaminose f

**181 avocado; avocado pear; alligator
pear**
Fruit of *Perseus* sp.
f avocat *m*
e aguacate *f*; avocado *m*
d Avokato-Birne *f*

* avocado pear → 181

182 azeotropic mixture
f azéotrope *m*
e mezcla *f* azeotrópica
d Azeotrop *n*

* azote → 1286

B

183 bacillus
f bacille *m*
e bacilo *m*
d Bacillus *m*

184 bacon
f lard *m*
e tocino *m*; lardo *m*
d Speck *n*

185 bacteria-propagation tank
f vase *m* clos de propagation des
bactéries
e depósito *m* para la propagación de
bacterias
d Bakterienfortpflanzungsbehälter *m*

186 bactericide
f bactéricide *m*
e bactericida *m*
d Bakterizid *n*

187 bacteriolysis
f bactériolyse *f*
e bacteriólisis *f*
d Bakteriolyse *f*

188 bacteriophage
f bactériophage *m*
e bacteriófago *m*
d Bakteriophag *m*

189 bacteriostat
f bactériostatique *m*
e bacteriostato *m*
d Bakteriostat *n*

190 bacteriostatic
f bactériostatique
e bacteriostático
d bakteriostatisch

191 bacterium
f bactérie *f*
e bacteria *f*
d Bakterie *f*

192 bagasse
f bagasse *f*
e bagazo *m*
d Bagasse *f*

193 bagasse roller
f cylindre *m* à bagasse
e rodillo *m* para bagazo
d Bagassenwalze *f*

194 bakery
f boulangerie *f*; pâtisserie *f*
e panadería *f*
d Bäckerei *f*

195 baking fault
f défault *m* des produits cuits au
four
e defecto *m* de horneado
d Gebäckfehler *m*

196 baking loss
f perte *f* à la cuisine
e pérdida *f* al hornear
d Ausbackverlust *m*; Gewichtsverlust
m beim Backen

197 baking powder
f levure *f* chimique; poudre *f* levante
chimique
e polvo *m* de hornear
d Backpulver *n*; Teiglockerungsmittel
n

* **baking soda** → 1712

198 ball mill
f broyeur *m* à boulets; moulin *m* à
galets
e molino *m* de bolas
d Kugelmühle *f*

199 balm
Melissa sp.
f mélisse *f*
e melisa *f*
d Melisse *f*

200 banana
Fruit of *Musa*.
f banane *f*
e plátano *m*; banana *f*
d Banane *f*

201 barley
Grain of *Hordeum vulgare*.
f orge *f*
e cebada *f*
d Gerste *f*

202 barley flakes
f flocons *mpl* d'orge
e hojuelas *fpl* de cebada
d Gerstenflocken *fpl*

203 barm
f levure f de bière; levain *m*
e giste *m*; jiste *m*
d Zeug *n*; Stellhefe f

204 barrel
f fût *m*; barrel *m*
e barril *m*; barrel *m*
d Fass *n*; Barrel *n*

205 barrel mixer
f mélangeur *m* à tonneau
e mezclador *m* de tambor giratorio
d Trommelmischer *m*

206 base
f base f
e base f
d Base f

207 basil
Ocimum basilicum, O. minimum.
f basilic *m*
e albahaca f
d Basilikum *n*

208 basket
f panier *m*
e rejilla f
d Korb *m*

209 bass
Morone labrax.
f bar *m*
e perca f; lobina f
d Meerbarsch *m*

210 batch
f fournée f; charge f; lot *m*
e lote *m*; partida f; tanda f
d Partie f; Charge f

211 batch freezer
f congélateur *m* discontinu
e congelador *m* discontinuo
d discontinuierlicher Chargenfreezer *m*

212 batch mixer
f mélangeur *m* en discontinu
e mezclador *m* para tratamiento por lotes
d Satzmischer *m*

213 batchwise operation
f opération f discontinue
e operación f por lotes
d Satzbetrieb *m*

214 bath
f bain *m*
e baño *m*
d Bad *n*

215 batter
A mix of flour etc.
f pâte f
e masa f
d Teig *m*

216 batter
A semi-liquid mixture mainly of eggs for coating food before frying.
f pâte f à frire
e empanado *m*
d geschlagener Teig *m*

217 Baudouin reaction
f réaction f de Baudouin
e reacción f de Baudouin
d Baudouin-Reaktion f

218 Baumé scale
f échelle f Baumé
e escala f Baumé
d Baumé-Skala f

* bay tree → 1091

219 beaker
f bécher *m*; vase *m*
e copa f
d Becherglas *n*

220 bean
f fève f
e haba f
d Bohne f

221 beef
f boeuf *m*
e carne f de vaca
d Rindfleisch *n*

222 beer
f bière f
e cerveza f
d Bier n

223 beer still
f alambic m pour la distillation de la
  bière
e alambique m de cerveza
d Bierdestillierapparat m

224 beer well
f cuve f à liquide fermenté
e cuba f para líquidos fermentados
d Bierbottich m

225 beeswax
f cire f d'abeilles
e cera f de abejas
d Bienenwachs n

226 beetroot
The crimson root of the beet plant,
Beta vulgaris, used as a vegetable.
f betterave f rouge
e remolacha f
d Runkelrübe f; rote Rübe f

227 beet sugar
f sucre m de betteraves
e azúcar m de remolacha
d Rübenzucker m

228 Benedict solution
f solution f de Benedict
e solución f de Benedict
d Benedikt-Lösung f

229 benzene hexachloride
f hexachlorure m de benzène
e hexacloruro m de benceno
d Benzolhexachlorid n

230 benzoic acid
f acide m benzoïque
e ácido m benzoico
d Benzoesäure f

231 benzoyl peroxide
f peroxyde m de benzoyle
e peróxido m de benzoilo
d Benzoylperoxyd n

232 benzyl cinnamate
f cinnamate m de benzyle
e cinamato m de bencilo
d Benzylcinnamat n

233 beriberi
f béribéri m
e beriberi f
d Beriberi f

234 beta-amylase
f bêta-amylase f
e beta-amilasa f
d Beta-Amylase f

* BHA → 334

* BHT → 335

* bicarbonate of sodium → 1712

235 bilberry; blueberry; wortleberry
Vaccinium sp.
f myrtille f; airelle f
e mírtilo m; arandano m
d Heidelbeere f

236 bile
f bile f
e bilis m; niel m
d Galle f

237 binding agent
f liant m
e aglutinante m; aglomerante m
d Bindemittel n

238 bindweed; black corn
Polygonum convolvulus.
f liseron m; liseron m des champs
e correguela f; correhuela f;
  enradera f; altabaquillo m
d Winde f; Ackerwinde f

**239 biochemical oxygen demand;
B.O.D.**
f demande f biochimique d'oxygène
e demanda f bioquímica de oxígeno
d biochemischer Sauerstoffverbrauch
  m

240 biological value
f valeur f biologique
e valor m biológico
d biologische Wertigkeit f

241 bioluminescence
f bioluminescence f
e bioluminescencia f
d Biolumineszenz f

242 biotin
f biotine f
e biotina f
d Biotin n

243 Birs dryer
f séchoir m de Birs
e secador m de Birs
d Birs Trockenturm m

244 biscuit; cookie
f biscuit m
e biscocho m; galleta f
d Keks m; Plätzchen n; Biscuit m

245 biscuit cutter
f découpoir m; emporte-pièce m
e cortador m de galletas; cortador m
de bizcochos
d Keksausstecher m

246 bitter
f amer
e amargo
d bitter

247 bitter almond
f amande f amère
e almendra f amarga
d Bittermandel f

248 bitter chocolate
f chocolat m amer
e chocolate m amargo
d herbe Schokolade f; Bitterschokolade f

249 bittering power
f pouvoir m d'amertume
e poder m de amargor
d Bitterwert m

250 biuret
f biuret m
e biuret m
d Biuret n

251 bixin
Pigment from seeds of *Bixa*
orellana.
f bixine f
e bixin m
d Bixin n

252 blackberry
Fruit of *Rubus fructicosus*.
f mûre f sauvage; mûre f de ronce
e zarzamora f; zarza f
d Brombeere f

* **black corn → 238**

* **black halibut → 877**

253 black malt
f malt m torréfié
e malta f colorante
d Röstmalz n; Farbmalz n

254 black pepper
Piper nigrum.
f poivre m noir
e pimienta f negra
d schwarzer Pfeffer m

255 black pudding
f boudin m noir
e morcilla f
d Blutwurst f

256 blackstem rust
Fungal disease due to *Puccinia
graminis tritici.*
f rouille f noire
e roya f negra
d Schwarzrost m

257 blackstrap molasses
f molasses fpl noires
e melazas fpl de mieles pobres
d Restmelasse f

258 blanch v
f blanchir
e blanquear
d blanchieren

259 blast freezing
f congélation f sous courant d'air
e congelamiento m por convección
forzada
d Luftgefrieren n

260 bleached flour
 f farine f blanchie
 e harina f blanqueada
 d gebleichtes Mehl n

261 bleaching
 f blanchiment m
 e blanqueo m
 d Bleichen n

262 bleaching powder; chlorinated lime
 f chaux f chlorée; poudre f à
  blanchir
 e cal f clorada; polvo m blanqueador
 d Bleichkalk m; Chlorkalk m; Bleichpulver n

* **bleaching powder** → 431

* **blend** v → 1237

* **blender** → 1238

263 blood albumin
 f albumine f du sang
 e albúmina f de sangre
 d Blutalbumin n

264 blood black
 f charbon m de sang
 e carbón m de sangre
 d Blutschwarz n

265 bloom
 White film on chocolate.
 f givre m gras; blanchiment m gras
 e lustre m
 d Fettreif m

266 bloom
 Superficial appearance of chilled or
 frozen meat.
 f givre m
 e lozania f
 d Reif m

267 bloom
 Powder covering on freshly picked
 fruit.
 f efflorescence f
 e pelusilla f; vello m
 d Blüte f; Ausblühung f

268 bloom
 Crust colour on bread.
 f brunissement m
 e lozania f
 d Bräunung f

269 blower
 f soufflante f
 e soplante m
 d Gebläse n

270 blowing of cans
 f bombement m de boîtes
 e abombamiento m de latas
 d Bombage f von Dosen

* **blueberry** → 235

271 blue whiting
 Micromesistius poutassou.
 f poutassou m
 e merlán m
 d blauer Wittling m

* **B.O.D.** → 239

272 bodying speed
 f vitesse f d'accroissement de la
  viscosité
 e velocidad f de aumento de
  viscosidad
 d Geschwindigkeit f des Anwachsens
  der Viskosität

273 boil down v
 f concentrer par ébullition; réduire
  par ébullition
 e concentrar por ebullición
 d verkochen; eindampfen

274 boiled sweets
 f bonbons mpl
 e caramelos mpl
 d Bonbons mpl/npl

275 boiler
 f chaudière f
 e caldera f
 d Kessel m

276 boiler scale
 f tartre m
 e incrustación f de calderas
 d Kesselsteinablagerung f

277 boiling
f ébullition f
e ebullición f
d Kochen n; Sieden n

278 boiling fermentation
f fermentation f bouleuse
e fermentación f tumultuosa
d kochende Gärung f

279 boiling point
f point m d'ébullition
e punto m de ebullición
d Siedepunkt m

280 bomb calorimeter
f bombe f calorimétrique;
calorimètre m de Berthelot
e calorímetro m de combustión
d kalorimetrische Bombe f

281 bone ash
f cendre f d'os
e ceniza f de huesos
d Knochenasche f

282 bone black; bone charcoal
f noir m d'os; noir m animal;
charbon m d'os
e carbón m de huesos; carbón m
animal
d Knochenkohle f; Knochenschwarz
n

* **bone charcoal** → 282

283 bone meal
f farine f d'os; engrais m d'os;
poudre f d'os
e harina f de huesos
d Knochenmehl n

284 borage
Borago officinalis.
f bourrache f
e borraja f
d Borretsch m

285 Bordeaux mixture
f bouillie f bordelaise
e caldo m bordelés; caldo m de
Burdeos
d Bordeaux-Brühe f

286 bottle v
f mettre en bouteilles
e embotellar
d abfüllen

287 bottle filler; bottling machine
f machine f à remplir les bouteilles;
embouteilleuse f; remplisseuse f de
bouteilles; soutireuse f à bouteilles
e envasadora f de botellas; llenadora
f de botellas
d Flaschenfüllmaschine f

288 bottleneck
f goulot m d'embouteillage
e congestionamiento m
d Engpass m

289 bottle washer
f laveuse f de bouteilles; machine f à
rincer les bouteilles
e lavadora f de botellas; máquina f
para lavar botellas
d Flaschenspülmaschine f

* **bottling machine** → 287

290 bottling tank
f tank m de soutirage
e tanque m a presión
d Drucktank m

291 bottoms
f residu m
e residuo m
d Rückstand m

292 bottom yeast
f levure f basse
e levadura f baja
d untergärige Hefe f

293 botulinum cook
f stérilisation f force 10
e cocimiento m botulínico
d Botulinum-Kochung f

294 botulism
Poisoning caused by *Clostridium*
botulinum.
f botulisme m
e botulismo m
d Botulismus m; Wurstvergiftung f

295 bouillon; broth; stock
f bouillon *m*
e caldo *m*
d Brühe f; Bouillon f

296 bound water
f eau f liée
e agua f enlazada
d gebundenes Wasser *n*

297 Boysenberry
f mûre f de Boysen
e zarzamora f de Boysen
d Himbeere-Brombeere-Kreuzung f

298 brackish
f saumatre
e salmastro
d brackig; halbsalzig

299 braise *v*
f braiser
e estofar
d schmoren

300 bran
f son *m*; sons *mpl*
e salvado *m*; afrecho *m*
d Kleie f; Mahlkleie f

301 brandy
f cognac *m*
e coñac *m*
d Branntwein *m*; Kognak *m*;
Fruchtschnaps *m*

302 bran finisher
f brosse f à son
e pulido *m* de salvado
d Kleiebürste f; Maschine f zum
Bürsten der Kleie

303 brawn
f fromage *m* de porc
e queso *m* de cerdo
d Presskopf *m*; Sülze f aus Schweinefleisch

304 brazil nut
Fruit of *Bertholletia excelsa.*
f noix f du Brésil; noix f d'Amérique
e nuez f del Brasil
d Paranuss f

305 bread
f pain *m*
e pan *m*
d Brot *n*

306 bread flour
f farine f panifiable
e harina f para pan
d Brotmehl *n*

307 bread texture
f porosité f de pain; alvéolage f de
pain
e textura f de pan
d Krummenbeschaffenheit f

308 breakfast cereals
f céréales *fpl* pour petit déjeuner
e cereales *mpl*
d Frühstücksnahrung f aus Weizen,
Mais usw.

309 break flour
f farine f de broyage
e harina f gruesa
d Schrotmehl *n*; Mehl *n* von den
Schrotpassagen

310 break rolls
f cylindres *mpl* de broyage;
cylindres *mpl* désagrégeurs
e molinos *mpl*
d Schrotwalzen *fpl*

311 bream
Fish of *Abramis* sp.
f brême f
e sargo *m*
d Brassen *m*; Brachsen *m*

312 brewer's grain
f drêche f de brasserie
e grano *m* de cervecero
d Biertreber *m*

313 brewery
f brasserie f
e cervecería f
d Brauerei f

314 brewing liquor
f eau f de brassage
e agua f de cocimiento
d Brauwasser *n*

315 **brill**
Marine flat fish *Scophthalmus rhombus*; in New Zealand *Caulopsetta scaphus*.
f barbue *f*
e mero *m*
d Glattbutt *m*

316 **brine**
f saumure *f*
e salmuera *f*
d Salzlösung *f*; Sole *f*; Salzlake *f*

317 **brine cooling**
f réfrigération *f* par saumure; refroidissement *m* par saumure
e enfriamiento con soluciones salinas
d Solekühlung *f*

318 **Brix scale**
f échelle *f* de Brix
e escala *f* de Brix
d Brix-Skala *f*

319 **broad bean**
Vicia faba.
f fève *f* de marais
e haba *f*
d Saubohne *f*

320 **bromelin**
f broméline *f*
e bromelina *f*
d Bromelin *n*

* **broth → 295**

321 **brown sugar**
f sucre *m* brut; sucre *m* roux
e azúcar *m* moreno
d Rohzucker *m*; Farin-Zucker *m*

322 **brucine**
f brucine *f*
e brucina *f*
d Brucin *n*

323 **Brussels sprouts**
Brassica oleracea gemmifera.
f choux *mpl* de Bruxelles
e bretones *mpl*; coles *fpl* de Bruselas
d Rosenkohl *m*

324 **bubble**
f bulle *f*
e burbuja *f*
d Blase *f*

325 **bubble-cap**
f cloche *f* de barbotage
e casquete *m* de burbujeo
d Blasenglocke *f*

326 **buffer salt**
f sel *m* tampon
e sal *f* tampón
d Puffersubstanz *f*

327 **buffer solution**
f solution *f* tampon
e solución *f* tampón
d Pufferlösung *f*

328 **bung**
f bouchon *m*
e tapón *m*
d Zapfen *m*

329 **bunghole**
f bonde *f* de bouchon
e agujero *m* del tapón
d Zapfenloch *n*; Spundloch *n*

330 **burbot**
Freshwater fish *Lota lota*; American variery *Lota maculosa.*
f lotte *f* de rivière
e mustela *f*
d Quappe *f*

331 **bushel**
f boisseau *m*
e fanega *f*
d Scheffel *m*

332 **butter**
f beurre *m*
e mantequilla *f*
d Butter *f*

333 **butter milk**
f lait *m* de beurre; babeurre *m*
e suero *m*
d Buttermilch *f*

334 **butylated hydroxyanisole; BHA**
f hydroxyanisol *m* butylé

e hidroxianisol *m* butilado
d Butylhydroxyanisol *n*

335 butylated hydroxytoluene; BHT
f hydroxytoluène *m* butylé
e hidroxitolueno *m* butilado
d Butylhydroxytoluol *m*

336 butyl ether
f éther *m* butylique
e éter *m* butílico
d Butyläther *m*

337 butyric acid
f acide *m* butyrique
e ácido *m* butírico
d Buttersäure *f*

338 by-product
f produit *m* secondaire; sous-produit
   m
e subproducto *m*; producto *m*
   secundario
d Nebenprodukt *n*

C

339 cabbage
Brassica oleracea.
f chou *m*
e col *f*; berza *f*
d Kohl *m*; Kraut *n*

* **cacao bean** → **460**

* **cacao butter** → **461**

340 caffeic acid
f acide *m* caféique
e ácido *m* cafeico
d Kaffeesäure *f*

341 caffeine
f caféine *f*
e cafeina *f*
d Coffein *n*; Koffein *n*

342 cake *v*
f grumeler (se)
e agrumarse
d klumpen (sich)

343 cake flour
f farine *f* de pâtisserie; farine *f* pâtissière
e harina *f* de pastelería
d Kuchenmehl *n*

* **cal.** → **348**

* **calamary** → **1783**

344 calandria
f calendre *f*
e calandria *f*
d Heizrohr *n*; Verdampfrohr *n*

* **calciferol** → **2015**

345 calcium carbonate
f carbonate *m* de calcium
e carbonato *m* cálcico
d Kalziumkarbonat *n*; kohlensaurer Kalk *m*

346 calcium pantothenate
f pantothénate *m* de calcium

e pantotenato *m* cálcico
d Kalziumpantothenat *n*

347 calcium phosphate
f phosphate *m* de calcium
e fosfato *m* cálcico
d Kalziumphosphat *n*

* **calcium sulphate (anhydrous)**
→ **130**

348 calorie; cal.
f calorie *f*
e caloría *f*
d Kalorie *f*

349 Campden process
f procédé *m* de Campden
e proceso *m* de Campden
d campdensches Verfahren *n*

350 can
Container.
f pot *m*; bidon *m*; cruche *f*; boille *f*
e vaso *m*; jarro *m*
d Kanne *f*

351 can
Tin can.
f boîte *f*
e lata *f*
d Büchse *f*; Blechdose *f*

352 candied fruit; crystallised fruit
f fruit *m* confit
e fruta *f* azucarada
d Kandisfrucht *f*

353 candied peel
f écorce *f* de fruits confit; zeste *f* confit
e confite *m*
d Zitronat *n*; Sukkade *f*; Kandisfrucht *f*

354 cane sugar
f sucre *m* de canne
e azúcar *m* de caña
d Rohrzucker *m*

355 canning
f mise *f* en boîtes
e enlatado *m*
d Eindosen *n*

356 canning industry
 f industrie f des conserves
 e industria f conservera
 d Konservenindustrie f

357 cape gooseberry
 Edible orange berry of *Physalis
 peruviana.*
 f alkékenge m; amour m en cage;
 coqueret m
 e alquequenje m
 d Judenkirsche f

358 capelin
 Mallotus rillosus.
 f capelan m
 e capelin m
 d Lodde f

359 capers
 Buds of *Capparis spinosa.*
 f câpres fpl
 e alcabarras fpl
 d Kapern fpl

360 capon
 f chapon m
 e capón m
 d Kapaun m

* capsicum → 400

361 captan
 f captan m
 e captano m
 d Captan n

362 caramel
 f caramel m
 e caramelo m
 d Karamell m

363 caraway
 Fruit of *Carum carvi.*
 f carvi m
 e colmino m
 d Kümmel m

364 carbohydrase
 f carbohydrase f
 e carbohidrasa f
 d Karbohydrase f

365 carbohydrate
 f hydrate m de carbone
 e carbohidrato m; hidrato m de
 carbono
 d Kohlenhydrat n

* carbolic acid → 1402

366 carbon cycle
 f cycle m du carbone
 e ciclo m del carbono
 d Kohlenstoffzyklus m

367 carbon dioxide
 f dioxyde m de carbone
 e dióxido m de carbono
 d Kohlendioxyd n

368 carboxymethylcellulose; C.M.C.
 f carboxyméthylcellulose f
 e carboximetilcelulosa f
 d Karboxymethylzellulose f

369 carboy
 f ballon f; dame-jeanne f
 e damajuana f; garrafa f
 d Ballon m; Korbflasche f

370 carcinogen
 f carcinogène m
 e carcinógeno m
 d Kanzerogen n; krebserzeugende
 Substanz f

371 cardamom
 Seed of *Elettaria cardamomum.*
 f cardamome m
 e cardamomo m
 d Kardamom m

372 cardamom oil
 f essence f de cardamome
 e aceite m de cardamomo
 d Kardamomöl n

**373 carob bean; locust bean; St. John's
 bread**
 Pod of *Ceratonia siliqua.*
 f caroube f
 e algaroba f
 d Johannisbrot n; Karub m; Karube
 f

374 carotene
f carotène *m*
e caroteno *m*
d Karotin *n*

375 carp
Freshwater fish *Cyprinus carpio.*
f carpe *f*
e carpa *f*
d Karpfen *m*

376 carrageenan; Irish moss
Chondrus crispus.
f mousse *f* perlée; mousse *f*
d'Irlande
e musgo *m* irlandés
d irlandisches Moos *n*; Perlmoos *n*;
Karrageen *n*

377 carrot
Root of *Daucus carota.*
f carotte *f*
e zanahoría *f*
d Mohrrübe *f*; Möhre *f*; Karotte *f*

378 casein
f caséine *f*
e caseína *f*
d Kasein *n*

379 casein glue
f colle *f* à base de caséine
e cola *f* a basa de caseína
d Kaseinleim *m*

380 casein hydrolysate
f hydrolysat *m* de caséine
e hidrolisado *m* de caseína
d Kaseinhydrolysat *n*

381 caseinogen
f caséinogène *m*
e caseinógeno *m*
d Kaseinogen *n*

382 cashew nut
Seed of *Anacardium occidentale.*
f noix *f* de cajou; noix *f* d'anacarde
e nuez *f* de merey
d Caschewnuss *f*; Kaschunuss *f*

383 cask
f tonneau *m*; foudre *m*; fût *m*
e barril *m*
d Fass *n*

384 cassava; manioc
Tuber of *Manihot utilissima.*
f cassave *f*
e cazabe *m*
d Kassawa *f*; Maniokwurzel *f*

385 cassia oil
Oil from *Cassia* tree (fam.
Papilionaceae).
f essence *f* de cannelle de Chine
e aceite *m* de casia
d Kassiaöl *n*

386 castor oil
Oil from *Ricinus communis.*
f huile *f* de ricin
e aceite *m* de ricino; aceite *m* de
castor
d Rizinusöl *n*

387 castor sugar
f sucre *m* en poudre
e azúcar *m* en polvo
d Staubzucker *m*; Puderzucker *m*

388 catalase
f catalase *f*
e catalasa *f*
d Katalase *f*

389 catalase test
f épreuve *f* de la catalase
e prueba *f* de catalasa
d Katalaseprobe *f*

390 catalysis
f catalyse *f*
e catálisis *f*
d Katalyse *f*

391 catalyst
f catalyseur *m*
e catalizador *m*
d Katalysator *m*

392 catering
f restauration *f*
e provisión *f*
d Verpflegung *f*

393 catfish; sea wolf
Marine fish *Anarhicas lupus*; in
America sub-order *Siluroidea* in
fresh water.

f chat m marin
e barbo m; siluro m
d Katfisch m; Seewolf m

394 cathepsin
f cathépsine f
e catepsina f
d Kathepsin n

395 cation
f cation m
e catión m
d Kation n

396 cauliflower
Brassica oleracea capitata.
f choufleur m
e coliflor f
d Blumenkohl m

397 caustic
f caustique
e cáustico
d ätzend

398 caustic potash
f potasse f caustique
e potasa f cáustica
d Ätzkali n

399 caustic soda
f soude f caustique
e sosa f cáustica
d Ätznatron n

**400 cayenne pepper; capsicum; red
    pepper; chilli pepper**
From fruit of *Capsicum frutescens*.
f poivre m de Cayenne; poivre m
    d'Inde; poivre m d'Espagne;
    capsicum m
e pimienta f de Cayena
d Cayennepfeffer m; Kapsikum n;
    spanischer Pfeffer m

401 celeriac
Apium graveolens rapaceum.
f céleri-rave f
e apio m napiforme
d Knollensellerie m/f

402 celery
Apium graveolens.
f céleri m

e apio m
d Sellerie m/f

403 celluloid
f celluloïde m
e celuloide f
d Zelluloid n

404 cellulose
f cellulose f
e celulosa f
d Zellulose f; Zellstoff m

405 cellulose ester
f ester m de cellulose
e éster m de celulosa
d Zelluloseester n

406 cell volume
f volume m des alvéoles
e volumen m de celdas; volumen m
    de alveolos
d Porenvolumen n

407 centigrade
f centigrade m
e centígrado m
d Celsiusskala f

408 centripetal pump
f pompe f centrepète
e bomba f centrípeta
d Zentripetalpumpe f; Greiferpumpe
    f

409 cereals
f céréales fpl; grains mpl
e cereales mpl; granos mpl
d Getreidearten fpl

410 cetyl alcohol
f alcool m cétylique
e alcohol m cetílico
d Zetylalkohol m

411 chaff
f balle f; glume f
e ahechadura f; zurrón m
d Spreu n; Spelze f

412 chain reaction
f réaction f en chaîne
e reacción f en cadena
d Kettenreaktion f

413 chalk
f craie f
e tiza f
d Kreide f

414 char
Salmo salvelinus.
f omble m; omble m chevalier
e umbra f
d Saibling m

415 char
Carbonisation product.
f matière f carbonisée
e carbón m animal; carbón m de huesos
d verkohltes Material n

416 charlock
Sinapis arvensis.
f moutarde f des champs; moutarde f sauvage
e mostaza f; silvestre m
d Ackersenf f

417 cheese
f fromage m
e queso m
d Käse m

418 cheese rind
f croûte f du fromage
e corteza f de queso
d Käserinde f

419 chemical leavening
f levée f de la pâte par agents chimiques
e fermentado m químico
d chemische Lockerung f des Teiges

420 cherry
Fruit of *Prunus avium* or *P. cerasus.*
f cerise f
e cereza f
d Kirsche f

421 chervil
Anthriscus cerefolium.
f cerfeuil m
e perifollo m
d Kerbel m

422 chestnut
Castanea sp.
f marron m; châtaigne f
e castaña f
d echte Kastanie f; Marone f

423 chewing gum
f chewing-gum m; pâte f à mâcher
e goma f para mascar
d Kaugummi m/n

424 chick pea
Cicer arietinum.
f pois m chiche
e garbanzo m; chícharo m
d Kichererbse f

425 chicle
Gum from *Achrus sapota*, used as main ingredient for chewing gum.
f chicle m
e llicle m
d Chiclegummi m/n

426 chicory
Chichorium intybus.
f endive f
e achicoria f
d Zichorie f

* **Chile saltpetre** → **1724**

427 chill v
f refroidir; réfrigérer
e helar; enfriar
d abkühlen; kühlen

* **chilli pepper** → **400**

* **China clay** → **1035**

* **chinic acid** → **1498**

428 chitterlings
f tripe f
e tripa f
d Kaldaune f; Kutteln f

429 chive
Allium schoenoprasum.
f civette f; ciboulette f
e cebolleta f
d Schnittlauch m

430 chlordane
f chlordane *m*
e clordán *m*
d Chlordan *n*

431 chloride of lime; bleaching powder
f chlorure *m* de chaux; poudre f à blanchir
e cloruro *m* de cal; polvo *m* para blanquear
d Bleichkalk *m*; Chlorkalk *m*; Bleichpulver *n*

* **chlorinated lime → 262**

432 chlorination
f chloration f
e cloración f
d Chlorierung f

433 chlorophyll
f chlorophylle f
e clorofila f
d Chlorophyll *n*

434 chocolate
f chocolat *m*
e chocolate *m*
d Schokolade f

435 chocolate coating machine
f machine f à enrober de chocolat
e máquina f para revestir de chocolate
d Schokoladen-Überziehmaschine f

436 chocolate milk
f lait *m* chocolaté; chocolat
e chocolate *m* de leche
d Kakaomilch f; Milchkakao *m*

437 cholesterol
f cholestérol *m*
e colesterol *m*
d Cholesterin *n*

438 cholic acid
f acide *m* cholique
e ácido *m* cólico
d Gallensäure f

439 choline
f choline f
e colina f
d Cholin *n*

440 chromatin
f chromatine f
e cromatina f
d Chromatin *n*

441 chromatography
f chromatographie f
e cromatografía f
d Chromatographie f

442 churn *v*
f baratter
e batir la leche
d buttern

443 churning
f barattage *m*
e batido *m*; agitación f
d Erschüttern *n*; Buttern *n*

* **chymosin → 1544**

444 chymotrypsin
f chymotrypsine f
e quimotripsina f
d Chymotrypsin *n*

445 cider
f cidre *m*
e sidra f
d Apfelmost *m*

446 cinnamon
Bark of *Cinnamomum* tree.
f canelle f
e canela f
d Zimt *m*

* **C.I.P. → 451**

447 circulation pump
f pompe f de circulation
e bomba f circulante
d Umwalzpumpe f

448 citric acid
f acide *m* citrique
e ácido *m* cítrico
d Zitronensäure f

449 clam
Mercenaria mercenaris.
f palourde f; clovisse f
e peine *m*; almeja f
d Sandklaffmuschel f

450 clarification
f clarification f
e clarificación f
d Klarung f; Abklarung f

451 cleaning in place; C.I.P.
f nettoyage m in situ
e limpieza f en al si⁺⁻
d geschlossene Rein._ .ng f

452 climacteric fruit
f fruit m climatérique
e fruta f climatérica
d klimakterische Frucht f

453 climbing film evaporator
f évaporateur m à grimpage
e evaporadora f de película
ascendiente
d Verdampfer m mit aufsteigendem
Film

454 clotted cream
f crème f préparée à l'anglaise
e nata f gruesa
d englischer Rahm m; englische
Sahne f

455 clove oil
f essence f de girofle
e esencia f de clavillos
d Nelkenöl n

456 cloves
Dried flower buds of *Eugenia
caryophyllus.*
f clous mpl de girofle
e clavillos mpl; clavos mpl de
especia
d Gewürznelken fpl

* C.M.C. → 368

457 coacervation
f coacervation f
e coacervación f
d Koazervation f

* coalfish → 1433

* cobalamin → 2013

458 cochineal
Red pigment of *Coccus cacti* beetle.

f cochenille f
e cochinilla f
d Koschenillefarbstoff m

459 cockle
Cardium edule.
f coque f
e bucarda f; caracol m de mar
d Herzmuschel f

460 cocoa bean; cacao bean
Seed of *Theobroma cacao* tree.
f fève f de cacao
e semilla f de cacao
d Kakaobohne f

461 cocoa butter; cacao butter
f beurre m de cacao
e manteca f de cacao
d Kakaobutter f

* cocoanut → 462

* cocoanut oil → 463

462 coconut; cocoanut
Fruit of *Cocos nucifera.*
f coco m
e coco m
d Kokosnuss f

463 coconut oil; cocoanut oil
f graisse f de copra; huile f de coco
e aceite m de coco
d Kokosfett n; Kokosnussöl n
(
464 code of principles (F.A.O.)
f code m de principles (F.A.O.)
e código m de principios (F.A.O.);
compilación f de leges (F.A.O.)
d Grundsatzbestimmungen fpl
(F.A.O.)

465 cod-liver oil
From various fish especially *Gadus*
sp.
f huile f de foie de morue
e aceite m de higado de bacalao
d Dorschlebertran m

466 coenzyme
An organic compound which, in
combination with a protein, can
form an enzyme system.

f coenzyme *f*
e coenzima *f*
d Koenzym *n*; Koferment *n*

467 coffee
Berries of *Coffea arabica* and *C. robusta* trees.
f café *m*
e café *m*
d Kaffee *m*

468 cold storage
f conservation *f* par le froid
e almacenamiento *m* a baja temperatura
d Kühllagerung *f*

* **cole-slaw → 1696**

469 coliform bacterium
Escherichia coli.
f bactérie *f* coliforme
e bacteria *f* coliforme
d Kolibakterie *f*

470 collagen
f collagène *m*
e colágeno *m*
d Kollagen *n*

471 colloid; macromolecular dispersion
f colloïde *m*; dispersion *f* macromoléculaire
e coloide *m*; dispersión *f* macromolecular
d Kolloid *n*; makromolekulare Lösung *f*

472 colloidal
f colloïdal
e coloidal
d kolloidal

473 colloid mill
f broyeur *m* pour colloïdes
e molino *m* para coloides
d Kolloidmühle *f*

474 colophony; rosin
f colophane *f*
e colofonia *f*
d Kolophonium *n*

* **colza oil → 1517**

475 combine harvester
f moissonneuse-batteuse *f*
e segador *m*
d Mähdrescher *m*

476 concentrate *v*
f concentrer
e concentrar
d konzentrieren

477 conche *v*
f concher
e conchar; batir
d konchieren

478 condensed milk
f lait *m* concentré sucré
e leche *f* condensada azucarada
d gezuckerte Kondensvollmilch *f*

479 condition *v*
f reposer; conditionner
e acondicionar
d konditionieren

480 confectionery (products)
f produit *m* sucré
e dulcería *f*; confitería *f*
d Süssware *f*; Konfekt *n*; Zuckerwerk *n*

481 conger eel
Conger conger.
f congre *m*
e congrio *m*
d Meeraal *m*

482 conjugated double bonds
f liaisons *fpl* doubles conjuguées
e enlaces *mpl* dobles conjugados
d konjugierte Doppelverbindungen *f pl*

483 consistency
f consistance *f*
e consistencia *f*
d Konsistenz *f*

484 consommé
f consommé *m*
e caldo *m*; consommé *m*
d Fleischbrühe *f*

485 constituent
f constituent *m*
e constituyente *m*
d Bestandteil *m*

486 contaminate v; taint v
f contaminer
e contaminar
d kontaminieren

487 contamination
f contamination *f*
e contaminación *f*
d Verunreinigung *f*; Kontamination *f*

488 continuous cooker
f autoclave *m* continu
e horno *m* continuo
d kontinuierlicher Autoklav *m*

489 continuous drying
f séchage *m* en continu
e secado *m* continuo
d kontinuierliche Trocknung *f*

490 continuous press
f presse *f* continue
e prensa *f* continua
d kontinuierliche Presse *f*

* controlled atmosphere storage
→ 823

491 conveyer
f transporteur *m*; benne *f* transporteuse
e portador *m*
d Förderanlage *f*

492 conveyer belt
f transporteur *m* à courroies
e cinturón *m* portador
d Förderband *n*

* cookie → 244

493 cooling section
f zone *f* de refroidissement
e parte *m* para enfriar
d Abkühlungszone *f*

494 cooling tunnel
f tunnel *m* de réfrigération
e tunel *m* de enfriamiento
d Kühltunnel *m*

495 coriander
Seed of *Coriandrum sativum.*
f coriandre *f*
e culantro *m*
d Koriander *m*

496 cork
Bark of *Quercus suber.*
f liège *m*
e corcho *m*
d Kork *m*

497 corn flakes
f flocons *mpl* de maïs; "cornflakes" *mpl*
e hojuelas *fpl* de maíz; copos *mpl* de maíz
d Maisflocken *fpl*; "Cornflakes" *fpl*

498 cornflour
f farine *f* de maïs
e harina *f* de maíz
d Maismehl *n*

499 corn syrup
f sirop *m* de maïs
e jarabe *m* de maíz
d Stärkesirup *m*

500 cosette
f cossette *f*
e rebanda *f* de remolacha en forma de V
d Zuckerrübenschnitzel *n*

501 cottonseed oil
Oil from seeds of *Gossypium* sp.
f huile *f* de coton
e aceite *m* de semillas de algodón
d Baumwollsamenöl *n*

502 counterflow heat exchanger
f échangeur *m* à contrecourant
e intercambiador *m* de calor por contracorriente
d Gegenstromwärmeaustauscher *m*

503 courgette
f courgette *f*
e calabaza *f* succhini
d Sukini *mpl*

504 couverture
f couverture *f*

e cubierta f
d Couverture f

505 **cover glass**
 f lamelle f couvre-objet
 e cubre objeto m; laminilla f
 d Deckgläschen n

506 **crab**
 Cancer paguras.
 f tourteau m
 e cangrejo m
 d Krabbe f

507 **cracker**
 f cracker m
 e galleta f de soda
 d Hartkeks m

508 **cranberry**
 Vaccinium sp.
 f canneberge f; airelle f rouge
 e arándano
 d Preiselbeere f; Moosbeere f;
   Kronsbeere f

509 **crawfish; spiny lobster; rock
   lobster**
 Palinurus sp., especially *P. vulgaris.*
 f langouste f
 e langosta f
 d Languste f

510 **crayfish**
 Astacus fluvialis, in America
 Cambarus affinis.
 f écrevisse f
 e cangrejo m de río
 d Flusskrebs m

511 **cream**
 f crème f
 e crema f; nata f
 d Sahne f; Rahm m

512 **cream of tartar; potassium tartrate;
   potassium bitartrate**
 f créme f de tartre; tartrate m de
   potassium
 e cremor m tártaro; tartrato m
   potásico
 d Weinstein m; Weinsteinrahm n;
   Kaliumtartrat n; weinsaures
   Kalium n

513 **cream separator**
 f écrémeuse f
 e separador m de crema
 d Entrahmungszentrifuge f

514 **crease**
 f sillon m
 e pliegue m
 d Furche f

515 **cress**
 Lepidium sativum.
 f cresson m
 e berro m
 d Kresse f

516 **crisp**
 f croustillant
 e crespo; rizado; tostado
 d rösch; spröd; knusperig

517 **critical temperature**
 f température f critique
 e temperatura f crítica
 d kritische Temperatur f

518 **cross beater mill**
 f broyeur m à marteaux
 e molino m batidor de martillos
 d Schlagkreuzmühle f

519 **cross linking**
 f réticulation f; liaison f transversale
 e reticulación f
 d Vernetzung f

520 **crouton**
 f croûton m
 e cubo m de pan tostado
 d gebackener Brotwürfel m

521 **crown cork**
 f bouchon-couronne m
 e tapa f de botillas de gaseosas
 d Kronkorken m

522 **crude fibre**
 f matière f cellulosique
 e fibra f cruda
 d Rohfaser f

523 **crude protein**
 f protéine f brute
 e proteína f cruda
 d Rohprotein n

524 crumb
f mie f
e miga f
d Krume f

525 crumb elasticity
f élasticité f de la mie; résilience f
de la mie
e elasticidad f de la miga
d Krumenelastizität f

526 crumb firmness
f fermeté f de la mie
e firmeza f de miga
d Krumenfestigkeit f

527 crumb formation
f formation f de la mie
e formación f de miga
d Krumenbildung f

528 crumb texture
f texture f de la mie
e textura f de miga
d Krummenbeschaffenheit f

529 crust
f croûte f
e corteza f; concha f
d Kruste f

530 crystallise v
f cristalliser
e cristalizar
d kristallisieren

* crystallised fruit → 352

531 crystallization
f cristallisation f
e cristalización f
d Kristallisation f

532 cucumber
Cucumis sp., especially *C. sativus.*
f concombre m
e pepino m; cohombro m
d Gurke f

533 cumin oil
Oil from *Cuminum cyminum.*
f essence f de cumin
e aceite m de comino
d Kuminöl n

534 cumquat; kumquat
Fruit of *Citrus aurantium.*
f kumquat m
e kumquat m
d Kumquat m; Zwergpomeranze f

535 curcuma; turmeric
Curcuma longa.
f curcuma m; safran m des Indes
e cúrcuma f
d Kurkuma f

536 curcumin
Dye from *Crocus longa.*
f curcumine f
e curcumina f
d Kurkumin n

537 curd
f caillé m
e cuajada f; requesón m
d Käsebruch m

538 cure v
To preserve food (usually meat) by
smoking, salting or pickling.
f saler; fumer; caquer (harengs)
e curar
d pökeln; einsalzen; räuchern;
trocknen; dörren; konservieren;
haltbar machen

539 cure v
To ripen a food.
f affiner; maturer
e curar
d reifen

540 currants
Fruit of *Ribes* species, bush fruits
with red, black or white berries.
f groseilles fpl
e groselas fpl
d Johannisbeeren fpl

541 currants
Dried black grapes.
f raisins mpl de Corinthe
e pasas fpl de Corinto
d Korinthen fpl

542 curry
f cari m; kari m
e curry m
d Curry m/n

543 custard
 f crème *f* cuite
 e flan *m*; natillas *fpl*
 d Krem *m*

544 cuticle
 f cuticle *f*
 e cutícula *f*
 d Kutikula *f*

545 cutlet
 f côtelette *f*
 e chuleta *f*
 d Kotelett *n*; Schnitzel *n*

546 cutting angle
 f angle *m* de tranchant
 e ángulo *m* de cortadura
 d Schneidewinkel *m*

547 cuttlefish; ink fish
   Sepia sp., *Sepiola* sp.
 f seiche *f*
 e jibia *f*; sepia *f*
 d Tintenfisch *m*

* **cyanocobalamin** → **2013**

548 cyclone
 f cyclone *m*
 e separador *m* ciclónico
 d Zyklonenscheider *m*

549 cysteine
 f cystéine *f*
 e cisteína *f*
 d Zystein *n*

550 cytochromes
 f cytochromes *mpl*
 e citocromos *mpl*
 d Zytochrome *npl*; Zellfarbstoffe *m*
   pl

D

551 dab
Limanda limanda.
f limande f
e barbada f
d Scharbe n; Blieschen n

* **dandelion** → 1881

552 date
f datte f
e dátil m
d Dattel f

553 de-aminase
f désaminase f
e desaminasa f
d Desaminase f

554 Dean and Stark apparatus
f appareil m de Dean et Stark
e aparato m de Dean y Stark
d Dean und Stark Apparat m

555 decantation
f décantation f
e decantación f
d Dekantierung f

556 decoction
f décoction f
e decocción f
d Absud m

557 decomposition
f décomposition f
e descomposición f; corrupción f
d Abbau m; Zerlegung f

558 decorticator
f décortiqueuse f
e descortezadora f mecánica
d Schälmaschine f; Entholzungsmaschine f

* **de-emulsifier** → 559

559 de-emulsifying agent; de-
emulsifier
f désémulsionnant m
e desemulsificador m
d Entemulgator m

560 deep frozen
f congelé à basse température
e congelado a baja temperatura
d tiefgefroren; gefrostet

561 deer
f cerf m; daim m
e ciervo m
d Reh n

562 defecation
Process of clarifying and purifying
solutions, e.g. by coagulation of the
soluble proteins and neutralization
with milk of lime of a sugar
solution.
f défécation f; clarification f
e clarificación f
d Klärung f

563 defoaming agent
f anti-mousse m
e antiespumante m
d Schaumzerstörungsmittel n

564 defrosting
f décongélation f; dégivrage m
e descongelación f
d Entfrostung f; Auftauen n

565 degrease v
f déhuiler; dégraisser
e desgrasar
d entölen

566 degreasing tank
f citerne f de dégraissage
e baño m desengrasante; depósito m
desengrasante
d Entfettungstank m

567 dehydrate v
f déshydrater
e deshidratar
d entwässern; trocknen

568 dehydration
f déshydratation f
e deshidratación f
d dehydrierung f; Wasserentziehung
f

569 dehydrofreezing
f réfrigération f par déshydration

e deshidrocongelamiento *m*
d Deshydrogefrieren *n*

570 dehydrogenase
 f déshydrogénase *f*
 e deshidrogenasa *f*
 d Dehydrogenase *f*

571 dehydrogenation
 f déshydrogénation *f*
 e deshidrogenación *f*
 d Dehydrierung *f*

572 deliquescence
 f déliquescence *f*
 e delicuecencia *f*
 d Flüssigwerden *n*; Verflüssigung *f*

573 delivery
 f débit *m*
 e entraga *f*
 d Förderleistung *f*

574 denaturation
 Irreversible change in proteins.
 f dénaturation *f*
 e desnaturalización *f*
 d Denaturierung *f*

575 denaturation
 Addition of denaturing agents to alcohol.
 f dénaturation *f*
 e desnaturalización *f*
 d Vergallung *f*

576 denatured alcohol; industrial alcohol
 f alcool *m* dénaturé
 e alcohol *m* desnaturalizado
 d denaturierter Alkohol *m*

577 density
 f densité *f*
 e densidad *f*
 d Dichte *f*

578 density grading
 f graduation *f* par densité
 e separación *f* por densidad
 d Dichtesortierung *f*

579 deodorant; deodorizer
 f désodorisant *m*

e desodorante *m*; desodorizante *m*
d Desodoriermittel *n*

580 deodorization
 f désodorisation *f*
 e desodorización *f*
 d Desodorisierung *f*

* **deodorizer** → 579

581 deoxy-; desoxy-
 f désoxy-
 e desoxi-
 d Desoxy-

582 deoxyribonucleic acid
 f acide *m* désoxyribonucléique
 e ácido *m* desoxirribonucléico
 d Desoxyribonukleinsäure *f*

583 depth of flute
 f profondeur *f* de la cannelure
 e profundidad *f* del canal
 d Riffeltiefe *f*

584 derivative
 f dérivé *m*
 e derivado *m*
 d Derivat *n*; Abkömmling *m*

585 desiccant
 f agent *m* dessiccateur
 e desecador *m*
 d Trocknungsmittel *n*

586 desiccate *v*
 f dessécher
 e desecar
 d austrocknen

587 desiccator
 f dessiccateur *m*; séchoir *m*
 e desecador *m*; secadero *m*
 d Entfeuchter *m*; Exsiccator *m*

588 desorption
 f désorption *f*
 e desorción *f*
 d Desorption *f*

* **desoxy-** → 581

589 detergent
 f détergent *m*

e detergente *m*
d Reinigungsmittel *n*; Detergens *n*

590 Dewar flask
f vase *m* Dewar
e frasco *m* Dewar
d Dewar-Gefäss *n*

591 dew point
f point *m* de rosée
e punto *m* de rocío
d Taupunkt *m*

592 dextrin
f dextrine *f*
e dextrina *f*
d Dextrin *n*

593 dextro-rotatory
f dextrogyre
e dextrorrotatorio; dextrógiro
d rechtsdrehend

* **dextrose** → 839

594 diacetyl
f diacétyle *m*
e diacetilo *m*
d Diacetyl *n*

595 dialysis
f dialyse *f*
e diálisis *f*
d Dialyse *f*

596 diaphragm; membrane
f diaphragme *m*; membrane *f*
e diafragma *m*; membrana *f*
d Diaphragma *n*; Membran *f*

597 diastase
f diastase *f*
e diastasa *f*
d Diastase *f*

598 diastatic activity
f pouvoir *m* diastasique
e actividad *f* diastática
d diastatische Kraft *f*; Zuckerbildungsvermögen *n*

* **diatomaceous earth** → 1049

* **diatomite** → 1049

599 dice *v*
f couper en dés
e cortar en cubos
d in Würfel schneiden; würfeln;
karieren

600 dieldrin
f dieldrine *f*
e dieldrina *f*
d Dieldrin *n*

601 dielectric heating
f chauffage *m* diélectrique
e calentamiento *m* dieléctrico
d dielektrische Erwärmung *f*

602 diene value
f valeur *f* diène
e valor *m* de dienos
d Dienzahl *f*

603 dietetic
f diététique
e dietético
d diätetisch

604 diffusion
f diffusion *f*
e difusión *f*
d Diffusion *f*

605 digestion
f digestion *f*
e digestión *f*
d Verdauung *f*

606 digitalin
Glycoside from *Digitalis purpurea.*
f digitaline *f*
e digitalina *f*
d Digitalin *n*

607 diglycol oleate
f oléate *m* de diglycol
e oleato *m* de diglicol
d Diglykololeat *n*

608 dilatation
f dilatation *f*
e dilatación *f*
d Ausdehnung *f*; Dilatation *f*

609 dill
Seeds of *Anethum graveolens.*

f aneth m
e eneldo m
d Dill n

610 dilute v
f diluer
e diluir
d verdünnen

611 dimorphic
f dimorphe
e dimórfico
d dimorph

* diose → 614

612 diphenyl
f diphényl m
e difenilo m
d Diphenyl n

613 directions for use
f mode f d'emploi
e instrucciones fpl
d Gebrauchsanweisung f

614 disaccharide; diose
f disaccharide m
e disacárico m
d Disaccharid n

615 disc mill
f broyeur m à disque
e molino m a disco
d Scheibenmühle f

616 disintegrator
f désintégrateur m; broyeur m
e desintegrador m; disgregador m
d Zerkleinerungsmaschine f

617 dispenser
f distributeur m
e dispensador m
d Verteiler m; Ausgabeapparat m

618 disperse v
f disperser
e dispersar
d dispergieren

619 dispersing agent
f agent m dispersant
e agente m dispersante
d Dispergiermittel n

620 dissociation
f dissociation f
e disociación f
d Dissoziation f; Aufspaltung f

621 distillery
f distillerie f
e destilería f
d Brennerei f

622 distillery residue
f vinasse f de distillerie
e residuo m de destilación
d Schlempe f

623 diterpene
f diterpène m
e diterpeno m
d Diterpen n

624 dithione
f dithione m
e ditión m
d Dithion n

625 dock v
f piquer
e picar
d stippen; einstechen

626 dockage
Foreign material in wheat.
f impuretés mpl
e impurezas fpl
d Fremdkörper mpl

627 dogfish; spur dog; smooth hound
Squalus family, especially Sq. acanthias.
f aiguillat m; émissole f; chien m de mer
e lija f
d Dornhai m; Glatthai m

* doree → 1028

* dosimeter → 1502

628 double drum drier
f séchoir m à deux cylindres
e secador m de doble tambor
d Zweiwalzentrockner m

629 dough aeration
f formation f de alvéoles dans la pâte
e aeración f de la masa
d Teiglockerung f

630 dough forming capacity
f aptitude f à former une pâte
e capacidad f para formar masas
d Teigbildungsvermögen n

631 dough kneading
f pétrissage m
e amasadura f de la masa
d Teigkneten n; Kneten n des Teiges

632 dough-making process
f conduite f de la pâte jusqu'au façonnage
e proceso m de hacer la masa
d Teigführung f

633 dough maturity
f maturité f de la pâte
e maduración f de la masa
d Teigreife f

634 dough yield
f rendement m en pâte
e rendimiento m de la masa
d Teigausbeute f

* **Dover sole → 1737**

635 Dragendorff's solution
f solution f de Dragendorff
e solución f de Dragendorff
d Dragendorffsche Lösung f

636 draught beer
f bière f en fût
e cerveza f de barril; cerveza f de sifón
d Bier n vom Fass; Schankbier n

637 drawn from the wood
f tiré au tonneau
e fresco de barril
d frisch vom Fass

* **dregs → 883**

638 dried milk
f lait m sec

e leche f desecada
d Trockenmilch f

639 dried yeast
f levure f sèche
e levadura f desecada
d Trockenhefe f

* **drier → 1680**

* **drinkable → 1441**

640 drip
Liquid which exudes from frozen meat when it is thawed.
f jus m de décongélation
e exudado m; jugo m
d Tropfsaft m

641 dripping
f graisse f de rôti
e grasa f de asado
d Bratenfett n

642 drum dryer
f séchoir m à tambour
e secador m rotativo
d Trommeltrockner m

643 drum-type magnetic separator
f séparateur m magnétique à tambour
e separador m magnético tipo tambor
d magnetischer Trommelscheider m

644 dry v
f sécher; dessécher
e secar; desecar
d trocknen; dörren

645 dry ice
f glace f carbonique; carboglace f
e hielo m seco
d Trockeneis n

646 drying oil
f huile f siccative
e aceite m secante
d trocknendes Öl n

647 drying oven
f étuve f de dessiccation
e estufa f de secado

d Trockenofen *m*; Trockenkasten *m*;
Trockenschrank *m*

648 drying section
f zone *f* de séchage
e zona *f* de secado
d Trockenabteil *n*

649 drying tower
f tour *f* de séchage
e torre *m* de secado
d Trockenturm *m*

650 drying tunnel
f séchoir-tunnel *m*
e tunel *m* de secado
d Trockentunnel *m*

651 dulcin
f dulcine *f*
e dulcina *f*
d Dulcin *n*

652 durum semolina
f semoule *f* de blé dur
e sémola *f* de trigo duro
d Durumweizengriess *m*

* **durum wheat** → **913**

E

* eau de Javelle → 1025

653 edge runner
f meule f verticale
e muela f vertical
d Läufer m

654 eel
Anguilla anguilla.
f anguille f
e anguila f
d Aal m

655 effervescence
f effervescence f
e efervescencia f
d Efferveszenz f; Aufbrausen n

656 efflorescence
f efflorescence f
e eflorescencia f
d Effloreszenz f

* egg albumin → 1339

* egg plant → 173

657 egg substitute
f succédané m d'oeuf
e substituto m del huevo
d Ei-Ersatz m

658 egg white; albumen
f blanc m d'oeuf; albumen m
e clara f de huevo; albumen m
d Eiweiss n; Eiklar n; Albumen n

659 egg yolk
f jaune m d'oeuf
e yema f de huevo
d Eigelb n; Eidotter m/n

660 elastin
f élastine f
e elastina f
d Elastin n

661 electrostatic separator
f séparateur m électrostatique
e separador m electrostático

d Vorrichtung f zur elektrostatischen Trennung

662 elutriation
f élutriation f
e elutriación f
d Auswaschung f; Schlämmung f

663 embryo
Germ or sporophyte in seeds.
f germe m
e germén m
d Keim m; Keimling m

664 embryo
Animal organism in early stages of growth.
f embryon m
e embrión m
d Embryo m

665 emulsifier
f émulsifiant m; émulsificateur m
e emulsificador m
d Emulgator m

666 emulsifying salt
f sel m de fonte; sel m émulsifiant
e emulsificador m; sal f emulsificante
d Schmelzsalz n

667 emulsion
f émulsion f
e emulsión f
d Emulsion f

668 emulsoid
f émulsoïde m
e emulsoide m
d Emulsoid n

669 encapsulation
f encapsulage m
e encapsulación f
d Verkapselung f

670 endive
Cichorium endivia.
f chicorée f
e endive f
d Endivie f

671 **endosperm**
f endosperme *m*
e endosperma *f*
d Endosperm *n*; Nährgewebe *n*

672 **end point**
f point *m* d'achèvement
e punto *m* final; punto *m* de
valoración
d Endpunkt *m*

673 **energy**
f énergie *f*
e energía *f*
d Energie *f*

* **ennoblement** → **674**

674 **enrichment; ennoblement;
fortification**
Term applied to the addition of
nutrients to food.
f enrichissement *m*
e enriquecimiento *m*; reforzamiento
m
d Bereicherung *f*; Anreicherung *f*

675 **enthalpy**
f enthalpie *f*
e entalpía *f*
d Enthalpie *f*

676 **entrainer**
f entraîneur *m*
e agente *m* arrastrante
d Mitschleppmittel *n*

677 **entrainment**
f entraînement *m*
e arrastre *m*
d Mitschleppen *n*

678 **entropy**
f entropie *f*
e entropía *f*
d Entropie *f*

679 **enzyme**
f enzyme *f*
e enzima *f*
d Enzym *n*

680 **eosin**
f éosine *f*

e eosina *f*
d Eosin *n*

681 **Epsom salts**
f sel *m* d'Epsom
e sal *f* de Epsom
d Epsomsalz *n*; Bittersalz *n*

682 **equilibrium humidity**
f humidité *f* relative d'équilibre
e humedad *f* en equilibrio
d Gleichgewichtsfeuchte *f*

683 **ergosterol**
f ergostérol *m*; ergostérine *f*
e ergosterol *m*
d Ergosterin *n*

684 **ergot**
Claviceps purpurea.
f ergot *m*
e cornezuelo *m*
d Mutterkorn *n*

685 **erucic acid**
f acide *m* érucique
e ácido *m* erucico
d Erucasäure *f*

686 **erythrodextrin**
f érythrodextrine *f*
e eritrodextrina *f*
d Erythrodextrin *n*

* **escallop** → **1626**

687 **essential fatty acid**
f acide *m* gras essentiel
e ácido *m* graso esencial
d essentielle Fettsäure *f*

688 **essential oil**
f huile *f* essentielle; huile *f* volatile
e aceite *m* esencial; aceite *m* volátil
d ätherisches Öl *n*

689 **ester**
f ester *m*
e éster *m*
d Ester *m*

690 **esterification**
f estérification *f*
e esterificación *f*
d Veresterung *f*

* **estrogen** → 1315

691 ether
f éther *m*
e éter *m*
d Äther *m*

* **ethyl acetate** → 15

692 ethyl alcohol
f alcool *m* éthylique
e alcohol *m* etílico
d Äthylalkohol *m*

693 ethyl cinnamate
f cinnamate *m* d'éthyle
e cinamato *m* de etilo
d Äthylcinnamat *n*

694 ethylene
f éthylène *m*
e etileno *m*
d Äthylen *n*

695 ethylene oxide
f oxyde *m* d'éthylène
e óxido *m* de etileno
d Äthylenoxyd *n*

696 ethyl-vanillin
f vanilline *f* d'éthyle
e vainillina *f* de etilo
d Äthylvanillin *n*

697 eucalyptus oil
Oil from *Eucalyptus* sp.
f huile *f* d'eucalyptus
e aceite *m* de eucalipto
d Eukalyptusöl *n*

698 eugenol
f eugénol *m*
e eugenol *m*
d Eugenol *n*

699 evaporated milk
f lait *m* concentré
e leche *f* evaporada
d evaporierte Milch *f*; Kondensmilch *f*

700 evaporated whole milk
f lait *m* entier concentré
e leche *f* completa evaporada
d evaporierte Vollmilch *f*

701 evaporation
f évaporation *f*
e evaporación *f*
d Verdampfung *f*

* **evaporation pond** → 1604

702 exhauster
f exhausteur *m*
e exhaustador *m*
d Exhaustor *m*; Absaugventilator *m*

703 exhaust fan
f ventilateur *m*
e ventilador *m* inhalador
d Lüfter *m*

704 exhaustion box
f boîte *f* sous vapeur
e caja *f* de escape
d Exhaustierbad *n*

705 exhaust steam
f vapeur *f* d'échappement
e vapor *m* de escape
d Abdampf *m*

706 exothermic
f exothermique
e exotérmico
d exotherm

707 expeller cake
f tourteau *m* dégraissé
e torta *f* residua
d Presskuchen *m*

708 extensograph
f extensographe *m*
e extensógrafo *m*
d Extensograph *m*

709 extensometer
f extensomètre *m*; indicateur *m* d'extension
e extensómetro *m*
d Extensometer *n*

710 extractant
f solvant *m* d'extraction
e solvente *m* de extracción
d Extraktionsmittel *n*

711 extraction
 f extraction *f*
 e extracción *f*
 d Extraktion *f*

712 extraction rate
 f taux *m* d'extraction
 e porcentaje *m* de extracción
 d Ausmahlungsgrad *n*; Ausbeute *f*

713 extraction thimble
 f enveloppe *f* d'extracteur
 e envoltura *f* de aparato de extracción
 d Auslaughülse *f*; Extraktionshülse *f*

714 extractive distillation
 Distillation method employing a fractioning column and an added substance which aids separation.
 f distillation *f* par extraction
 e destilación *f* extractiva
 d Extraktivdestillation *f*

* **eyepiece** → **1310**

F

715 Fahrenheit scale
f échelle f Fahrenheit
e escala f Fahrenheit
d Fahrenheit-Skala f

716 falling back
f ralentissement m
e disminuición f; descenso m
d Zurückgehen n

* **farina → 766**

717 farinograph
f farinographe m
e farinógrafo m
d Farinograph m

718 farnesol
f farnésol m
e farnesol m
d Farnesol n

719 fatty acid
f acide m gras
e ácido m graso
d Fettsäure f

* **fatty acid glyceride → 19**

720 fatty alcohol
f alcool m gras
e alcohol m graso
d Fettalkohol m

721 fatty amine
f amine f alipathique
e amina f alifática
d aliphatisches Amin n

722 fatty ester
f ester m d'acide gras
e éster m graso
d Fettester m

723 feed roller
Used in sugar industry.
f rouleau m alimenteur
e cilindro m de alimentación
d Speisewalze f

724 feed rolls
Used in flour industry.
f cylindres mpl d'alimentation
e cilindros mpl de alimentación
d Speisewalzen fpl

725 Fehling's solution
f liqueur f de Fehling
e solución f de Fehling
d Fehlingsche Lösung f

726 fennel
Foeniculum vulgare.
f fenouil m
e hinojo m
d Fenchel m

727 fenugreek
Trigonella foenumgraecum.
f fenu-grec m
e fenogreco m; alholva f
d Bockshornkraut n

728 ferment
f ferment m
e fermento m
d Ferment n

729 ferment v
f fermenter
e fermentar
d fermentieren; gären

730 fermentation
f fermentation f
e fermentación f
d Fermentation f; Gärung f

731 fermenter
f cuve f de fermentation
e cuba f de fermentación
d Gärbottich m

732 fermenting cellar
f cave f de fermentation
e bodega f de fermentación
d Gärkeller m

733 fermenting tank
f cuve f de fermentation
e tanque m de fermentación
d Gärtank m

734 fermentograph
f fermentographe *m*
e fermentógrafo *m*
d Fermentograph *m*

735 ferric ammonium citrate
f citrate *m* de fer ammoniacal
e citrato *m* férrico-amónico
d Ferriammoniumcitrat *n*; Eisenammoniumcitrat *n*

736 ferrous sulphate
f sulfate *m* ferreux
e sulfato *m* ferroso
d Ferrosulfat *n*

737 fertilizer
f engrais *m*
e fertilizante *m*
d Düngemittel *n*; Kunstdünger *m*

738 fibre
f fibre *f*; crin *m*
e fibra *f*
d Faser *f*; Fiber *f*

739 ficin
f ficine *f*
e ficina *f*
d Ficin *n*

740 fig
Ficus sp., particularly *F. carica.*
f figue *f*
e higo *m*
d Feige *f*

741 filter
f filtre *m*
e filtro *m*
d Filter *m*

742 filter paper
f papier-filtre *m*
e papc⁖ *m* de filtro
d Filterpapier *n*

743 filter press
f presse *f* à filtrer
e prensa *f* para filtrar
d Filterpresse *f*

744 filth; hairs
The filth test originated in the

U.S.A., for determining the
contamination of a food with
rodent hairs and insect fragments.
f traces *fpl* de prédatures; "filth" *m*;
souillures *fpl*
e suciedad *f*
d "Filth" *m*

745 filtrate
f produit *m* filtré
e líquido *m* filtrado
d Filtrat *n*

746 fine v
f clarifier
e aclarar; clarificar
d abklären

747 fines herbes
f fines herbes *fpl*
e hierbas *fpl* finas
d gemischte Kräuter *npl*

* **finings** → 1015

748 finished beer
f bière *f* prête au débit
e cerveza *f* lista para consumo
d fertiges Bier *n*

749 fire v
f brûler
e quemar
d verfeuern

750 firkin
f demi petit fût *m*
e barrilito *m* medio
d halbes Fässchen *n*

751 first runnings; fore-runnings
f têtes *fpl*; produit *m* de tête
e producto *m* de cabeza
d Vorlauf *m*; Vorprodukt *n*

752 Fischer's reagent
f réactif *m* de Fischer
e reactivo *m* de Fischer
d Fischerisches Reagens *n*

* **fish-glue** → 1015

753 fish oil
f huile *f* de poisson

e aceite *m* de pescado
d Fischöl *n*

754 flash distillation
f distillation *f* flash
e destilación *f* en corriente de vapor
d Gleichgewichtsdestillation *f*

755 flash evaporation
f évaporation *f* instantanée
e evaporación *f* instantanea
d Expansionverdampfung *f*

756 flash heating
f chauffage *m* rapide
e calentamiento *m* rápido
d Schnellerhitzung *f*

757 flash point
f point *m* d'inflammabilité
e punto *m* de inflamabilidad
d Flammpunkt *m*

758 flask
f ballon *m*; flacon *m*
e frasco *m*; matraz *m*
d Flasche *f*; Kolben *m*

759 flatulence
f flatulence *f*; flatuosité *f*
e flatulencia *f*
d Blähung *f*

760 flavone
f flavone *f*
e flavona *f*
d Flavon *n*

761 flavoprotein
f flavoprotéine *f*
e flavoproteina *f*
d Flavoprotein *n*

762 flavour
f saveur *f*; goût *m*
e sabor *m*; gusto *m*
d Geschmack *m*

763 flavour potentiator
f exhausteur *m* d'arôme
e potenciador *m* de sabor
d Geschmackverstärker *m*;
  Geschmackversteigerer *m*

764 flocculation
f floculation *f*
e floculación *f*
d Ausflockung *f*; Flockenbildung *f*

765 flounder; fluke
  Platichthys flesus, in U.S.A.
  Epimotis gibbosus.
f flet *m*
e lenguado *m*
d Flunder *m*

766 flour; farina
f farine *f*
e harina *f*
d Mehl *n*

767 flow chart
f schéma *m* de fabrication
e diagrama *m* de flujo
d schematischer Arbeitsplan *m*;
  Fabrikationsschema *n*

768 fluidised bed drier
f séchoir *m* à lit fluidisé
e secador *m* a cama fluidizada
d Einrichtung *f* zum Trocknen durch
  Fluidisieren

* **fluke** → 765

769 fluorescein
f fluorescéine *f*
e fluoresceína *f*
d Fluoreszein *n*

770 fluorescence
f fluorescence *f*
e fluorescencia *f*
d Fluoreszenz *f*

771 foaming agent
f agent *m* moussant
e agente *m* espumador; espumante
  m
d Schaummittel *n*

772 foam mat drying
  Drying of foods by whipping a
  liquid concentrate to a foam,
  spreading on a tray and drying in a
  stream of warm air.
f séchage *m* de mousse
e secado *m* a espuma
d Schaumtrocknung *f*

47 — fortification

773 foam vacuum drying
Drying of foods from solution
under vacuum, where foam
formation assists in the process by
giving greater surface area
available for drying.
f séchage m de mousse sous vide
e secado m a espuma al vacío
d Schaumsprühtrocknung f

774 foil
f feuille f
e lámina f
d Folie f

775 folic acid
f acide m folique
e ácido m fólico
d Folinsäure f

776 fondant
f fondant m
e fundente m
d Fondant m

777 food additive
f additif m alimentaire
e aditivo m alimenticio
d Lebensmittelzusatz m

778 food adulteration
f falsification f des produits
alimentaires
e adulteración f de alimentos
d Lebensmittelverfälschung f

779 food colour
f colorant m alimentaire
e colorante m alimenticio
d Lebensmittelfarbe f

780 food labelling
f étiquetage m des produits
alimentaires; désignation f
spécifique des produits alimentaires
e descripción f de alimentos
d Lebensmittelkennzeichnung f

781 food poisoning
f intoxication f alimentaire
e envenenamiento m alimenticio
d Nahrungsmittelvergiftung f

782 food requirements
f besoins mpl nutritifs; besoins mpl
alimentaires
e requerimientos mpl alimenticios
d Nahrungsbedarf m

783 foodstuffs
f produits mpl alimentaires
e alimentos mpl
d Lebensmittel npl; Nahrungsmittel
npl

784 food value
f valeur f alimentaire
e valor m alimenticio
d Nährwert m

785 forage crops
f plantes fpl fourragères
e forraje m
d Futterpflanzen fpl

786 foreign matter
f matière f étrangère; substance f
étrangère
e materia f extraña
d Fremdstoff m

* **fore-runnings → 751**

787 fork lift truck
f benne f à fourche; élévateur m à
fourche; lève-palette f
e montacarga f; elevadora f de
horquilla
d Gabelstapler m; Hubstapler m

788 formaldehyde sulphoxylate
f formaldéhyde-sulfoxylate m
e formaldehido-sulfoxilato m
d Formaldehydsulfoxylat n

789 formalin
f formaline f
e formalina f
d Formalin n

790 formic acid
f acide m formique
e ácido m fórmico
d Ameisensäure f

* **fortification → 674**

791 **fortified**
f enrichi
e fortificado
d angereichert

792 **fortify** v
f fortifier
e fortificar
d verstärken

793 **fractional crystallization**
f cristallisation f fractionnée
e cristalización f fraccionada
d Umkristallisation f

794 **fractional distillation**
f distillation f fractionnée
e destilación f fraccionada
d fraktionierte Destillation f

795 **free radical**
f radical m libre
e radical m libre
d freies Radikal n

* **freeze dehydration** → 796

796 **freeze drying; freeze dehydration;
lyophilisation**
f lyophilisation f
e liofilización f
d Gefriertrocknung f; Lyophilisieren
n

797 **freezer**
f congélateur m
e congelador m
d Gefrieranlage f

798 **freezer burn**
f brulûre f de congélation
e quemadura f por frío
d Gefrierbrand m

799 **freezing point**
f point m de congélation
e punto m de congelación
d Gefrierpunkt m

* **French dressing** → 1597

800 **friability**
f friabilité f
e friabilidad f
d Brüchigkeit f

801 **fructose; laevulose**
f fructose f; lévulose m; sucre m de
fruit
e fructosa f; levulosa f
d Fruktose f; Lävulose f; Fruchtzucker m; Schleimzucker m

802 **fruit juice**
f jus m de fruit
e zumo m de frutas
d Fruchtsaft m

803 **fruit pulp**
f purée f de fruits
e pulpa f de frutas
d Fruchtmark n

804 **frying**
f friture f
e frito m; fritura f
d Braten n; Backen n

805 **fudge**
f bonbon m; caramel m moux
e bombón m
d weicher Bonbon m; Praline f

806 **full cream milk**
f lait m entier
e leche f completa
d Vollmilch f

807 **fuller's earth**
f terre f à foulon
e tierra f decolorante
d Fullererde f

808 **fume cupboard**
f hotte f; canal m d'aspiration
e campana f de gasos; conducto m
de ventilación
d Abzug m

809 **fumigant**
f produit m fumigatoire
e fumigante m
d Räuchermittel n

810 **fumigation**
f fumigation f
e fumigación f
d Begasung f

811 fungal amylase
From *Aspergillus orizae.*
  f amylase *f* fongique
  e amilasa *f* de hongos
  d Pilzamylase *f*

812 fungicide
  f fongicide *m*
  e fungicida *m*
  d Fungizid *n*; Schimmelvernichtungs-
    mittel *n*

813 fungistat
  f fongostat *m*
  e fungistato *m*
  d Fungistat *n*

814 furfural
  f furfural *m*
  e furfural *m*
  d Furfural *n*

815 fusel oil
  f huile *f* de fusel
  e aceite *m* de fusel
  d Fuselöl *n*

G

816 galactose
f galactose f
e galactosa f
d Galaktose f

817 galantine
f galantine f
e galantina f
d gewickeltes Kalbsfleisch n in
Gelee; Huhn n in Gelee

818 gallic acid
f acide m gallique
e ácido m gálico
d Gallussäure f

819 gallon
f gallon m
e galón m
d Gallone f

820 garlic
f ail f
e ajo m
d Knoblauch n

821 gas chromatography
f chromatographie f en phase
gazeuse
e cromatografía f de gases
d Gaschromatographie f

822 gassing power
f pouvoir m de formation des gaz
e capacidad f para formar gas
d Gasbildungsvermögen n

**823 gas storage; controlled atmosphere
storage**
f stockage m sous atmosphère
controllée
e almacenamiento m bajo atmósfera
controlada
d Gaslagerung f

824 gel
f gel m
e gel m
d Gel n

825 gelatin
f gélatine f
e gelatina f
d Gelatine f

826 gene
f géne m
e gen m; gene m
d Gen n

827 geraniol
f géraniol m
e geraniol m
d Geraniol n

828 Gerber test
f épreuve f de Gerber
e prueba f de Gerber
d Gerberprobe f

829 germicide
f germicide m
e germicida m
d Keimtötungsmittel n

* giant perch → 1413

830 gibberellic acid
f acide m gibbérellique
e ácido m giberélico
d Gibberellinsäure f

831 ginger
Zingiber officinale.
f gingembre m
e ginabra f
d Ingwer m

832 glacial acetic acid
f acide m acétique cristallisable
e ácido m acético glacial
d Eisessig m

* gland → 1824

833 Glauber's salt
f sel m de Glauber
e sal f de Glauber
d Glaubersalz n

834 glaze v
f glacer
e glasear
d glasieren

835 glazing
f glace f
e glasé m
d Glasur f; Zuckerguss m

836 gliadin
f gliadine f
e gliadina f
d Gliadin n

837 globulin
f globuline f
e globulina f
d Globulin n

838 gluconic acid
f acide m gluconique
e ácido m glucónico
d Glukonsäure f

839 glucose; dextrose
f glucose f; dextrose f
e glucosa f; dextrosa f
d Glukose f; Dextrose f; Traubenzucker m

840 glucose syrup
f sirop m de glucose
e jarabe m de glucosa
d Stärkesirup m

841 glue
f colle f
e cola f
d Leim m; Klebstoff m; Kleister m

842 glutamic acid
f acide m glutamique
e ácido m glutámico
d Glutaminsäure f

843 glutamine
f glutamine f
e glutamina f
d Glutamin n

844 gluten
f gluten m; phytocolle f
e gluten m
d Gluten n; Glutin n

845 gluten extensibility
f extensibilité f de gluten
e extensibilidad f del gluten
d Kleberdehnbarkeit f

846 glutenin
f gluténine f
e glutenina f
d Glutenin n

847 glyceride
f glycéride m
e glicérido m
d Glyzerid n

* **glycerin → 848**

848 glycerol; glycerin
f glycérol m; glycérine f
e glicerina f; glicerol m
d Glyzerin n

849 glycerol monostearate
f monostéarate m de glycérine
e monoestearato m de glicerina
d Glyzerinmonostearat n

850 glycerophosphoric acid
f acide m glycérophosphorique
e ácido m glicerofosfórico
d Glyzerinphosphorsäure f

* **glyceryl monoacetate → 18**

851 glycine; glycocoll
f glycine f; glycocolle m
e glicina f; glicocola f
d Glyzin n; Glykokoll n

* **glycocoll → 851**

852 glycogen
f glycogène m
e glicógeno m
d Glykogen n

853 glycol(l)ic acid
f acide m glycolique
e ácido m glicólico
d Glykolsäure f

854 glycoside
f glycoside m
e glicósido m
d Glykosid n

* **glycyrrhiza → 1111**

855 goitre
f goitre *m*
e bocio *m*; papera *f*
d Kropf *m*

856 "golden" syrup
f sirop *m* de sucre
e jarabe *m* de azúcar
d Zuckersirup *m*

857 gooseberry
Fruit of *Ribes grossularia.*
f groseille f verte; groseille f à
maquereau
e grosella f espinosa
d Stachelbeere f

858 gossypol
f gossypol *m*
e gosipol *m*
d Gossypol *n*

859 grade *v*
f cribler; tamiser
e calificar; clasificar
d sortieren

860 grade
f degré *m*
e grado *m*
d Güte f; Qualität f; Sorte f

861 graduated pipette
f pipette f graduée
e pipeta f graduada
d Messpipette f

862 grain
f grain *m*
e grano *m*; cereal *m*
d Getreidekorn *n*; Korn *n*

863 graining point
f point *m* de cristallisation; point *m*
de granulation
e punto *m* de cristalización
d Granulierpunkt *m*

864 grain weevil; granary weevil
f charançon *m*; calandre f du grain
e gorgojo *m*
d Kornkäfer *m*; Kornkrebs *m*;
schwarzer Kornwurm *m*

865 gram-equivalent
f gramme-équivalent *m*
e equivalente-gramo *m*
d Grammäquivalent *n*

866 gramicidin
f gramicidine f
e gramicidina f
d Gramicidin *n*

867 gram-molecule
f molécule-gramme *m*
e molécula-gramo *m*
d Grammolekul *n*; Mol *n*

868 gram-negative
f gram-négatif
e gram-negativo
d gram-negativ

869 gram-positive
f gram-positif
e gram-positivo
d gram-positiv

870 granadilla; passion fruit
Fruit of *Passiflora quadrangularis.*
f grenadille f
e granadilla f
d Passionsfrucht f

* **granary weevil** → 864

871 granulated sugar
f sucre *m* cristallisé
e azúcar *m* granulado
d Kristallzucker *m*

872 grape
Fruit of genus *Vitis.*
f grain *m* de raisin; raisin *m*
e uva f
d Weinbeere f; Weintraube f; Traube
f

873 grapefruit
Fruit of *Citrus paradisi.*
f pamplemousse f
e toronja f
d Pampelmuse f

874 grayling
Thymallus thymallus.
f ombre *m*

e umbla *f*
d Asche *f*

875 greasing oil
 f huile *f* lubrifiante
 e aceite *m* lubricante
 d Schmieröl *n*

* **green cod → 1433**

876 greengage
 Green fruit of *Prunus* sp.
 f prune *f* de reine-claude
 e ciruela *f* verdal; claudia *f*
 d Reine-Claude *f*

877 Greenland halibut; black halibut; mock halibut
 Rheinhardtius hippoglossoides.
 f flétan *m* noir
 e mero *m* negro
 d Schwarzer Heilbutt *m*

878 green malt; long malt
 f malt *m* vert
 e malta *f* verde
 d Grünmalz *n*

879 grenadine
 f grenadine *f*
 e granadina *f*
 d Grenadine *f*

880 grey mullet; striped mullet
 Mugil chelo.
 f mulet *m*
 e mújil *m*
 d Meerasche *f*

881 grill *v*
 f griller
 e asar a la parilla
 d grillen; rösten

* **grinding mill → 1231**

882 groats
 f gruau *m* d'avoine
 e grano *m* de avena
 d Hafergrütze *f*

* **groundnut → 1374**

883 grounds; dregs
 f dépôt *m*
 e depósito *m*; sedimento *m*
 d Geläger *n*

884 ground state
 f état *m* normal
 e estado *m* fundamental
 d Grundzustand *m*

885 growth inhibiting factor
 f inhibiteur *m* de croissance
 e inhibidor *m* del crecimiento
 d Wachstumshemmungsfaktor *m*

886 growth promoting substance
 f stimulateur *m* de croissance
 e estimulador *m* del crecimiento
 d Wuchsstoff *m*

887 growth stimulation
 f accélération *f* de la croissance
 e estimulación *f* del crecimiento
 d Wachstumsförderung *f*; Wachstums-beschleunigung *f*

888 guaiac resin
 f résine *f* de guaïac
 e goma *f* de guayaco
 d Guajakharz *n*

889 guanine
 f guanine *f*
 e guanina *f*
 d Guanin *n*

890 guano
 f guano *m*
 e guano *m*
 d Guano *m*

891 guanosine
 f guanosine *f*
 e guanosina *f*
 d Guanosin *n*

892 guar gum
 f gomme *f* guar
 e goma *f* guar
 d Guarangummi *n*

893 guava
 Fruit of *Psidium guajava.*
 f goyave *f*

e guayaba *f*
d Guajabe *f*

894 gum
f gomme *f*
e goma *f*
d Gummi *n*

895 gum arabic
f gomme *f* arabique
e goma *f* arábica
d Gummiarabikum *n*

896 gum tragacanth; tragacanth gum
Gum from *Astragalus*.
f gomme *f* adragante; gomme *f*
   adraganthe
e goma *f* de adraganto; goma *f* de
   tragacanto
d Tragantgummi *n*

897 gurnard; gurnet
Trigla hirundo.
f grondin *m*
e trigla *f*
d Knurrhahn *m*

* **gurnet → 897**

* **gustation → 1887**

898 Gutzeit test
f épreuve *f* de Gutzeit
e prueba *f* de Gutzeit
d Gutzeitprobe *f*; Gutzeittest *n*

899 gyratory crusher
f broyeur *m* giratoire; concasseur *m*
   giratoire
e quebrantadora *f* giratoria
d Kreiselbrecher *m*; Glockenmühle *f*

H

900 haddock
Melanogrammus aeglefinus.
f aiglefin *m*; églefin *m*; aigrefin *m*
e besugo *m*; róbalo *m*
d Schellfisch *m*

901 haematin
f hématine *f*
e hematina *f*
d Hämatin *n*

902 haematoxylin
f hématoxyline *f*
e hematoxilina *f*
d Hämatoxylin *n*

903 haemoglobin
f hémoglobine *f*
e hemaglobina *f*
d Hämoglobin *n*

* **hairs** → 744

904 hake
Merluccius sp.
f merlu *m*; merlus *m*; merluche *f*
e merlango *m*; merluza *f*
d Hechtdorsch *m*; Seehecht *m*; Meerhecht *m*

905 halibut
Hippoglossus.
f flétan *m*
e mero *m*
d Heilbutt *m*

906 halibut liver oil
f huile *f* de foie de flétan
e aceite *m* de higado de mero
d Heilbuttlebertran *m*

907 halite
f halite *f*
e halita *f*
d Halit *m*; Steinsalz *n*

908 ham
f jambon *m*
e jamón *m*
d Schinken *m*

909 hammer mill
f broyeur *m* à marteaux
e triturador *m* de martillos
d Hammermühle *f*

910 handwheel
f volant *m*
e volante *m*
d Handrad *n*

911 hardened fat; hydrogenated fat
f graisse *f* durcie; graisse *f*
hydrogénée
e grasa *f* endurecida; grasa *f*
hidrogenada
d gehärtetes Fett *n*

912 hardness
f dureté *f*
e dureza *f*
d Härte *f*

* **hard roe** → 1568

913 hard wheat; durum wheat
f froment *m* vitreux; blé *m* vitreux;
blé *m* dur
e trigo *m* duro
d Hartweizen *m*; Durumweizen *m*

914 hare
f lièvre *m*
e liebre *f*
d Hase *m*

915 haricot bean
Phaseolus vulgaris.
f haricot *m*
e judía *f* verde
d Speckbohne *f*; Fleischbohne *f*

916 harvest
f moisson *f*
e cosecha *f*
d Ernte *f*

917 head space
f espace *m* de tête
e espacio *m* vacío
d Kopfraum *m*

918 heat exchanger
f échangeur *m* de chaleur
e intercambiador *m* de calor;

termointercambiador *m*; termopermutador *m*
d Wärmeaustauscher *m*

919 heat of formation
f chaleur f de formation
e calor *m* de formación
d Bildungswärme f

920 heat of solution
f chaleur f de dissolution
e calor *m* de solución
d Lösungswärme f; Auflösungswärme f

921 hedonic scale
f échelle f hédonique
e escala f hedónica
d hedonische Skala f

922 hemicellulose
f hémicellulose f
e hemicelulosa f
d Hemizellulose f

923 hemlock bark
Bark from *Tsuga canadensis.*
f écorce f de sapin-ciguë
e corteza f de abeto
d Hemlockrinde f

924 hemp
f chanvre *m*
e cáñamo *m*
d Hanf *m*

925 heparin
f héparine f
e heparina f
d Heparin *n*

926 heptachlor
f heptachlore *m*
e heptacloro *m*
d Heptachlor *n*

927 herb
f herbe f
e hierba f
d Kraut *n*

928 herbal extract
f extrait *m* d'herbes aromatiques
e extracto *m* de hierbas
d Kräuter-Extrakt *m*

* **herbicide** → 2041

929 herring
Clupea harengus.
f hareng *m*
e arenque *m*
d Hering *m*

930 hesperidin
f hespéridine f
e hesperidina f
d Hesperidin *n*

931 heterocyclic
f hétérocyclique
e heterocíclico
d heterozyklisch

932 hexachlorocyclohexane
f hexachlorocyclohexane *m*
e hexaclorociclohexano *m*
d Hexaclorzyklohexan *n*

933 hexaclorobenzene
f hexachlorobenzène *m*
e hexaclorobenceno *m*
d Hexaclorbenzol *n*

934 hexaethyl tetraphosphate
f tétraphosphate *m* d'hexaéthyle
e tetrafosfato *m* de hexaetilo
d Hexaäthyltetraphosphat *n*

935 hexose
f hexose *m*
e hexosa f
d Hexose f

* **high-frequency cooking** → 1222

936 high-speed mixing
f pétrissage *m* rapide; pétrissage *m* intensifié
e mezclado *m* a alta velocidad
d Schnellkneten *n*; Intensivkneten *n*

937 high temperature short time; H.T.S.T.
Refers to the high temperature short time process for pasteurization of liquids. See also U.H.T.
f pasteurisation f H.T.S.T.
e alta temperatura f por corto tiempo
d H.T.S.T. Erhitzung f

938 hip
Fruit of *Rosa canina.*
f cynorrhodon *m*
e fruto *m* del rosal
d Hagebutte *f*

939 histamine
f histamine *f*
e histamina *f*
d Histamin *n*

940 histidine
f histidine *f*
e histidina *f*
d Histidin *n*

941 hock
Joint of hind leg in quadrupeds.
f jarret *m*
e tobillo *m*
d Sprunggelenk *n*

942 hock
Rhine wine.
f vin *m* blanc du Rhin
e vino *m* blanco del Rhin
d Rheinwein *m*

943 hogget
f agnelet *m* d'un an
e borrego *m*
d einjähriges Schaf *n*

944 homogenization
f homogénéisation *f*
e homogenización *f*
d Homogenisierung *f*

945 honey
f miel *m*
e miel *f*
d Honig *m*

946 hop
Humulus lupulus.
f houblon *m*
e lúpulo *m*
d Hopfen *m*

947 hormone
f hormone *f*
e hormona *f*
d Hormon *n*

948 horseradish
Armoracia lapathifolia.
f raifort *m*
e rábano *m* silvestre
d Meerrettich *m*

* H.T.S.T. → 937

949 humectant
f humectant *m*
e humectante *m*
d Benetzungsmittel *n*; Anfeuchter *m*

950 humidity
f humidité *f*
e humedad *f*
d Feuchtigkeit *f*

951 humus
f humus *m*
e humus *m*
d Humus *m*

952 husk
f cosse *f*; enveloppe *f*
e cáscara *f*; váina *f*
d Hülse *f*; Schrote *f*

953 hyaluronidase
f hyaluronidase *f*
e hialuronidasa *f*
d Hyaluronidase *f*

954 hydatid
Taenia echinococcus.
f hydatide *f*
e hidátide *f*
d Blasenwurm *m*

955 hydnocarpic acid
f acide *m* hydnocarpique
e ácido *m* hidnocárpico
d Hydnokarpussäure *f*

956 hydration
f hydratation *f*
e hidratación *f*
d Hydration *f*

957 hydraulic lime
f chaux *f* hydraulique
e cal *f* hidráulica
d Wasserkalk *m*

958 hydrazone
f hydrazone f
e hidrazona f
d Hydrazon n

959 hydrocellulose
f hydrocellulose f
e hidrocelulosa f
d Hydrozellulose f

* **hydrogenated fat** → 911

960 hydrogenated oil
f huile f hydrogénée
e aceite m hidrogenado
d gehärtetes Öl n

961 hydrogenation
f hydrogénation f
e hidrogenación f
d Hydrierung f; Wasserstoffanlagerung f

962 hydrogenator
f appareil m d'hydrogénation
e tanque m hidrogenador
d Härtungskessel m

963 hydrogen sulphide
f hydrogène m sulfuré
e sulfuro m de hidrógeno
d Schwefelwasserstoff m

964 hydrolysis
f hydrolyse f
e hidrólisis f
d Hydrolyse f

965 hydrometer
f hydromètre m; aréomètre m
e hidrómetro m; areómetro m
d Hydrometer n; Areometer n;
Senkwaage f

966 hydrophilic
f hydrophile
e hidrófilo
d hydrophil

967 hydrophobic
f hydrophobe
e hidrófobo
d hydrophob

968 hydrostatic cooker
f autoclave m hydrostatique
e autoclave m hidrostático
d hydrostatischer Autoklav m

969 hydroxymercurichlorophenol
f hydroxymercurichlorophénol m
e hidroximercuriclorofenol m
d Hydroxymerkurichlorophenol n

970 hydroxymercuricresol
f hydroxymercuricrésol m
e hidroximercuricresol m
d Hydroxymerkurikresol n

971 hygiene
f hygiène f
e higiene f
d Gesundheitspflege f; Hygiene f;
Hygenik f

972 hygrometer
f hygromètre m
e higrómetro m
d Hygrometer n

973 hygroscopic
f hygroscopique
e higroscópico
d wasseraufnehmend; hygroskopisch

974 hypochlorous acid
f acide m hypochloreux
e ácido m hipocloroso
d unterchlorige Säure f; Unterchlorsäure f

I

975 ice cream
f glace f; crème f glacée
e helado m
d Speiseeis n; Sahneeis n; Eiskrem f

976 icing sugar
f sucre m glace
e azúcar m de nevar
d Staubzucker m; Puderzucker m

977 immiscible
f non-miscible
e inmiscible
d unmischbar

978 immunity
f immunité f
e inmunidad f
d Immunität f

979 impregnate v
f imprégner
e impregnar
d imprägnieren

980 improver
f améliorant m
e mejorador m
d Verbesserungsmittel n

981 in-can immersion cooler
f refroidisseur-plongeur m
e enfriador m por inmersión
d Kanneneintauch-Kühler m

* **Indian corn → 1157**

982 indicator
f indicateur m
e indicador m
d Indikator m

983 indolebutyric acid
f acide m indolbutyrique
e ácido m indolbutírico
d Indolbuttersäure f

984 induction heating
f chauffage m par induction
e calentamiento m por inducción
d induktive Heizung f

985 induction period
f période f d'induction
e período m de inducción
d Induktionsperiode f

* **industrial alcohol → 576**

986 inedible
f inconsommable
e incomestible
d ungeniessbar; verdorben

987 inert
f inerte
e inerte
d inert; träge

988 infuse v
f infuser
e poner en infusión
d aufgiessen; auslaugen

989 infusion
f infusion f
e infusión f
d Aufguss m; Infusion f

990 ingredient
f ingrédient m
e ingrediente m
d Bestandteil m; Zutat f

991 inhibitor
f inhibiteur m
e inhibidor m
d Inhibitor m

992 initiator
f initiateur m
e iniciador m
d Initiator m; Reaktionseinleiter m

* **ink fish → 547**

993 inoculate v
f inoculer; ensemencer
e inocular
d impfen; abimpfen; beimpfen;
   okulieren

994 inosine
f inosine f
e inosina f
d Inosin n

995 inositol
  f inositol *m*
  e inositol *m*
  d Inositol *n*; Muskelzucker *m*

996 insecticide
  f insecticide *m*
  e insecticida *m*
  d Insektizid *m*; Insektenbekämpfungs-
    mittel *n*

997 instantize *v*
  f instantanéiser
  e instantaneizar
  d instantisieren

998 instrumentation
  f instrumentation *f*
  e instrumentación *f*
  d Instrumentierung *f*

999 insulin
  f insuline *f*
  e insulina *f*
  d Insulin *n*

1000 interesterification
  f interestérification *f*
  e interesterificación *f*
  d Umesterung *f*

1001 interfacial tension
  f tension *f* interfaciale
  e tensión *f* interfacial
  d Grenzflächenspannung *f*

1002 inulin
  Polysaccharide from *Dahlia* and
  Helianthus tuberosus.
  f inuline *f*
  e inulina *f*
  d Inulin *n*

1003 inversion
  f inversion *f*
  e inversión *f*
  d Inversion *f*; Umkehrung *f*

1004 invertase; sucrase; saccharase
  f invertase *f*
  e invertasa *f*
  d Invertase *f*

1005 invert sugar
  f sucre *m* inverti
  e azúcar *m* invertido
  d Invertzucker *m*

1006 iodine number; iodine value
  f indice *m* d'iode
  e índice *m* de yodo
  d Jodzahl *f*

  * iodine value → 1006

1007 ion exchange
  f échange *f* d'ions
  e intercambio *m* de iones
  d Ionenaustausch *m*

1008 ion exchange resin
  f résine *f* à échanges d'ions
  e resina *f* intercambiadora de iones
  d Ionenaustauschharz *n*

1009 ionic strength
  f force *f* ionique
  e fuerza *f* iónica
  d Ionenstärke *f*

1010 ionization
  f ionisation *f*
  e ionización *f*
  d Ionisation *f*; Ionenspaltung *f*;
    Ionisierung *f*

1011 ionone
  f ionone *f*
  e ionona *f*
  d Jonon *n*

1012 ipecacuanha
  From root of *Cephaelis*
  ipecacuanha.
  f ipécacuana *m*
  e ipecacuana *f*
  d Ipekakuanha *n*; Brechwurzel *f*

  * Irish moss → 376

1013 irradiation
  f irradiation *f*
  e irradiación *f*
  d Bestrahlung *f*; Irradiation *f*

1014 irreversible reaction
  f réaction *f* irréversible

  e reacción *f* irreversible
  d irreversible Reaktion *f*

1015 isinglass; finings; fish-glue
  f colle *f* de poisson
  e colapez *f*; cola *f* de pescado
  d Fischleim *m*

1016 isoelectric point
  f point *m* isoélectrique
  e punto *m* isoeléctrico
  d isoelektrischer Punkt *m*

1017 isoeugenol
  f isoeugénol *m*
  e isoeugenol *m*
  d Isoeugenol *n*

1018 isoleucine
  f isoleucine *f*
  e isoleucina *f*
  d Isoleucin *n*

1019 isopropyl alcohol
  f alcool *m* isopropylique
  e alcohol *m* isopropílico
  d Isopropylalkohol *m*

1020 isosafrole
  f isosafrol *m*
  e isosafrol *m*
  d Isosafrol *n*

1021 isothiocyanate
  f isothiocyanate *m*
  e isotiocianato *m*
  d Isothiocyanat *n*

1022 isovaleric acid
  f acide *m* iso-valérianique
  e ácido *m* isovalérico
  d Isovaleriansäure *f*

J

1023 jam
f confiture f
e mermelada f
d Marmelade f; Konfitüre f

* **Japanese medlar** → 1138

1024 jasmine oil
Oil from *Jasminum grandiflorum.*
f essence f de jasmin
e aceite m de jazmín
d Jasminöl n

1025 Javelle water; eau de Javelle
f eau f de Javel
e agua f de Javel
d Eau n de Javelle; Javellesche
Lauge f

1026 jelly
f gelée f
e gelatina f
d Gelee n; Sulze f (bei Fleisch)

1027 Jerusalem artichoke
Tuber of *Helianthus tuberosus.*
f topinambour m
e cotufa f; pataca f; aquaturma f
d Topinambur f; Batate f

1028 John Dory; doree
Zeus faber.
f Saint Pierre m
e fabro m
d Petersfisch m

1029 joule
Unit of energy, now being used
instead of calories.
f joule m
e joule m
d Joule n

1030 juice
f jus m; suc m
e zumo m; jugo m
d Saft m

1031 juniper oil
Oil from *Juniperus communis.*

f essence f de genièvre
e aceite m de enebro
d Wachholderöl n

1032 junket
f lait m emprésuré
e cuajada f; requesón m
d Dickmilch f

1033 jute
Fibres from *Corchorus* sp.
f jute m
e yute m
d Jute f

K

* kail → 1034

1034 kale; kail
f chou *m* frisé
e bretón *m*
d Grünkohl *m*

1035 kaolin; China clay
f kaolin *m*; terre *f* à porcelaine
e caolín *m*; arcilla *f*
d Kaolin *n*; Porzellanerde *f*

1036 karaya gum
Gum from *Sterculia* sp.
f gomme *f* de karaya
e goma *f* de karaya
d Karayagummi *n*

1037 Karl Fischer reagent
f réactif *m* de Karl Fischer
e reactivo *m* de Karl Fischer
d Karl Fischer Reagens *n*

1038 kebab
f kebâb *m*
e pinchos *mpl*; kebab *m*
d Kebab *n*

1039 kelp
Laminaria and *Fucus* seaweeds.
f varec *m*
e quelpo *m*
d Kelp *n*

1040 keratin
f kératine *f*
e queratina *f*
d Keratin *n*; Hornstoff *m*

1041 kerosene; kerosine
f kérosène *m*; pétrole *m* lampant
e keroseno *m*; petróleo *m* de
lámpara
d Kerosin *n*; Leuchtpetroleum *n*

* kerosine → 1041

1042 ketone
f cétone *f*
e cetona *f*
d Keton *n*

1043 ketose
f cétose *m*
e cetosa *f*
d Ketose *f*

1044 kettle
f marmite *f*; bouilleur *m*
e marmita *f*; caldereta *f*
d Kochkessel *m*; Kessel *m*

1045 Keyes process
f procédé *m* Keyes
e proceso *m* Keyes
d Keyesches Verfahren *n*

1046 kibbler
f égrugeoir *m*
e triturador *m*
d Zerkleinerungsmaschine *f*

1047 kid
f chevreau *m*
e cabrito *m*
d Zicklein *n*; Ziegenhamm *n*

1048 kidney
f rognon *m*
e riñón *m*
d Niere *f*

**1049 kieselguhr; diatomaceous earth;
diatomite**
f kieselgur *m*; terre *f* d'infusoires
e kieselgur *m*; tierra *f* de diatomas
d Kieselgur *f*; Diatomenerde *f*;
Infusorienerde *f*

1050 kilderkin
Cask holding 18 gallons.
f barril *m*
e barrilito *m*
d Fässchen *n*

1051 kiln
f touraille *f*; séchoir *m*
e tostador *m*; secadero *m*
d Darre *f*; Trockner *m*

1052 kiln *v*; kiln-dry *v*
To dry in a kiln.
f dessécher; sécher
e desecar; secar
d ausdarren; darren

* kiln-dry *v* → 1052

1053 kiln malt
f malt *m* touraillé
e malta *f* tostada
d Darrmalz *n*

1054 kipper
f hareng *m* salé et fumé
e arenque *m* ahumado
d Räucherhering *m*

1055 Kjeldahl flask
f flacon *m* de Kjeldahl
e frasco *m* de Kjeldahl
d Kjeldahlkolben *m*

1056 Kjeldahl's method
f méthode *f* de Kjeldahl
e método *m* de Kjeldahl
d Kjeldahlsche Methode *f*

1057 knead v
f malaxer; pétrisser
e amasar
d kneten; durcharbeiten

1058 kneading
f pétrissage *m*; malaxage *m*
e amasadura *f*
d Kneten *n*

* **koji** → 1872

1059 kosher
f cawcher
e kosher
d koscher

1060 Kreis test
f épreuve *f* de Kreis
e prueba *f* de Kreis
d Kreisprobe *f*

* **kumquat** → 534

L

1061 labile
 f labile
 e lábil; inestable
 d labil

1062 lachrymatory
 f lacrymogène
 e lacrimógeno
 d tränenerregend

1063 lacquer
 f laque *m*
 e laca *f*
 d Lack *m*

1064 lactalbumin
 f lactalbumine *f*
 e lactalbúmina *f*
 d Laktalbumin *n*

1065 lactam
 f lactame *m*
 e lactama *f*
 d Laktam *n*

1066 lactase
 f lactase *f*
 e lactasa *f*
 d Laktase *f*

1067 lactate
 f lactate *m*
 e lactato *m*
 d Laktat *n*; milchsaures Salz *n*

 * **lacteous** → 1230

1068 lactic acid
 f acide *m* lactique
 e ácido *m* láctico
 d Milchsäure *f*

1069 lactobutyrometer
 f lactobutyromètre *m*
 e lactobutirómetro *m*
 d Laktobutyrometer *n*

 * **lactoflavin** → 2011

1070 lactone
 f lactone *m*
 e lactona *f*
 d Lakton *n*

1071 lactose; milk sugar
 f lactose *m*; sucre *m* de lait
 e lactosa *f*
 d Laktose *f*; Milchzucker *m*

1072 laevorotatory
 f lévogyre
 e levorrotatorio; levógiro
 d linksdrehend

 * **laevulose** → 801

1073 lag *v*
 f revêtir
 e revestir
 d ummanteln

1074 lager beer
 f bière *f* de fermentation basse
 e cerveza *f* de fermentación baja
 d Lagerbier *n*

1075 lamb
 f agneau *m*
 e cordero *m*
 d Lamm *n*

1076 lamella; lamina
 f lamelle *f*
 e laminilla *f*; lámina *f*
 d Lamelle *f*; Blättchen *n*

 * **lamina** → 1076

1077 laminar flow
 f flux *m* laminaire
 e flujo *m* laminar
 d laminare Strömung *f*

1078 laminate
 f laminée *f*
 e laminado *m*
 d Folie *f*; Laminate *f*

1079 laminate *v*
 f conrecoller; doubler; cacheter;
    laminer
 e laminar
 d kaschieren

1080 **lanceolate**
  f lancéolé
  e lanceolado
  d lanzenförmig

1081 **lanolin; wool fat**
  f lanoléine f; lanoline f; graisse f de laine
  e lanolina f
  d Lanolin n; Wollfett n

1082 **lanosterol**
  f lanostérol m
  e lanosterol m
  d Lanosterin n

1083 **lap sealing**
  f fermeture f par recouvrement
  e sellado m por superposición de solapas
  d Überlappsiegeln n

1084 **lap weld**
  f soudure f à recouvrement
  e soldadura f de recubrimiento; soldadura f a solape
  d Überlappungsschweissung f

1085 **lard**
  f saindoux m; panne f
  e manteca f; sain m
  d Schweine-Schmalz n

1086 **lascar; sand sole**
  Pegusa lascaris.
  f sole f
  e lenguado m
  d Sandzunge f

1087 **latent heat**
  f chaleur f latente
  e calor m latente
  d latente Wärme f; bleibende Wärme f

1088 **latex**
  Fluid obtained from *Hevea brasiliensis.*
  f latex m
  e látex m
  d Latex m; Kautchukmilch f; Milchsaft m

1089 **lather** v
  f savonner
  e producir espuma
  d schäumen

1090 **lather booster**
  f exalteur m de mousse
  e agente m de mejoración de espuma
  d Schaumverbesserer m

  * **laughing gas** → 1292

1091 **laurel; bay tree; sweet bay**
  Laurus nobilis.
  f laurier m
  e laurel m
  d Lorbeer n

1092 **lauric acid**
  f acide m laurique
  e ácido m láurico
  d Laurinsäure f

1093 **lauryl alcohol**
  f alcool m laurique
  e alcohol m láurico
  d Laurylalkohol m

1094 **lavender**
  Lavandula officinalis.
  f lavende f
  e espliego m; lavanda f
  d Lavendel f

  * **lavender spike** → 1766

1095 **laver**
  f laitue f de mer
  e ova f
  d Meerlattich m

1096 **leaching**
  f lessivage m
  e lixiviación f
  d Auslaugen n; Laugung f

1097 **leak**
  f fuite f
  e grieta f
  d Leck n

1098 **leaven**
  f levain m
  e hez m
  d Hefe f; Sauerteig m

1099 lecithin
f lécithine f
e lecitina f
d Lecithin n

1100 leek
Allium porrum.
f poireau m
e puerro m
d Lauch m; Porree m

1101 lemon
Fruit of *Citrus limon.*
f citron m
e limón m
d Zitrone f

1102 lemon-grass oil
f essence f de lemongrass
e esencia f de lemongras
d Lemongrasöl n; Grasöl n; Zitronengrasöl n

1103 lemon oil
f essence f de citron
e esencia f de limón
d Zitronenöl n

1104 lemon sole
Microstomus.
f limande f
e lenguado m
d Limande f

1105 lentil
Seed of *Lens esculenta.*
f lentille f
e lenteja f
d Linse f

1106 lethal dose
f dose f mortelle
e dosis f letal
d tödliche Dosis f

1107 lettuce
Lactuca sativa.
f laitue f
e lechuga f
d Lattich m; Kopfsalat m

1108 leucine
f leucine f
e leucina f
d Leuzin n

1109 liberate v
f libérer
e liberar
d befreien

1110 lichen
f lichen m
e liquen m
d Flechte f

1111 licorice; liquorice; glycyrrhiza
Extract of *Glycyrrhiza glabra.*
f réglisse f
e regaliz m; orozuz m
d Lakritze f; Süssholz n

1112 Liebig condenser
f condensateur m Liebig
e condensador m de Liebig
d Liebigkühler m

1113 lights
Lungs of slaughtered cattle, pigs or
sheep.
f mou m
e bofes mpl
d Lungen fpl

1114 lignin
f lignine f
e lignina f
d Lignin n; Holzfaserstoff m

1115 lime
Fruit of *Citrus aurantifolia.*
f limon m
e lima f
d Limone f

1116 lime defecation
Clarification of juice with milk of
lime.
f défécation f au lait de chaux
e clarificación f con lechada de cal
d nasse Scheidung f

1117 limpet
Patella caerulea.
f patelle f; bernique f
e lapa f
d Napfschnecke f

1118 linoleic acid
f acide m linoléique

e ácido m linoléico
d Linolsäure f

1119 linolein
f linoléine f
e linoleína f
d Linolein n

1120 linolenic acid
f acide m linolénique
e ácido m linolénico
d Linolensäure f

1121 linseed
Seed of *Linum usitatissimum.*
f lin m; graine f de lin
e linaza f
d Leinsamen m; Leinsaat f

1122 linseed oil
f huile f de lin
e aceite m de linaza
d Leinöl n; Baumöl n

1123 linters
f linters mpl
e linteres mpl; borra f de algodón
d Linters npl

1124 Lintner value
f valeur f de Lintner
e valor m de Lintner
d Lintnerwert m

1125 lipase
f lipase f
e lipasa f
d Lipase f

1126 lipolysis
f lipolyse f
e lipólisis f
d Lipolyse f; Fettspaltung f

* **lipoxydase → 1127**

1127 lipoxygenase; lipoxydase
f lipoxygenase f; lipoxydase f
e lipoxigenasa f; lipoxidasa f
d Lipoxygenase f; Lipoxydase f

1128 liquefaction
f liquéfaction f
e licuefacción f
d Verflüssigung f

1129 liquid-liquid extraction
f extraction f par partage
e extracción f por partición
d Flüssig-Flüssig-Extraktion f

1130 liquor
f eau f de brassage
e agua f de cocimiento; licor m
d Brauwasser n

* **liquorice → 1111**

1131 litmus
f tournesol m
e tornasol m
d Lackmus m

1132 litre
f litre m
e litro m
d Liter n

1133 liver
f foie m
e hígado m
d Leber f

1134 loaf sugar
f sucre m mélis
e azúcar m de pilón
d Melis m; Meliszucker m

1135 loaf volume
f rendement m en volume
e volumen m del pan
d Volumenausbeute f

1136 lobster
Homarus sp.
f homard m
e langosta f de mar
d Hummel m

* **locust bean → 373**

1137 loganberry
Rubus ursinus loganobaccus.
f ronce-framboise f
e mora f
d Himbeere-Brombeere-Kreuzung f

* **long malt → 878**

1138 loquat; Japanese medlar
Fruit of *Eriobotrya japonica.*
f nèfle *f*
e níspola *f*
d japanische Mispel *f*

1139 Lovibond tintometer
f colorimètre *m* de Lovibond
e tintómetro *m* de Lovibond
d Lovibond-Kolorimeter *n*

1140 low calorie
f pauvre en calories
e bajo contenido *m* calorífico
d kalorienarm

1141 lumen
f lumen *m*
e lumen *m*
d Lumen *n*

1142 lutein
f lutéine *f*
e luteína *f*
d Lutein *n*

1143 lye
f lessive *f*
e lejía *f*
d Lauge *f*

* **lyophilisation → 796**

1144 lysine
f lysine *f*
e lisina *f*
d Lysin *n*

1145 lysosome
f lysosome *f*
e lisosoma *f*
d Lysosom *n*

1146 lysozyme
f lysozime *m*
e lisozima *f*
d Lysozym *n*

* **lythe → 1433**

M

1147 macaroni
f macaroni *m*
e macarrones *mpl*
d Makkaroni *mpl*

1148 mace
Outer covering of *Myristica fragrans.*
f macis *m*
e macia *f*
d Muskatblüte *f*

1149 macedoine
f macédoine *f*
e ensalada *f*; ensalada *f* de frutas
d mazedoine *f*

1150 mace oil
f huile *f* de muscade
e aceite *m* de macis
d Mazisöl *n*; Muskatblütenöl *n*

1151 macerate *v*
f macérer
e macerar
d einweichen

1152 mackerel
Scomber scombrus.
f maquereau *m*
e escombro *m*
d Makrele *f*

* **macromolecular dispersion** → **471**

1153 macromolecule
f macromolécule *f*
e macromolécula *f*
d Makromolekül *n*

1154 macroscopic
f macroscopique
e macroscópico
d makroskopisch

1155 maggot
f ver *m*; asticot *m*; lubie *f*
e cresa *f*
d Made *f*

1156 Maillard reaction; non-enzymic browning
f réaction *f* de Maillard
e oscurecimiento *m* no enzimático
d Amino-Karbonyl-Bräunung *f*; Bräunungsreaktion *f*

1157 maize; Indian corn
Seed of *Zea mays.*
f maïs *m*; blé *m* de Turkie
e maíz *m*
d Mais *m*

1158 make-up water
f eau *f* d'appoint
e agua *f* de relleno; agua *f* adicional
d Zusatzwasser *n*

1159 malathion
f malathion *m*
e malatión *m*
d Malathion *n*

1160 maleic hydrazide
f hydrazide *f* maléique
e hidracida *f* del ácido maléico
d Maleinsäurehydrazid *n*

1161 malic acid
f acide *m* malique
e ácido *m* málico
d Apfelsäure *f*

1162 malnutrition
f malnutrition *f*; alimentation *f* défectueuse
e malnutrición *f*
d Unterernährung *f*; Fehler-ernährung *f*; falsche Ernährung *f*

1163 malt
f malt *m*
e malta *f*
d Malz *n*

1164 malt *v*
f malter
e maltear
d mälzen

1165 maltase
f maltase *f*
e maltasa *f*
d Maltase *f*

1166 malted milk
 f lait *m* malté
 e leche *f* malteada
 d Malzmilch *f*

1167 malthouse
 f malterie *f*
 e maltería *f*
 d Malzerei *f*

1168 malting barley
 f orge *m* de brasserie
 e cebada *f* de maltear
 d Braugerste *f*

1169 maltose
 f maltose *m*; sucre *m* de malt
 e maltosa *f*
 d Maltose *f*; Malzzucker *m*

1170 malt piece
 f tas *m* de malt
 e pila *f* de malta
 d Malzhaufen *m*

1171 mandarin
 Fruit of *Citrus reticulata.*
 f mandarine *f*
 e naranja *f* mandarina
 d Mandarine *f*

1172 mandarin oil
 f essence *f* de mandarine
 e esencia *f* de mandarina
 d Mandarinenöl *n*

1173 manhole
 f trou *m* d'homme; trou *m* de visite
 e agujero *m* de visita; agujero *m* de hombre
 d Mannloch *n*

 * **manioc → 384**

1174 manometer
 f manomètre *m*
 e manómetro *m*
 d Manometer *n*; Druckmesser *m*

1175 manure
 f engrais *m*
 e abono *m* fertilizante
 d Dünger *m*

1176 marc; pomace; spent grains
 f marc *m*; drêche *f*
 e orujo *m*; bagazo *m*
 d Treber *m*; Trester *m*; Malztreber

1177 margarine
 f margarine *f*
 e margarina *f*
 d Margarin *f*; Margarine *f*

1178 marinade
 f marinade *f*
 e escabeche *m*; vinagreta *f*
 d Marinade *f*

1179 marjoram
 Origanum marjorana.
 f marjolaine *f*
 e mejorana *f*; marjorana *f*
 d Majoran *m*

1180 marmalade
 f confiture *f* d'oranges
 e mermelada *f*
 d Orangenmarmelade *f*; Orangenkonfitüre *f*

1181 marrow
 Fruit of *Cucurbita* sp.
 f courge *f* à la moelle
 e cucúrbita *f* ovífera
 d Markkürbis *m*

1182 marzipan
 f massepain *m*
 e mazapán *m*
 d Marzipan *n*

1183 mash
 f maische *m*; trempe *f*
 e mosto *m*
 d Maische *f*

1184 masher
 f hydrateur *m*
 e cuba *f* mezcladora; premezclador *m*
 d Maischepfanne *f*

1185 mashing
 f brassage *m*
 e braceaje *m*
 d Maischen *n*

1186 **mash tun**
 f cuve-matière f
 e tina f de mezcla; cuba f de mosto
 d Maischbottich m

1187 **mass production**
 f fabrication f en série
 e fabricación f en serie
 d Massenproduktion f

1188 **masticate** v
 f mâcher; mastiquer
 e mascar; masticar
 d kauen; zerkleinern

1189 **mastic gum**
 From *Pistacia lentiscus.*
 f gomme f mastic
 e almáciga f
 d Mastix m; Gummi-Mastiche n

1190 **maturation**
 f maturation f
 e maduración f
 d Alterung f; Reifen n

1191 **matzo**
 f matzo m
 e matzo m
 d Matze m

1192 **mayonnaise; salad cream**
 f mayonnaise f
 e mayonesa f; mahonesa f
 d Mayonnaise f; Salatsosse f

1193 **meat**
 f viande f
 e carne f
 d Fleisch n

1194 **meat extract**
 f extrait m de viande
 e extracto m de carne
 d Fleischextrakt m

1195 **meat inspection**
 f inspection f des viandes
 e inspección f de carne
 d Fleischbeschau f

1196 **mechanical press**
 f presse f mécanique
 e prensa f mecánica
 d mechanische Presse f

1197 **medlar**
 Fruit of *Mespilus germanica.*
 f nèfle f
 e níspola f
 d Mispel f

1198 **megrim**
 Lepidorhombus whiff.
 f cardine f
 e jacqueca f
 d Scheefsnut m

1199 **melanin**
 f mélanine f
 e melanina f
 d Melanin n

* **melitriose** → 1200

1200 **mellitose; raffinose; melitriose**
 f mélitose m; raffinose m
 e melitosa f; rafinosa f
 d Melitose f; Raffinose f

1201 **mellorine**
 f mellorine f
 e melorina f
 d Mellorine f

1202 **melon**
 Cucurbiticea fam.
 f melon m
 e melón m
 d Melone f

* **membrane** → 596

1203 **menthol**
 f menthol m
 e mentol m
 d Menthol n

1204 **menthone**
 f menthone f
 e mentona f
 d Menthon n

1205 **mercaptan; thiol**
 f mercaptan m; thioalcool m
 e mercaptano m
 d Merkaptan n; Thioalkohol m

1206 **meringue**
 f méringue f

e merengue *m*
d Meringe *f*

1207 **mesh**
f maille *f*
e malla *f*
d Masche *f*

1208 **mesityl oxide**
f oxyde *m* de mésityle
e óxido *m* de mesitilo
d Mesityloxyd *n*

1209 **mesophilic bacterium**
f bactérie *f* mésophile
e bacteria *f* mesófila
d mesophile Bakterie *f*

1210 **metabolism**
f métabolisme *m*
e metabolismo *m*
d Stoffwechsel *m*

1211 **metal detector**
f détecteur *m* de métal
e detector *m* de metal
d Metalldetektor *m*

1212 **metallic**
f métallique
e metálico
d metallisch

1213 **methionine**
f méthionine *f*
e metionina *f*
d Methionin *n*

1214 **methylated spirit**
f alcool *m* dénaturé
e alcohol *m* metilado
d denaturierter Spiritus *m*

1215 **methyl cinnamate**
f cinnamate *m* de méthyle
e cinamato *m* de metilo
d Methylcinnamat *n*

1216 **methylene blue**
f bleu *m* de méthylène
e azul *m* de metileno
d Methylenblau *n*

1217 **methyl red**
f rouge *m* de méthyle
e rojo *m* de metilo
d Methylrot *n*

1218 **methylstyrene**
f méthylstyrolène *m*
e metilestireno *m*
d Methylstyrol *n*

1219 **micelle**
f micelle *f*
e micela *f*
d Mizelle *f*

1220 **micron**
f micron *m*
e micrón *m*
d Mikron *n*

1221 **microscopic**
f microscopique
e microscópico
d mikroskopisch

1222 **microwave cooking; high-frequency
cooking**
f cuisson *f* à micro-ondes; cuisson *f*
à haute fréquence
e cocinado *m* por microondas
d Mikrowellenkochen *n*

1223 **middlings**
f recoupe *f*
e salvado *m*
d Mittelmehl *n*

1224 **middlings bran**
f recoupettes *fpl*
e salvado *m*; alfrecho *m*
d Griesskleie *f*

1225 **migration**
f migration *f*
e migración *f*
d Migration *f*; Wanderung *f*;
Umsetzung *f*

1226 **mild**
f doux
e suave
d mild

1227 **mildew**
Erysiphe graminis.
f mildiou *m*
e mildiu *m*
d Mehltau *m*

1228 **milk**
f lait *m*
e leche *f*
d Milch *f*

* **milk sugar** → **1071**

1229 **milk texture**
f texture *f* de lait
e consistencia *f* de leche
d Gefüge *n* der Milch

1230 **milky; lacteous**
f laiteux
e lechozo; lácteo
d milchig

1231 **mill; grinding mill**
f moulin *m*; broyeur *m*
e molino *m*
d Mühle *f*

1232 **millet**
Panicum miliaceum.
f millet *m*; mil *m*; melica *m*;
mélique *f*
e mijo *m*
d Hirse *f*

1233 **milling**
f meunerie *f*; minoterie *f*
e molienda *f*
d Mahlen *n*

1234 **milt; soft roe**
Male gonads of fish.
f laitance *f*; laite *f*
e lecha *f*; lechaza *f*
d Milch *f*

* **milt** → **1772**

1235 **mincing machine**
f hachoir *m*
e máquina *f* picadora de carne
d Wolf *m*; Fleischwolf *m*

1236 **mint**
Mentha sp.
f menthe *f*
e menta *f*
d Minze *f*

1237 **mix** *v*; **blend** *v*
f mélanger; mêler; malaxer
e mezclar; mixturar; amasar
d mischen; vermengen; zusammenrühren

1238 **mixer; blender**
f mélangeur *m*
e mezclador *m*
d Mischer *m*

1239 **mixture**
f mélange *m*
e mezcla *f*
d Gemisch *n*; Mischung *f*

1240 **mocha**
f moka *m*
e café *m*; moca
d Mokka *m*

* **mock halibut** → **877**

1241 **mock-up**
f maquette *f*; modéle *m*
e maqueta *f*
d Attrappe *f*; Baumodell *n*

1242 **moisture content**
f teneur *f* en humidité
e contenido *m* de humedad
d Feuchtigkeitsgehalt *n*

1243 **molar solution**
f solution *f* molaire
e solución *f* molar
d molare Lösung *f*

1244 **molasses; treacle**
f mélasse *f*
e melaza *f*
d Melasse *f*

1245 **molecular heat**
f chaleur *f* moléculaire
e calor *m* molecular
d Molekularwärme *f*

1246 molecular rotation
 f rotation *f* moléculaire
 e rotación *f* molecular
 d Molekulardrehung *f*

 * **monkeynut → 1374**

1247 monk fish; angel fish
 Lophius piscatoris.
 f baudroie *f*; lotte *f* de mer
 e angelote *m*
 d Seeteufel *m*

1248 monoglyceride
 f monoglycéride *m*
 e monoglicérido *m*
 d Monoglyzerid *n*

1249 monomolecular
 f monomoléculaire
 e monomolecular
 d monomolekular

 * **monosodium glutamate → 1721**

1250 mother liquor
 f eau-mère *f*
 e agua *f* madre
 d Mutterlaufge *f*

1251 motility
 f mobilité *f*; motilité *f*
 e motilidad *f*
 d Beweglichkeit *f*

1252 mould
 f moisissure *f*
 e moho *m*; hongo *m*
 d Schimmelpilz *m*; Schimmel *m*

 * **M.S.G. → 1721**

1253 mulberry
 Morus sp.
 f mûre *f*
 e mora *f*
 d Maulbeere *f*

1254 multiple-effect evaporator
 f évaporateur *m* à multiple effet
 e evaporador *m* de efecto múltiple
 d Mehrfachverdampfapparat *m*

1255 muscatel
 f raisin *m* sec muscatel
 e moscatel *m*
 d Muskatrosine *f*

1256 muscatel
 Sweet wine from muscat grape.
 f vin *m* muscat
 e vino *m* moscatel
 d Muskatellerwein *m*

1257 muscle
 f muscle *m*
 e músculo *m*
 d Muskel *m*

1258 mushroom
 f champignon *m*
 e seta *f*; hongo *m*
 d Champignon *m*; Pilz *m*

1259 mussel
 Mytilus edulis.
 f moule *f*
 e almeja *f*; marisco *m*
 d Miesmuschel *f*

1260 must
 f moût *m*; vin *m* doux
 e mosto *m*
 d Most *m*

1261 mustard oil
 f sénévol *m*; essence *f* de moutarde
 e aceite *m* de mostaza
 d Senföl *n*

1262 musty
 f à odeur de moisi
 e enmohecido
 d muffig

1263 mutton
 f mouton *m*
 e carnero *m*; oveja *f*
 d Hammelfleisch *n*; Schöpfenfleisch
   n; Schaffleisch *n*

1264 mycelium
 f mycélium *m*; mycélion *m*
 e micelio *m*
 d Myzelium *n*

1265 mycotoxin
   f mycotoxine *f*
   e micotoxina *f*
   d Mykotoxin *n*

1266 myoglobin
   f myoglobine *f*
   e mioglobina *f*
   d Myoglobin *n*

N

1267 narcotic
f narcotique *m*
e narcótico *m*
d Betäubungsmittel *n*; Rauschgift *n*

1268 natural fibre
f fibre *f* naturelle
e fibra *f* natural
d Naturfaser *f*

1269 natural gas
f gaz *m* naturel
e gas *m* natural
d Erdgas *n*

1270 nauseous
f nauséabond
e nauseabundo
d ekelhaft; widerlich

1271 nectarine
Fruit of *Prunus persica nectarina.*
f nectarine *f*
e nectarina *f*
d Nektarine *f*

1272 needle valve
f robinet *m* à pointeau
e válvula *f* de aguja
d Nadelventil *n*

1273 nephelometer
f opacimètre *m*
e nefelómetro *m*
d Trübungsmesser *m*

1274 neroli oil; orange flower oil
Oil from *Citrus aurantium.*
f essence *f* de néroli; essence *f* de
fleurs d'orange
e aceite *m* de neroli
d Neroliöl *n*

1275 Nessler's reagent
f réactif *m* de Nessler
e reactivo *m* de Nessler
d Nesslersches Reagens *n*

1276 neurine
f neurine *f*

e neurina *f*
d Neurin *n*

1277 neutral
f neutre
e neutro
d neutral

1278 neutralise v
f neutraliser
e neutralizar
d neutralisieren

1279 Newtonian flow
f flux *m* newtonien
e flujo *m* Newtoniano
d Newtonsche Strömung *f*

* **niacin → 1283**

* **niacinamide → 1281**

1280 Nicol prism
f prisme *m* Nicol
e Nicol *m*
d Nicolsches Prisma *n*

**1281 nicotinamide; niacinamide;
vitamin PP**
f nicotinamide *f*; niacinamide *f*;
vitamine *f* PP
e nicotinamida *f*; niacinamida *f*;
vitamina *f* PP
d Nikotinamid *n*; Niazinamid *n*;
Vitamin *n* PP

1282 nicotine
f nicotine *f*
e nicotina *f*
d Nikotin *n*

1283 nicotinic acid; niacin; vitamin PP
f acide *m* nicotinique; niacine *f*;
vitamine *f* PP
e ácido *m* nicotínico; niacina *f*;
vitamina *f* PP
d Nikotinsäure *f*; Niazin *n*; Vitamin
n PP

1284 ninhydrin test
f épreuve *f* de ninhydrine
e prueba *f* de ninhidrina
d Ninhydrinprobe *f*; Ninhydrinreaktion *f*

1285 nisin
Antibiotic from *Streptococcus lactis.*
f nisine *f*
e nisina *f*
d Nisin *n*

* **nitre → 1445**

1286 nitrogen; azote
f nitrogène *f*; azote *m*
e nitrógeno *m*
d Stickstoff *m*

1287 nitrogenase
f nitrogénase *f*
e nitrogenasa *f*
d Nitrogenase *f*

1288 nitrogen fixation
f azotation *f*
e fijación *f* del nitrógeno
d Stickstoffbindung *f*

1289 nitrogen trichloride; agene
f trichlore *m* d'azote
e tricloruro *m* de nitrógeno; ageno *m*
d Stickstofftrichlorid *n*

1290 nitrosamine
f nitrosamine *f*
e nitrosamina *f*
d Nitrosamin *n*

1291 nitroso compound
f composé *m* nitrosé
e compuesto *m* nitroso
d Nitrosoverbindung *f*

1292 nitrous oxide; laughing gas
f oxide *m* nitreux; gaz *m* hilarent
e óxido *m* nitroso; gas *m* hilarante
d Stickoxydul *n*; Lachgas *n*

* **non-enzymic browning → 1156**

1293 non-fat
f non-gras; dégraissé
e no graso
d fettfrei

1294 noodles
f nouilles *fpl*
e pasta *f*
d Nudeln *fpl*

1295 norleucine
f norleucine *f*
e norleucina *f*
d Norleucin *n*

1296 norm
f norme *f*
e norma *f*
d Norm *f*

1297 normal
f normal
e normal
d normal

1298 normal solution
f solution *f* normale
e solución *f* normal
d Normallösung *f*

* **Norway lobster → 1451**

1299 notatin
f notatine *f*
e notatina *f*
d Notatin *n*

1300 noxious
f nocif
e nocivo
d schädlich

1301 nucleic acid
f acide *m* nucléique
e ácido *m* nucléico
d Nukleinsäure *f*

1302 nucleoprotein
f nucléoprotéine *f*
e nucleoproteína *f*
d Nukleoprotein *n*

1303 nut
f noix *f*
e nuez *f*
d Nuss *f*

1304 nutmeg
Seed of *Myristica fragrans.*
f noix *f* muscade
e nuez *f* moscada
d Muskatnuss *f*

1305 nutrient
  f aliment *m*
  e nutrimento *m*
  d Nährstoff *m*

1306 nutritive value
  f valeur *f* nutritionnelle
  e valor *m* nutritivo
  d Nährwert *m*

O

1307 oak bark
f écorce f de chêne
e corteza f de roble
d Eichenrinde f

1308 oats
Grain from *Avena sativa*.
f avoine f
e avena f
d Hafer m

1309 octopus
Octopus sp.
f poulpe m
e pulpo m
d Krake m

1310 ocular; eyepiece
f oculaire m
e ocular m
d Okular n; Augenlinse f

1311 odoriferous
f odorant; odoriférant
e odorante; odorífero
d riechend

1312 odorimetry
f odorimétrie f
e odorimetría f
d Geruchsmessung f

1313 odour; smell; scent
f odeur f
e olor m; aroma f
d Geruch m

1314 odourless
f inodore
e inodoro
d geruchlos

* oenometer → 2004

1315 oestrogen; estrogen
f oestrogène m
e estrógeno m
d Östrogen n

1316 offal
By-products of milling.
f issues fpl
e desperdicios mpl
d Abfälle fpl

1317 offal
Viscera and trimmings of a
butchered animal removed in
dressing.
f tripaille f
e menudillos mpl
d Schlachtabfälle mpl; Innereien fpl

1318 off-flavour
f mauvais goût m; goût m
défectueux
e malo sabor m
d abfallender Geschmack m; fehlerhafter Geschmak m; Geschmackfehler m

1319 oil palm
Elaeis quineensis.
f éteide f de guinée
e palmera f de aceite
d Ölpalme f

1320 olefin
f oléfine f
e olefina f
d Olefin n

1321 oleic acid
f acide m oléique
e ácido m oléico
d Ölsäure f

1322 olfactory epithelium
f épithélium m olfactif
e epitelio m olfacterio
d Geruchsorgan-Epithel n

1323 olive oil
Oil from *Olea europaea.*
f huile f d'olive
e aceite m de oliva
d Olivenöl n

1324 one-way valve
f soupape f de retenue
e válvula f de retención
d Rückströmventil n

1325 onion
Allium cepa.
f onion *m*
e cebolla *f*
d Zwiebel *f*

1326 on stream
f en marche
e en marcha
d in Betrieb

1327 opalescence
f opalescence *f*
e opalescencia *f*
d Opaleszenz *f*; Schiller *m*

1328 opaque
f opaque
e opaco
d undurchsichtig

1329 optical activity
f activité *f* optique
e actividad *f* óptica
d optische Aktivität *f*

1330 optical isomer
f isomère *m* optique
e isómero *m* óptico
d optisches Isomer *n*

1331 orange
Citrus sinensis.
f orange *f*
e naranja *f*
d Orange *f*

* orange flower oil → 1274

1332 organoleptic examination
f examen *m* organoleptique; contrôle
m organoleptique
e examen *m* organoléptico
d Sinnenprüfung *f*

1333 orientate *v*
f orienter
e orientar
d orientieren

1334 orifice
f orifice *m*
e orificio *m*; abertura *f*
d Mündung *f*; Öffnung *f*

* ormer → 1

1335 ornithine
f ornithine *f*
e ornitina *f*
d Ornithin *n*

1336 orotic acid
f acide *m* orotique
e ácido *m* orótico
d Orotsäure *f*

1337 osmosis
f osmose *f*
e ósmosis *f*
d Osmose *f*

1338 ossein
f osséine *f*
e oseína *f*
d Knockengallerte *f*

1339 ovalbumin; egg albumin
f ovalbumine *f*
e ovoalbúmina *f*; albúmina *f* de
huevo
d Eieralbumin *n*; Ovalbumin *n*

1340 oven
f four *m*
e estufa *f*; horno *m*
d Ofen *m*; Backofen *m*; Trockenofen
m

1341 overhaul *v*
f réviser
e revisar
d überholen

1342 overrun
Increase in volume by whipping air
into ice cream during freezing.
f foisonnement *m*; "overrun" *m*
e sobrecrecimiento *m*
d Aufschlag *m*; "Overrun" *m*

1343 ox
f boeuf *m*
e buey *m*
d Ochse *m*

1344 oxidase
f oxydase *f*
e oxidasa *f*
d Oxydase *f*

1345 oxidation
 f oxydation *f*
 e oxidación *f*
 d Oxydation *f*

1346 oxidation-reduction indicator
 f indicateur *m* d'oxydo-réduction
 e indicador *m* de oxidación-
  reducción
 d Oxydations-Reduktionsindikator *m*

1347 oxidizing agent
 f agent *m* oxydant
 e agente *m* de oxidación; oxidante *m*
 d Oxydationsmittel *n*

1348 oxytetracycline
 f oxytétracycline *f*
 e oxitetraciclina *f*
 d Oxytetracyclin *n*

1349 oyster
 Ostrea sp. or *Crassostrea* sp.
 f huître *f*
 e ostra *f*
 d Auster *f*

1350 ozone
 f ozone *m*
 e ozono *m*
 d Ozon *n*

P

1351 packaging
f emballage *m*
e embalaje *m*
d Packung *f*

1352 palm
f palmier *m*
e palma *f*; palmera *f*
d Palme *f*

1353 palmitic acid
f acide *m* palmitique
e ácido *m* palmítico
d Palmitinsäure *f*

1354 palmitoleic acid
f acide *m* palmitoléique
e ácido *m* palmitoléico
d Palmitoleinsäure *f*

1355 palm kernel oil
Oil from *Elaesis guineensis.*
f huile *f* de palmiste
e aceite *m* de nuez de palma
d Palmkernöl *n*

1356 palm oil
Oil from pulp of several palms.
f huile *f* de palme
e aceite *m* de palma
d Palmöl *n*

1357 panary fermentation
f fermentation *f* panaire
e fermentación *f* de la masa
d Brotgärung *f*; Brotteiggärung *f*

1358 pancreatin
f pancréatine *f*
e pancreatina *f*
d Pankreatin *n*

1359 pan mill
f broyeur *m* à meules verticales
e molino *m* de rodillos
d Kollergang *m*; Kollermühle *f*

1360 pantothenic acid
f acide *m* pantothénique
e ácido *m* pantoténico
d Pantothensäure *f*

1361 papain
f papaïne *f*
e papaína *f*
d Papain *n*

1362 papaya; paw paw
Fruit of *Carica papaya.*
f papaye *f*
e papaya *f*; lechoza *f*
d Papaya *f*

1363 paprika; sweet pepper
Fruit of *Capsicum annuum.*
f piment *m*; poivron *m*
e pimienta *f* dulce
d Paprika *m*

1364 parboil *v*
f échauder; faire bouiller légèrement
e hervir parcialmente
d brühen; nicht-garkochen

1365 parchment paper
f papier *m* parcheminé
e papel *m* vitela
d Pergamentpapier *n*

1366 parsley
Petroselinum crispum.
f persil *m*
e perejil *m*
d Petersilie *f*

1367 parsnip
Pastineca sativa.
f panais *m*
e chirivia *f*
d Pastinak *m*; Pastinake *f*; Zuckerwurzel *f*

1368 particle size analysis
f analyse *f* granulométrique
e análisis *m* del tamaño de partículas
d Teilchengrössenbestimmung *f*

* **passion fruit** → 870

* **pasta** → 88

1369 pasteurization
f pasteurisation *f*
e pasteurización *f*
d Pasteurisierung *f*

1370 patent
f brevet *m*
e patente *f*
d Patent *n*

1371 patent flour
f farine *f* de qualité; farine *f* fleur
e harina *f* patente
d helles Weizenmehl *n*

1372 pathogenic bacterium
f bactérie *f* pathogène
e bacteria *f* patógena
d pathogene Bakterie *f*

* **paw paw → 1362**

1373 pea
Garden pea is the seed of the
legume *Pisum sativum.* Used as a
vegetable.
f pois *m*; petit pois *m*
e garbanzo *m*; guisante *m*
d Erbse *f*

1374 peanut; groundnut; monkeynut
Seed of *Arachis hypogaea.*
f arachide *f*; cacuéte *f*
e cacahuete *f*; maní *m*
d Erdnuss *f*

1375 peanut butter
f beurre *m* d'arachide; pâte *f*
d'arachide
e crema *f* de cacahuete; mantequilla
f de maní
d Erdnussbutter *f*; Erdnussmasse *f*

1376 peanut oil; arachis oil
f huile *f* d'arachide
e aceite *m* de maní; aceite *m* de
cacahuete
d Erdnussöl *n*; Arachisöl *n*

1377 pear
Pyrus sp.
f poire *f*
e pera *f*
d Birne *f*

1378 pecan nut
Carya illinoensis.
f pécan *m*
e nuez *f* del nogal americano
d Hickorynuss *f*

1379 pectin
f pectine *f*
e pectina *f*
d Pektin *n*

1380 pellucid; transparent
f pellucide; transparent
e diáfano; transparente; pelúcido
d durchsichtig

1381 penetrometer
f pénétromètre *m*
e penetrómetro *m*
d Penetrationsmesser *m*; Härtemesser *m*

1382 penicillin
Antibiotic from *Penicillium
notatum* or *P. chrysogenum.*
f pénicilline *f*
e penicilina *f*
d Penicillin *n*

1383 pentose
f pentose *f*
e pentosa *f*
d Pentose *f*

1384 pepper
f poivre *m*
e pimienta *f*
d Pfeffer *m*

1385 peppermint oil
f essence *f* de menthe
e aceite *m* de menta
d Pfefferminzöl *n*

1386 pepsin
f pepsine *f*
e pepsina *f*
d Pepsin *n*

1387 peptization
f peptisation *f*
e peptización *f*
d Peptisieren *n*

1388 peptone
f peptone *f*
e peptona *f*
d Pepton *n*

1389 perch
  Perca.
  f perche f
  e perca f
  d Barsch m

1390 percolation
  f percolation f; suintement m
  e percolación f; infiltración f
  d Durchsickern n

1391 pericarp
  f péricarpe m
  e pericarpio m
  d Perikarp n; Fruchthülse f

* **periwinkle → 2061**

1392 permanent hardness
  f crudité f permanente
  e dureza f permanente
  d bleibende Härte f

1393 permeability
  f perméabilité f
  e permeabilidad f
  d Durchlässigkeit f; Permeabilität f

1394 peroxidase
  f peroxydase f
  e peroxidasa f
  d Peroxydase f

1395 peroxide value
  f indice m d'oxydation
  e valor m de peróxidos
  d Oxydationszahl f

1396 perry
  f poiré m
  e vino m de peras
  d Birnenwein m

1397 pesticide
  f pesticide m
  e pesticida f
  d Pestizid n; Schädlingsbekämpfungs-
    mittel n

1398 pest infestation
  f infestation f par les prédateurs
  e infestación f por pestes
  d Schädlingsfrass m

1399 Petri dish
  f boîte f de Pétri
  e capsula f de Petri
  d Petrischale f

1400 petroleum wax
  f cire f de pétrole
  e cera f del petróleo
  d Petroleumwachs n

1401 pH value
  f valeur f pH
  e valor m pH
  d pH-Wert m

1402 phenol; carbolic acid
  f phénol m; acide m phénylique
  e fenol m; ácido m carbólico
  d Phenol n; Karbolsäure f

1403 phosphatase test
  f test m de la phosphatase
  e prueba f de fosfatasa
  d Phosphatasetest m

1404 phosphatide
  f phosphatide m
  e fosfátido m
  d Phosphatid n

1405 phospholipid
  f phospholipide m
  e fosfolípido m
  d Phospholipid n

1406 photosynthesis
  f photosynthèse f
  e fotosíntesis f
  d Photosynthese f

1407 phytic acid
  f acide m phytique
  e ácido m fítico
  d phytinsäure f

1408 phytochemical
  f phytochimique
  e fitoquímico
  d pflanzenchemisch; phytochemisch

1409 phytol
  f phytol m
  e fitol m
  d Phytol n

1410 phytosterol
f phytostérol *m*
e fitosterol *m*
d Phytosterin *n*

1411 pickle *v*
f saumurer
e escabechar
d pökeln

1412 pike
Esox lucius.
f brochet *m*
e lucio *m*
d Hecht *m*

1413 pike perch; giant perch
Lucio perca lucio perca.
f sandre *f*
e sollo *m*
d Zander *m*; Sander *m*

* **pilchard** → 1616

1414 pineapple
Ananas comosus.
f ananas *m*
e piña *f*; ananás *m*
d Ananas *f*

1415 pipette
f pipette *f*
e pipeta *f*
d Pipette *f*

1416 pistachio
Pistacia vera.
f pistache *f*
e pistacho *m*
d Pistazie *f*

1417 pitching yeast
f levain *m*
e levadura *f* de siembra
d Anstellhefe *f*

1418 pitting
f corrosion *f*; piqûre *f*
e picado *m*
d Korrosion *f*; Lochfrass *m*

1419 plaice
Pleuronectes platessa, in U.S.A.
Paralichthys dentatus.
f plie *f*
e platija *f*
d Scholle *f*

1420 plankton
f plancton *m*
e plancton *m*
d Plankton *n*

1421 plantation white
f sucre *m* colonial
e azúcar *m* colonial; azúcar *m* blanco
d Kolonialzucker *m*; Weisszucker *m*

1422 plasma
f plasma *m*
e plasma *m*
d Plasma *n*

1423 plastic
f matière *f* plastique
e plástico *m*
d Kunststoff *n*

1424 plasticizer
f agent *m* plastifiant
e plastificante *m*
d Plastifiziermittel *n*

1425 plate cooler
f réfrigérant *m* à plaques
e enfriador *m* de platos
d Plattenkühler *m*

1426 plate evaporator
f évaporateur *m* à plaques
e evaporador *m* de platos
d Plattenverdampfer *m*

1427 plate heater
f réchauffeur *m* à plaques
e calentador *m* de platos
d Plattenhitzer *m*

1428 plate heat exchanger
f échangeur *m* de chaleur à plaques
e termointercambiador *m* de platos
d Plattenwärmeaustauscher *m*

1429 plum
Fruit of *Prunus domestica.*
f prune *f*
e ciruela *f*
d Pflaume *f*; Zwetsche *f*; Zwetschge *f*

1430 pneumatic dryer
f séchoir m à gaz
e secador m neumático
d Gastrockner m

1431 poach v
f pocher
e escalfar
d pochieren

1432 polarimeter
f polarimètre m
e polarímetro m
d Polarisationsmesser m

1433 pollack; lythe; coalfish; green cod
Pollachius pollachius.
f jaune m lieu
e abadejo m; pescadilla f
d Pollack m

1434 polyethylene; polythene
f polyéthylène m
e polietileno m
d Polyäthylen n

1435 polymorphism
f polymorphisme m
e polimorfismo m
d Polymorphismus m; Vielgestältigkeit f

1436 polyose
f polyose m
e poliosa f
d Polyose f

1437 polyphosphate
f polyphosphate m
e polifosfato m
d Polyphosphat n

1438 polypropylene
f polypropylène m
e polipropileno m
d Polypropylen n

* **polythene** → **1434**

* **pomace** → **1176**

1439 pomegranate
Fruit of *Punica granatum.*
f grenada f

e granada f
d Granatapfel m

1440 porphyrin
f porphyrine f
e porfirina f
d Porphyrin n

1441 potable; drinkable
f potable
e potable
d trinkbar

* **potassium bitartrate** → **512**

1442 potassium bromate
f bromate m de potassium
e bromato m potásico
d Kaliumbromat n

1443 potassium hydroxide
f hydroxyde m de potassium; potasse
f caustique
e hidróxido m potásico
d Kaliumhydroxyd n; Ätzkali n

1444 potassium metabisulphite
f métabisulfite m de potassium
e metabisulfito m potásico
d Kaliummetabisulfit n

1445 potassium nitrate; saltpetre; nitre
f nitrate m de potassium; salpêtre
m ; nitre m
e nitrato m potásico; salitre m
d Kaliumnitrat n; Kalisalpeter m;
Salpeter m

1446 potassium nitrite
f nitrite m de potassium
e nitrito m potásico
d Kaliumnitrit n

* **potassium tartrate** → **512**

1447 potato
Solanum tuberosum.
f pomme f de terre
e patata f
d Kartoffel f

1448 potato spirit
f eau-de-vie f de pommes de terre
e aguardiente m de patatas
d Kartoffelspiritus m

1449 pot still; still
f alambic *m*
e alambique *m*
d Destillationsapparat *m*

1450 pout
Trisopterus luscus.
f tacaud *m*
e mustela *f* de río; faneca *f*
d Franzosendorsch *m*

1451 prawn; scampi; Norway lobster
Any of several species of decapod
crustaceans.
f langoustine *f*
e gamba *f*
d Kaisergranat *m*; Kaiserhummer *m*

1452 precipitate
f précipité *m*
e precipitado *m*
d Niederschlag *m*

1453 predrier
f préséchoir *m*
e presecador *m*
d Vortrockner *m*

1454 preheater
f préchauffeur *m*
e precalentador *m*
d Vorwärmer *m*

1455 premixing
f prémélange *m*
e premezclado *m*
d Vormischung *f*

1456 preservation
f conservation *f*
e conservación *f*; preservación *f*
d Konservierung *f*

1457 preservative
f conservateur *m*
e preservativo *m*
d Konservierungsmittel *n*

1458 pressure cooker; autoclave
f marmite *f* à pression
e olla *f* a presión
d Dampfdrucktopf *m*

1459 pressure reducing valve
f détendeur *m*
e válvula *f* reductora de presión
d Druckreduzierventil *n*

1460 pretreatment
f traitement *m* préalable
e tratamiento *m* preliminar
d Vorbehandlung *f*

1461 process
f procédé *m*; traitement *m*
e proceso *m*; método *m*;
procedimiento *m*
d Herstellungsverfahren *n*

1462 processed cheese
f fromage *m* fondu
e queso *m* procesado
d Schmelzkäse *m*

1463 production line
f chaîne *f* de production; voie *f* de
production
e línea *f* de producción
d Arbeitsstrasse *f*

1464 productivity
f productivité *f*
e productividad *f*
d Ertragsfähigkeit *f*

1465 proline
f proline *f*
e prolina *f*
d Prolin *n*

1466 promoter
f activeur *m*
e activador *m*
d Aktivierungsmittel *n*;
Beschleuniger *m*; Promoter *m*

1467 proof spirit
f esprit preuve *m*
e grado *m* alcohólico
d Normalweingeist *m*

1468 pro-oxidant
f pro-oxydant *m*
e prooxidante *m*
d Prooxydans *n*; oxydationsförderndes Mittel *n*

1469 propanol
f propanol *m*
e propanol *m*
d Propanol *n*

1470 propionic acid
f acide *m* propionique
e ácido *m* propiónico
d Propionsäure *f*

1471 protease
f protéase *f*
e proteasa *f*
d Protease *f*

1472 protein
f protéine *f*
e proteína *f*
d Eiweiss *n*; Protein *n*

1473 protoplasm
f protoplasme *m*
e protoplasma *m*
d Protoplasma *n*

1474 prove *v*
    To leave bread dough to rise.
f laisser reposer la pâte
e deixar; crescer
d aufgehen lassen

1475 proving cabinet
f étuve *f* à fermentation
e cámara *f* de fermentación
d Gärschrank *m*

1476 prune
f pruneau *m*
e ciruela *f* pasa
d gedörrte Pflaume *f*

1477 pseudo-acid
f pseudo-acide *m*
e pseudoácido *m*
d Pseudosäure *f*

1478 pseudo-base
f pseudo-base *f*
e pseudobase *f*
d Pseudobase *f*

1479 psychrophilic bacterium
f bactérie *f* psychrophile
e bacteria *f* psicrofílica
d psychrophile Bakterie *f*

1480 ptomaine
f ptomaïne *f*
e ptomaína *f*
d Ptomain *n*

1481 puf *v*
f faire gonfler
e asar
d puffen

1482 pulse
    Seed of *Leguminosae* fam.
f légumineuse *f*
e legumbre *f*
d Hülsenfrüchte *f*

1483 pumpkin; squash
    Cucurbita sp.
f citrouille *f*
e calabaza *f*; calabacera *f*
d Kürbis *m*

1484 purine
f purine *f*
e purina *f*
d Purin *n*

1485 purslane
    Portulaca oleracea.
f pourpier *m*
e verdolaga *f*
d Portulak *m*

1486 putrefaction
f putréfaction *f*
e putrefacción *f*
d Fäulnis *f*

1487 putrefy *v*
f putréfier (se)
e putreficar
d verfaulen; vermodern

1488 putrid
f putride
e pútrido; podrido
d verfault

1489 pyrethrin
f pyréthrine *f*
e piretrina *f*
d Pyrethrin *n*

*   **pyridoxin** → **2012**

1490 pyroligneous acid
   f acide *m* pyroligneux
   e ácido *m* piroleñoso
   d Holzessigsäure *f*

1491 pyrolysis
   f pyrolyse *f*
   e pirólisis *f*
   d Pyrolyse *f*

Q

1492 quality control
f contrôle *m* de la qualité
e control *m* de cualidad
d Qualitätskontrolle *f*

1493 quality evaluation
f appréciation *f* de la qualité
e evaluación *f* de cualidad
d Qualitätsbeurteilung *f*

1494 quaternary ammonium compound
f composé *m* d'ammonium
  quaternaire
e compuesto *m* amónico cuaternario
d quaternäre Ammoniumverbindung
  f

1495 quercetin
f quercétine *f*
e quercetina *f*
d Quercetin *n*

1496 quick freezing
f congélation *f* rapide
e congelamiento *m* rápido
d Schnellgefrieren *n*

1497 quince
  Cydonia oblonga.
f coing *m*
e membrillo *m*
d Quitte *f*

1498 quinic acid; chinic acid
f acide *m* quinique
e ácido *m* quínico
d Chinasäure *f*

1499 quinine
  Alkaloid from *Cinchona* sp.
f quinine *f*
e quinina :'
d Chinin *n*

R

1500 rabbit
f lapin *m*
e conejo *m*
d Kaninchen *n*

1501 radiation
f rayonnement *m*
e radiación *f*
d Strahlung *f*

1502 radiation dosimeter; dosimeter
f dosimètre *m*
e dosímetro *m*
d Dosimeter *n*; Dosimesser *m*

1503 radiation loss
f perte *f* par rayonnement
e pérdida *f* por radiación
d Strahlungsverlust *m*

1504 radio-active
f radioactif
e radiactivo
d radioaktiv

1505 radio-activity
f radioactivité *f*
e radiactividad *f*
d Radioaktivität *f*

1506 radish
Root of *Raphanus sativus.*
f radis *m*
e rábano *m*
d Rettich *m*

1507 radurization
Treatment of food by radiation.
f irradiation *f*
e radurización *m*
d Radurisation *f*

* **raffinose → 1200**

1508 raise steam *v*
f produire de la vapeur
e producir vapor
d Dampf erzeugen

1509 raisin
f raisin *m* sec
e pasa *f*
d Rosine *f*

1510 raising agent
f agent *m* levant
e fermento *m*
d Backtriebmittel *n*

1511 rancid
f rance
e ráncido
d ranzig

1512 rancidity
f rancidité *f*; rancissement *m*;
rancissure *f*
e rancidez *f*
d Ranzigkeit *f*

1513 random
f par hasard
e fortuito; casual; al azar
d zufällig

1514 random sample
f échantillon *m* prélevé au hasard
e muestra *f* al azar
d Stichprobe *f*

1515 Raoult's law
f loi *f* de Raoult
e ley *f* de Raoult
d Raoultsches Gesetz *n*

1516 rape
Brassica napus.
f colza *m*
e colza *f*
d Raps *m*

1517 rape seed oil; colza oil
f huile *f* de colza
e aceite *m* de colza
d Rüböl *n*; Rapsöl *n*

1518 rarefaction
f raréfaction *f*
e rarefacción *f*; enrarecimiento *m*
d Verdünnung *f*

1519 raspberry
Fruit of *Rubus idaeus.*

f framboise f
e frambueza f
d Himbeere f

1520 **raw**
  f brut
  e crudo
  d roh

1521 **razor clam**
  Solen sp.
  f couteau m
  e navaja f
  d Meerscheide f

1522 **reaction**
  f réaction f
  e reacción f
  d Reaktion f

1523 **reactivation**
  f réactivation f
  e reactivación f
  d Reaktivierung f

1524 **Reaumur scale**
  f échelle f Réaumur
  e escala f de Reaumur
  d Reaumur-Skala f

1525 **receiver**
  f récipient m
  e recipiente m
  d Sammelbehälter m

1526 **recirculation**
  f recyclage m
  e recirculación f
  d Umlauf m

1527 **recommended intake**
  f ration f journalière
  e consumo m recomendado
  d empfohlene Aufnahme f

1528 **recorder**
  f enregistreur m
  e registrador m; contador m
  d Registrierapparat m

1529 **rectification**
  f rectification f
  e rectificación f
  d Rektifikation f

1530 **rectifier**
  f redresseur m
  e rectificador m
  d Gleichrichter m

1531 **red mullet**
  Mullus surmeletus.
  f rouget-barbet m
  e mujol m; barbo m de mar
  d Meerbarbe f

* **red pepper** → **400**

1532 **reduction**
  f réduction f
  e reducción f
  d Reduktion f

1533 **reference electrode**
  f électrode f de réference
  e electrodo m de referencia
  d Bezugselektrode f

1534 **refinery**
  f raffinerie f
  e refinería f
  d Raffinerie f

1535 **reflux**
  f reflux m
  e reflujo m
  d Rückfluss m; Rückstrom m

1536 **refractive index**
  f indice m de réfraction
  e índice m de refracción
  d Brechungsexponent m; Refraktions-
    zahl f

1537 **refrigerant**
  f réfrigérant m
  e refrigerante m
  d Kühlmittel n

1538 **refrigeration**
  f refroidissement m; réfrigération f
  e refrigeración f
  d Kühlung f

1539 **relative humidity**
  f humidité f relative
  e humedad f relativa
  d relative Feuchtigkeit f

1540 relative viscosity
f viscosité f relative
e viscosidad f relativa
d relative Viskosität f

1541 relief valve
f vanne f de détente; détendeur m
e válvula f de seguridad
d Überdruckventil n

1542 rennet
f présure f
e cuajo m
d Lab n

1543 rennet casein
f caséine f caillée
e caseína f al cuajo
d Labkasein n

1544 rennin; chymosin
f rénine f; présure f
e renina f
d Labferment n; Rennin n; Chymosin n

1545 resilience
f résilience f
e resiliencia f
d Rückprallelastizität f

1546 resin
f résine f
e resina f
d Harz n

1547 resorcinol test
f essai m à la résorcinel
e prueba f de resorcinol
d Resorcinprobe f

* **retinol → 2009**

1548 retort
f cornue f
e retorta f
d Retorte f; Destillationskolben m

* **retrogradation → 1786**

1549 revivification
Re-activation of charcoal.
f réduction f
e reactivación f
d Wiederbelebung f

1550 rH value
f valeur f rH
e valor m rH
d rH-Wert m

1551 rheological instrumentation
f instrumentation f rhéologique
e instrumentación f reológica
d rheologische Instrumentierung f

1552 rheology
f rhéologie f
e reología f
d Rheologie f; Fliesskunde f; Fliesslehre f

1553 rheometer
f consistomètre m
e reómetro m
d Rheometer n; Konsistenzmesser m

1554 rheopexy
f rhéopexie f
e reopexia f
d Rheopexie f

1555 rhodopsin
f rhodopsine f
e rodopsina f
d Rhodopsin n

1556 rhubarb
Rheum fam.
f rhubarbe f
e ruibarbo m
d Rhabarber m

* **riboflavin → 2011**

1557 ribonucleic acid
f acide m ribonucléique
e ácido m ribonucléico
d Ribonukleinsäure f

1558 ribose
f ribose m
e ribosa f
d Ribose f

1559 rice
Oryza sativa.
f riz m
e arroz m
d Reis m

1560 ricin
Poison from *Ricinus communis*.
f ricine *f*
e ricina *f*
d Rizin *n*

1561 ricinoleic acid
f acide *m* ricinoléique
e ácido *m* ricinoléico
d Rizinolsäure *f*

1562 rickets
f rachitisme *m*
e raquitismo *m*
d Rachitis *f*; englische Krankheit *f*

1563 rigor mortis
f rigidité *f* cadavérique
e rigor mortis *m*
d Leichenstarre *f*; Rigor mortis *f*

1564 ripen *v*
f maturer; affiner; mûrir
e madurar
d reifen

1565 rising power
f levée *f*; pousse *f*
e potencia *f* del fermento
d Trieb *m*; Teiglockerung *f*

1566 roast *v*
f rôtir; cuire au four
e asar; tostar
d braten; rosten; schmorren

1567 Rochelle salt
f sel *m* de Seignette
e sal *f* de Rochelle
d Rochellesalz *n*

* **rock lobster** → 509

1568 roe; hard roe
Eggs of fish.
f rogue *f*
e hueva *f*
d Rogen *m*

1569 roller dryer
f séchoir *m* à cylindres
e secador *m* de cilindros
d Walzentrockner *m*

1570 roller mill
f malaxeur *m*; mélangeur *m* à cylindres
e moledora *f* de cilindros
d Walzenmühle *f*; Mischwalzwerk *n*

1571 ropiness
In bread and milk.
f viscosité *f*
e pegajosidad *f*; viscosidad *f*
d Fadenziehen *n*; Viskosität *f*

1572 rosemary
Rosmarinus officinalis.
f romarin *m*
e romero *m*
d Rosmarin *m*

1573 rosemary oil
f essence *f* de romarin
e aceite *m* de romero
d Rosmarinöl *n*

* **rosin** → 474

1574 rotameter
f débitmètre *m*
e rotámetro *m*
d Rotadurchflussmesser *m*

1575 rotary dryer
f séchoir *m* rotatif
e secador *m* rotatorio
d Trommeltrockner *m*

1576 rotary filter
f filtre *m* rotatif
e filtro *m* rotatorio
d Drehfilter *m*; Trommelfilter *m*

1577 rotenone
f roténone *f*
e rotenona *f*
d Rotenon *n*

1578 roughage
f fourrage *m* grossier
e forraje *m*
d Raufutter *n*

1579 rouse *v*
f activer la fermentation
e activar la fermentación
d Gärung beleben

1580 roux
  f roux *m*
  e hermejo *m*
  d Mehlschwitze *f*

1581 royalty
  f redevance *f*
  e regalía *f*; derecho *m*
  d Lizenzabgabe *f*

1582 rumen
  f panse *f*; rumen *m*
  e omaso *m*; panza *f*
  d Pansen *m*; Vordermagen *m*

1583 runner bean
  Phaseolus coccineus.
  f haricot *m* d'Espagne
  e judía *f* verde trepadora; judía *f*
    escarlata
  d Feuerbohne *f*; Prunkbohne *f*

1584 rusk; zwieback
  f biscotte *f*
  e bizcocho *m*
  d Zwieback *m*

1585 rust
  Parasitic micro-organisms on plants
  of *Basidiomycetes* group.
  f rouille *f*
  e rust *m*
  d Rost *m*

  * **rutabaga → 1851**

1586 rye
  Secale cereale.
  f seigle *m*
  e centeno *m*
  d Roggen *m*

S

* **saccharase** → **1004**

1587 saccharimeter
f saccharimètre *m*
e sacarímetro *m*
d Saccharimeter *n*

1588 saccharin
f saccharine *f*
e sacarina *f*
d Saccharin *n*

1589 saccharometer
f saccharimètre *m*
e sacarómetro *m*
d Saccharometer *n*

1590 saccharose; sucrose
f saccharose *m*; sucrose *m*
e sacarosa *f*; sucrosa *f*
d Saccharose *f*; Sukrose *f*

1591 safe
Relating to food additives.
f inoffensif
e seguro; no tóxico
d unbedenklich

1592 safety
Applied to food additives.
f innocuité *f*
e securidad *f*; no tóxicidad *f*
d Unbedenklichkeit *f*

1593 safety valve
f soupape *f* de sûreté
e válvula *f* de seguridad
d Ablassventil *n*; Sicherheitsventil *n*

1594 saffron
f safran *m*
e azafrán *m*
d Safran *m*

1595 sage
Salvia officinalis.
f sauge *f*
e salvia *f*
d Salbei *m/f*

1596 sago
Starch from *Metroxylon sago* and
other tropical palms.
f sagou *m*
e sagú *m*
d Sago *m*

* **salad cream** → **1192**

1597 salad dressing; French dressing
f sauce *f* vinaigrette
e salsa *f* de ensalada; vinagreta *f*
d Salatsosse *f*

1598 saline
f salin
e salino
d salzig; salzhaltig

1599 saliva
f salive *f*
e saliva *f*
d Speichel *m*

1600 salmon
Salmonides sp.
f saumon *m*
e salmón *m*
d Lachs *m*

1601 salmonella
Any of a genus (*Salmonella*) of
aerobic bacteria.
f salmonelle *f*
e salmonela *f*
d Salmonella *f*

1602 salsify
Tragopogon porrifolius.
f salsifis *m*
e salsifí *m*
d Haferwurz *f*

1603 salt
f sel *m*
e sal *f*
d Salz *n*

1604 saltern; evaporation pond
f saunerie *f*; bassin *m* d'évaporation
e salina *f*; estanque *m* de
evaporación
d Saline *f*; Abdampfbecken *n*

* **saltpetre** → **1445**

1605 salty
f salé
e salado
d salzig

1606 sample
f échantillon m; spécimen m
e muestra f; prueba f
d Muster n; Probe f

1607 sampler
A person who tests samples.
f échantillonneur m
e catador m; muestrador m
d Probenehmer m

1608 sampling
f échantillonnage m
e catadura f
d Probieren n; Probenahme f

1609 sand filter
f filtre m à sable
e filtro m de arena
d Sandfilter m

* **sand sole → 1086**

1610 sanitary quality
f qualité f hygiénique
e cualidad f sanitaria
d hygienische Qualität f

1611 sanitation
f amélioration f sanitaire
e mejoramiento m sanitario
d hygienische Qualitätsverbesserung f

1612 saponification
f saponification f
e saponificación f
d Verseifung f

1613 saponification number
f nombre m de saponification
e número m de saponificación
d Verseifungszahl f

1614 saponin
f saponine f
e saponina f
d Saponin n

1615 sarcosine
f sarcosine f
e sarcosina f
d Sarkosin n

1616 sardine; pilchard
Sardinia pilchardus.
f sardine f
e sardina f
d Sardine f

1617 sarsparilla
Shoots of Smilax sp.
f sassaparille f
e zarzaparilla f
d Sassaparille f; Heilwurz f

1618 saturated solution
f solution f saturée
e solución f saturada
d gesättigte Lösung f

1619 saturation
f saturation f
e saturación f
d Sättigung f

1620 sauerkraut
f choucroute f
e sauerkraut m; chucrut m
d Sauerkraut n

1621 sausage
f saucisse f; saucisson m
e embutido m; morcilla f; salchichón m; salchicha f; chorizo m
d Wurst f

1622 sauté v
f sauter
e freir
d braten

1623 savory
Satureia sp., especially S. hortensis and S. montana.
f sarriette f
e ajedrea f
d Bohnenkraut n

1624 scald v
f échauder; chauffer
e hervir; escaldar
d ausbrühen; auskochen

1625 scale
f tartre m
e incrustación f
d Kesselstein m

1626 scallop; escallop
Pecten sp.
f coquille f St.-Jacques
e venera f; pechina f
d Kamm-Muschel f

* **scampi** → 1451

* **scent** → 1313

* **scleroprotein** → 71

1627 scorch v
f roussir
e chamuscar
d versengen

1628 scraper
f racloir m
e rascador m
d Abstreifer m

1629 screening test
f épreuve f de triage rapide
e prueba f rápida
d Schnelltest m zum Aussieben

1630 screw conveyor
f transporteur m à vis sans fin
e tornillo m sin fin
d Förderschnecke f

1631 screw extruder
f presse f hélicoïdale
e prensa f helicoidal
d Schneckenpresse f

1632 scum
f écume f
e espuma f de impurezas
d Abschaum m

1633 scurvy
f scorbut m
e escorbuto m
d Skorbut m

1634 scutellum
f scutellum m

e scutellum m
d Schildchen n; Getreideschildchen
n

1635 sea bream
Parellus centrodontus or Sparidae
fam.
f dorada f; daurada f
e besugo m
d Meerbrassen m

* **sea ear** → 1

1636 sea-kale
Crambe maritima.
f chou m marin
e berza f marina
d Seekohl m

1637 seal ring
f joint m
e anillo m sellador
d Dichtungsring m

1638 seamless
f sans couture; sans soudure
e inconsútil
d nahtlos

1639 seasoning
f assaisonnement m
e sazón f; aliño m; condimento m
d Würze f; Gewürz n

* **sea wolf** → 393

1640 sediment
f sédiment m
e sedimento m
d Absatz m; Bodensatz m

1641 seed v
To sprinkle with seed.
f ensemencer
e sembrar
d einsähen

1642 seeding
Inoculation by introduction of
crystal nuclei.
f ensemencement m
e siembra f
d Impfen n; Beimpfen n; Einsähen n

1643 **seep** *v*
 f suinter
 e rezumar; infiltrarse
 d durchsickern

1644 **Seitz filter**
 f filtre *f* Seitz
 e filtro *m* de Seitz
 d Seitzfilter *m*

1645 **self-raising flour**
 f farine *f* autolevante
 e harina *f* autolevantadora
 d Fertigmehl *n*

1646 **semi-permeable**
 f semi-perméable
 e semipermeable
 d halbdurchlässig

1647 **semi-preserved**
 f semi-conservé
 e semipreservado
 d halb-konserviert

1648 **semolina**
 Middlings of *Triticum durum.*
 f semoule *f*
 e sémola *f*
 d Griess *m*

1649 **senescence**
 f vieillissement *m*; sénescence *f*
 e envejecimiento *m*
 d Älterung *f*; Altern *n*

1650 **sensing element**
 f organe *m* sensible
 e sensor *m*
 d Fühler *m*

1651 **sensitivity**
 f sensibilité *f*
 e sensitividad *f*
 d Empfindlichkeit *f*

1652 **sensory evaluation**
 f évaluation *f* sensorielle
 e evaluación *f* sensorial; prueba *f*
 sensorial
 d sensorische Prüfung *f*

1653 **sensory perception**
 f perception *f* sensorielle

 e percepción *f* sensorial
 d sensorische Wahrnehmung *f*;
 Sinneswahrnehmung *f*

1654 **sensory receptor**
 f récepteur *m* sensoriel
 e receptor *m* sensorial
 d sensorischer Rezeptor *m*

1655 **separate** *v*
 f séparer; isoler
 e separer; aislar
 d trennen; ausschneiden

* **separated milk** → **1695**

1656 **separator**
 f écrémeuse *f*
 e separador *m*
 d Separator *m*

1657 **septic tank**
 f fosse *f* septique
 e pozo *m* séptico
 d Faulraum *m*

1658 **sequestration**
 f séquestration *f*
 e secuestración *f*
 d Absonderung *f*; Sequestration *f*

1659 **serendipity berry**
 Extremely sweet fruit of
 Dioscoreophyllum cumminsii.
 f baie *f* de *Dioscoreophyllum*
 cumminsii
 e baya *f* de *Dioscoreophyllum*
 cumminsii
 d Beere *f* des *Dioscoreophyllum*
 cumminsii

1660 **serine**
 f sérine *f*
 e serina *f*
 d Serin *n*

1661 **sesame oil**
 Oil from *Sesamum indicum.*
 f huile *f* sésame
 e aceite *m* de ajonjolí
 d Sesamöl *n*

1662 **settling tank**
 f cuve *f* de sédimentation; décanteur

m
e tanque *m* de sedimentación
d Absetzbecken *n*; Klarbecken *n*

1663 sewage
f eaux *fpl* résiduelles; eaux *fpl*
   d'égout
e aguas *fpl* cloacales
d Abwasser *n*

1664 sewage disposal
f évacuation *f* des eaux résiduelles
e evacuación *f* de aguas cloacales
d Abwasserbeseitigung *f*

1665 sewage sludge
f boue *f* d'égouts
e fango *m* cloacal
d Abwasserschlamm *m*

1666 sewer
f égout *m*
e albañal *m*; cloaca *f*
d Abwasserkanal *m*

1667 shad
   Alosa sapidissima.
f alose *f*
e alosa *f*
d Alse *f*; Maifisch *m*

1668 shallot
   Allium ascalonicum.
f échalote *f*
e chalote *m*; ascalonia *f*; escaloña *f*
d Schalotte *f*

1669 shark
   Squali sp.
f requin *m*
e tiburón *m*
d Hai *m*

1670 shark liver oil
f huile *f* de foie de requin
e aceite *m* de hígado de tiburón
d Haifischtran *m*

1671 shearing strength
f résistance *f* au cisaillement
e resistencia *f* al desgarro
d Scheuerfestigkeit *f*

1672 shear press
f texturomètre *m*; presse *f* de
   cisaillement
e prensa *f* de esfuerzo
d Scherpresse *f*

* **sherbet** → **1744**

1673 shoddy
f shoddy *m*
e lana *f* de desecho
d Lumpenwolle *f*; Shoddywolle *f*

1674 shoot; sprout
f rejet *m*
e brote *m*
d Schössling *m*

1675 shortening
   American term for soft fats.
f matière *f* gras
e manteca *f*
d Backfett *n*

1676 shredder
f délisseuse *f*
e triturador *m*; desmenuzador *m*
d Zerkleinerungsmaschine *f*;
   Zerfaserer *m*

1677 shrimp
   Crangon sp. and *Pandalus* sp.
f crevette *f*; salicoque *f*
e gámbaro *m*
d Garnele *f*; Krabbe *f*

1678 shrinkage
   Extent of loss on storage.
f rétrécissement *m*; perte *f* au
   stockage
e encogimiento *m*
d Schwund *m*

* **shrink film** → **1679**

1679 shrinking film; shrink film
f feuille *f* rétractile
e lámina *f* encogible
d Schrumpffolie *f*

1680 siccative; drier
f siccatif *m*
e secante *m*; secativo *m*
d Trockenmittel *n*; Sikkativ *n*

1681 sieve
f tamis *m*
e tamíz *m*; criba *f*
d Sieb *n*

1682 sieve *v*
f cribler; tamiser
e tamizar; cribar
d sieben

1683 silica gel
f gel *m* de silice
e gel *f* de sílice
d Silikagel *n*

1684 silicone rubber
f caoutchouc *m* silicone
e goma *f* silicónica
d Silikonkautschuk *m*

1685 simmer *v*
f mijoter; mitonner
e hervir a fuego lento
d brodeln

1686 single cell protein
f protéine *f* monocellulaire
e proteína *f* unicelular
d Einzellerprotein *n*

1687 single effect evaporator
f évaporateur *m* à simple effet
e evaporador *m* de un solo paso
d Einstufen-Eindampfer *m*

1688 sinker
f grain *m* plongeur
e grano *m* pesado
d Sinker *m*

1689 siphon off *v*
f siphonner
e sifonar
d abhebern

1690 sisal
Fibre from *Agave sisalana.*
f sisal *m*; agave *f* d'Amérique
e sisal *m*
d Sisalhanf *m*

1691 sitosterol
f sitostérol *m*
e sitosterol *m*
d Sitosterin *n*

1692 skate
Raja sp.
f raie *f*
e raya *f*
d Riche *m*

1693 skatole
f scatol *m*
e escatol *m*
d Skatol *n*

1694 skim *v*
f écumer
e espumar
d abschäumen

1695 skim-milk; separated milk
f lait *m* écrémé; petit lait *m*
e leche *f* descremada; leche *f*
separada
d Magermilch *f*; entrahmte Milch *f*

* **slaughter house → 2**

1696 slaw; cole-slaw
f salade *f* de chou
e ensalada *f* de col
d Kohlsalat *m*

1697 sludge
f boue *f*
e fango *m*
d Schlamm *m*

1698 slurry
f boue *f*; bouillie *f*
e lechada *f*
d Brei *m*; Schlamm *m*

* **smell → 1313**

1699 smell defect
f défaut *m* d'odeur
e mal olor *m*
d Geruchsfehler *m*

1700 smelt
Osmerus sp.
f éperlan *m*
e esperlán *m*
d Stint *m*

1701 smoked ham
f jambon *m* fumé; quartier *m* de

lard
e tocino *m* ahumado; lardo *m*
ahumado
d geräucherter Schinken *m*

1702 **smoking**
f fumage *m*
e ahumado *m*
d Räuchern *n*

* **smooth hound** → 627

1703 **smooth roller mill**
f convertisseur *m*
e molino *m* de rodillas lisas
d Glattwalzenstuhl *m*

1704 **smut**
Basidiomycetes, especially *Ustilago
tritici* and *Tilletia tritici.*
f rouille *f*
e ustílago *m*; tizón *m*
d Faulbrand *m*

1705 **snibbing**
f étâge-équeutage *m*
e mondadura *f*
d Schnippeln *n*

1706 **soak** *v*; **steep** *v*
f tremper
e embeber
d trenken; einweichen

1707 **soap**
f savon *m*
e jabón *m*
d Seife *f*

* **soda** → 1714

1708 **soda bread**
f pain *m* fait avec du bicarbonate de
soude
e pan *m* de soda
d Brot *n* mit Natriumbikarbonat
gemacht

1709 **sodium alginate**
f alginate *m* de sodium
e alginato *m* sódico
d Natriumalginat *n*

1710 **sodium ascorbate**
f ascorbate *m* de sodium
e ascorbato *m* sódico
d Natriumaskorbat *n*

1711 **sodium benzoate**
f benzoate *m* de sodium
e benzoato *m* sódico
d Natriumbenzoat *n*

1712 **sodium bicarbonate; bicarbonate of
sodium; baking soda**
f bicarbonate *m* de sodium
e bicarbonato *m* sódico
d Natriumbikarbonat *n*

1713 **sodium bromate**
f bromate *m* de sodium
e bromato *m* sódico
d Natriumbromat *n*

1714 **sodium carbonate; soda**
f carbonate *m* de sodium; soude *f*
e carbonato *m* sódico; sosa *f*
d Natriumkarbonat *n*; Soda *f*

1715 **sodium chlorate**
f chlorate *m* de sodium
e clorato *m* sódico
d Natriumchlorat *n*

1716 **sodium chloride; table salt**
f chlorure *m* de sodium; sel *m* de
cuisine
e cloruro *m* sódico; sal *f* de mesa
d Natriumchlorid *n*; Kochsalz *n*

1717 **sodium chlorite**
f chlorite *m* de sodium
e clorito *m* sódico
d Natriumchlorit *n*

1718 **sodium cyclamate**
f cyclamate *m* de sodium
e ciclamato *m* sódico
d Natriumzyklamat *n*

1719 **sodium fluoroacetate**
f fluoroacétate *m* de sodium
e fluoroacetato *m* sódico
d Natriumfluoracetat *n*

1720 **sodium gluconate**
f gluconate *m* de sodium

e gluconato *m* sódico
d Natriumglukonat *n*

1721 sodium glutamate; monosodium glutamate; M.S.G.
f glutamate *m* de sodium; glutamate *m* monosodique
e glutamato *m* sódico; glutamato *m* monosódico
d Natriumglutamat *n*; Mononatrium-glutamat *n*

1722 sodium iron pyrophosphate
f pyrophosphate *m* sodique de fer
e pirofosfato *m* sódico de hierro
d Natriumeisenpyrophosphat *n*

1723 sodium lauryl sulphate
f lauryl-sulfate *m* de sodium
e laurilsulfato *m* sódico
d Natriumlaurylsulfat *n*

1724 sodium nitrate; Chile saltpetre
f nitrate *m* de sodium; salpêtre du Chili
e nitrato *m* sódico; nitrato *m* de Chile; salitre *m* de Chile
d Natriumnitrat *n*; Chilesalpeter *m*

1725 sodium nitrite
f nitrite *m* de sodium
e nitrito *m* sódico
d Natriumnitrit *n*

1726 sodium perborate
f perborate *m* de sodium
e perborato *m* sódico
d Natriumperborat *n*

1727 sodium persulphate
f persulfate *m* de sodium
e persulfato *m* sódico
d Natriumpersulfat *n*

1728 sodium propionate
f propionate *m* de sodium
e propionato *m* sódico
d Natriumpropionat *n*

1729 sodium silicate; water glass
f silicate *m* de sodium; verre *m* soluble
e silicato *m* sódico; vidrio *m* soluble
d Natriumsilikat *n*; Wasserglas *n*

1730 soft drinks
f boissons *fpl* non-alcoholiques
e refrescos *mpl*
d alkoholfreie Getränke *mpl*

1731 softening point
f point *m* de remollissement
e temperatura *f* de reblandecimiento
d Erweichungspunkt *m*

* **soft roe** → **1234**

1732 soft soap
f savon *m* mou
e jabón *m* blando
d Schmierseife *f*

1733 soiling
f souillure *f*; salissure *f*; contamination *f*
e contaminación *f*
d Verschmutzung *f*; Verunreinigung *f*

1734 sol
f sol *m*
e sol *m*
d Sol *n*

1735 soldered seam of tins
f soudure *f* de boîtes métalliques
e costura *f* de latas
d Lötnaht *f* bei Dosen

1736 soldering
f soudure *f*
e soldadura *f*
d Löten *n*

1737 sole; Dover sole
Solea solea.
f sole *f*
e lenguado *m*
d Seezunge *f*

1738 solubility
f solubilité *f*
e solubilidad *f*
d Löslichkeit *f*

1739 solute
f substance *f* dissoute
e soluto *m*
d aufgelöster Stoff *m*; Gelöstes *n*

1740 solution
 f solution *f*
 e solución *f*
 d Lösung *f*

1741 solvent
 f solvant *m*; dissolvant *n*
 e solvente *m*
 d Lösungsmittel *n*

1742 solvent extraction
 f extraction *f* par dissolvant
 e extracción *f* por solvente
 d Flüssigkeitsextraktion *f*

1743 solvent recovery
 f récupération *f* du solvant
 e recuperación *f* de solvente
 d Lösungsmittelwiedergewinnung *f*

1744 sorbet; sherbet
 Semi-frozen water ice.
 f sorbet *m*
 e sorbete *m*
 d Scherbet *n*; Sorbett *m*

1745 sorbic acid
 Acid occurring in unripe fruit of
 Sorbus aucuparia.
 f acide *m* sorbique
 e ácido *m* sórbico
 d sorbinsäure *f*

1746 sorbitol
 Occurring in *Pyrus aucuparia.*
 f sorbitol *m*
 e sorbitol *m*; sorbita *f*
 d Sorbit *n*; Zuckeralkohol *m*

1747 sorbose
 f sorbose *m*
 e sorbosa *f*
 d Sorbose *f*

1748 sorghum
 Sorghum vulgare.
 f sorgho *m*
 e sorgo *m*
 d Sorghum *m*; Mohrenhirse *f*

1749 sour
 f acide
 e agrio; ácido; acedo
 d sauer

1750 sour cream
 f créme *f* acide
 e crema *f* agria; nata *f* agria
 d Sauerrahm *m*

1751 sour dough
 f levain *m*
 e masa *f* fermentada
 d Sauerteig *m*

1752 souse *v*
 f mariner
 e marinar
 d marinieren

1753 soya bean; soybean
 Glycine sp.
 f soja *m*; soya *m*
 e soja *f*; haba *f* de soja
 d Sojabohne *f*

1754 soya bean oil
 f huile *f* de soja
 e aceite *m* de habas de soja
 d Sojabohnenöl *n*

1755 soya sauce
 f sauce *f* au soja
 e salsa *f* de soja
 d Sojasosse *f*

 * soybean → 1753

1756 sparge pipe
 f tuyau *m* perforé
 e tubo *m* rociador
 d Zerstäuberrohr *n*

1757 specific gravity
 f poids *m* spécifique
 e peso *m* específico
 d spezifisches Gewicht *n*

1758 specific heat
 f chaleur *f* spécifique
 e calor *m* específico
 d spezifische Wärme *f*

1759 specificity
 f spécificité *f*
 e especifidad *f*; especificidad *f*
 d Spezifität *f*

1760 specific viscosity
f viscosité f spécifique
e viscosidad f especifica
d spezifische Viskosität f

1761 specific volume
f volume m spécifique
e volumen m específico
d spezifisches Volumen n

1762 spectrum
f spectre m
e espectro m
d Spektrum n

* spent grains → 1176

1763 spent wash
f lessive f résiduaire
e vinaza f
d Ablauge f

1764 sperm oil
f huile f de baleine
e aceite m de esperma
d Spermöl n

1765 spice
f épice f
e condimento m; especia f
d Gewürz n

1766 spike oil; lavender spike
Oil from *Lavandula spica.*
f huile f de spic
e esencia f de espliego
d Spiköl n

1767 spinach
Spinacia oleracea.
f épinard m
e espinaca f
d Spinat m

1768 spindle
f axe m; arbre m
e eje m
d Spindel f

* spiny lobster → 509

1769 spiral heater
f réchauffeur m hélicoïdal
e calentador m helicoidal
d Spiralhitzer m

1770 spirits of salt
f esprit m de sel
e espíritu m de sal
d Salzsäure f

1771 spirits of wine
f esprit m de vin
e espíritu m de vino
d Weingeist m

1772 spleen; milt
f rate f
e bazo m
d Milz f

1773 spontaneous combustion
f combustion f spontanée
e combustión f espontánea
d Selbstverbrennung f

1774 spore formation
f sporulation f
e formación f de esporas
d Sporenbildung f

1775 sprat
Sprattus sprattus.
f sprat m
e sardineta f; arenque m pequeño
d Sprotte f

1776 spray chamber
f chambre f d'atomisation
e cámara f de atomización
d Zerstäubungsraum m

1777 spray cooling
f refroidissement m par atomisation
e enfriamiento m por atomización
d Zerstäubungskühlung f

1778 spray drying
f séchage m par atomisation
e secado m por atomización
d Zerstäubungstrocknung f

1779 spray tower
f tour f d'atomisation
e torre f de atomización
d Zerstäubungsturm m

1780 sprout v
f germer
e germinar
d keimen

* sprout → 1674

1781 sprout inhibitor
   f anti-germinant *m*
   e antigerminante *m*
   d Keimhemmungsmittel *n*

* spur dog → 627

1782 squalene
   f squalène *f*
   e esqualeno *m*
   d Squalen *n*

* squash → 1483

1783 squid; calamary
   f encornet *m*; calmar *m*
   e calamar *m*
   d Kalmar *m*

1784 stabilizer
   f stabilisateur *m*
   e estabilizador
   d Stabilisator *m*

1785 stainless steel
   f acier *m* inoxydable
   e acero *m* inoxidable
   d rostfreier Stahl *m*

1786 staling; retrogradation
   f rassissement *f*; rétrogradation *f*
   e retrogradación *f*
   d Altbackenwerden *n*; Retrogradation
   f

1787 standard solution
   f solution *f* normale
   e solución *f* normal
   d Normallösung *f*

1788 staphylococcus
   f staphylocoque *m*
   e estafilococo *m*
   d Staphylokokkus *m*

1789 staple
   Principal product or commodity of
   a region.
   f denrée *f* principale
   e producto *m* principal
   d Haupterzeugnis *n*; Hauptprodukt *n*

1790 stapler; stapling machine
   f agrafeuse *f*
   e engrapadora *f*
   d Heftmaschine *f*

* stapling machine → 1790

1791 starch
   f amidon *m*
   e almidón *m*
   d Stärke *f*

1792 starch content
   f teneur *m* en amidon
   e contenido *m* en almidón
   d Stärkegehalt *m*

1793 starter
   Bacterial culture used to inoculate
   milk.
   f levain *m*
   e iniciador *m*
   d Säurewecker *m*

1794 statutory order
   f réglementation *f* légale
   e orden *f* estatutoria
   d gesetzliche Verordnung *f*

1795 stave
   f douve *f*
   e duela *f*
   d Daube *f*

1796 steam
   f vapeur *f*
   e vapor *m*
   d Dampf *m*

1797 steam distillation
   f distillation *f* à la vapeur
   e destilación *f* por vapor
   d Wasserdampfdestillation *f*

1798 steam ejector
   f éjecteur *m* à vapeur
   e aspirador *m* accionado por vapor
   d Dampfstrahlapparat *m*

1799 steam extraction
   f extraction *f* à la vapeur
   e extracción *f* por vapor
   d Dampfextraktion *f*

1800 steam generator
f chaudière f; générateur m de vapeur
e generador m de vapor
d Dampferzeuger m

1801 steam injection heating
f chauffage m par injection de vapeur
e calentamiento m por injección de vapor
d Dampfinjektionserhitzung f

1802 steam jacket
f chemise f de vapeur
e camisa f de vapor
d Dampfmantel m

1803 steam pressure
f pression f de vapeur; tension f de vapeur
e presión f de vapor
d Dampfdruck m

1804 stearic acid
f acide m stéarique
e ácido m esteárico
d Stearinsäure f

1805 stearin
f stéarine f
e estearina f
d Stearin n

1806 steep v
To immerse barley to induce germination for malting.
f trempfer
e remojar
d weichen

* **steep** v → **1706**

1807 steer
f bouvillon m
e buey m joven
d junger Ochse m

1808 Steffens process
f procédé m Steffens
e proceso m Steffens
d Steffensches Verfahren n

1809 stereoisomer
f stéréo-isomère m
e estereoisómero m
d Stereoisomer n

1810 stereospecific
f stéréospécifique
e estereoespecífico
d stereospezifisch

1811 sterile
f stérile
e estéril
d steril; keimfrei

1812 sterile air
f air m stérile
e aire m esterilizado
d sterile Luft f

1813 sterilize v
f stériliser
e esterilizar
d sterilisieren

1814 stiff
f consistant; épais
e consistente
d steif

* **still** → **1449**

1815 stimulus
f stimulus m
e estímulo m
d Reiz m; Reizmittel n; Stimulans n

* **St. John's bread** → **373**

* **stock** → **295**

1816 stockfish
f stockfisch m; morue f sèche
e estocafís m; bacalao m seco
d Stockfisch m

1817 stone-fruit
f fruit m à noyau
e fruta f de hueso
d Steinobst n; Kernfrucht f

1818 stop cock
f robinet m d'arrêt
e llave f; grifo m
d Absperrhahn m

1819 storage
f emmagasinage *m*
e almacenamiento *m*
d Lagerung *f*

1820 stout
f stout *m*
e cerveza *f* negra
d Starkbier *n*

1821 straight-through can washer
f machine *f* rectiligne à laver des bidons
e lavador *m* continuo de latas
d Langskannenwaschmaschine

1822 strawberry
Fragasia fam.
f fraise *f*
e fresa *f*
d Erdbeere *f*

1823 streptomycin
f streptomycine *f*
e estreptomicina *f*
d Streptomycin *n*

* **striped mullet** → 880

1824 stuffing box; gland
Seal around a shaft.
f boîte *f* à bourrage
e capa *f* de empaquetadura
d Stopfbüchse *f*

1825 stun *v*
f étourdir
e ensordecer; aturdir
d betäuben

1826 sturgeon
Acipenser sp.
f esturgeon *m*
e esturión *m*
d Stör *m*

1827 sublimation
f sublimation *f*
e sublimación *f*
d Sublimation *f*

1828 substitute
f succédané *m*
e substituto *m*; succedáneo
d Ersatz *m*

1829 subtilin
Antibiotic from *Bacillus subtilis*.
f subtiline *f*
e subtilina *f*
d Subtilin *n*

* **sucrase** → 1004

* **sucrose** → 1590

1830 suction pump
f pompe *f* aspirante
e bomba *f* aspirante
d Saugpumpe *f*

1831 suet
f graisse *f* de rognon
e grasa *f* de riñón
d Nierentalg *m*; Nierenfett *n*

1832 sugar
f sucre *m*
e azúcar *m*
d Zucker *m*

1833 sugar beet
Beta vulgaris.
f betterave *f* à sucre
e remolacha *f* azucarera
d Zuckerrübe *f*

1834 sugar cane
Saccharum officinarum.
f canne *f* à sucre
e caña *f* de azúcar
d Zuckerrohr *n*

1835 sugar crusher
f broyeur *m* de cannes de sucre
e machacador *m* de azúcar
d Zuckerrohrquetsche *f*

1836 sugar cube; sugar lump
f morceau *m* de sucre
e terrón *m* de azúcar
d Zuckerwürfel *m*

* **sugar lump** → 1836

1837 sugar of lead
f sucre *m* de saturne
e azúcar *m* de plomo
d Bleizucker *m*

1838 sulphonated oil
f huile f sulfonée
e aceite m sulfonado
d geschwefeltes Öl n

1839 sulphur dioxide
f dioxyde m de soufre
e dióxido m de azufre
d Schwefeldioxyd n

1840 sulphurous acid
f acide m sulfureux
e ácido m sulfuroso
d schwefelige Säure f

1841 sultana
f raisin m sec de Smyrne
e sultana f; pasita f
d Sultanine f

1842 sunflower oil
Oil from *Helianthus annuus*.
f huile f de tournesol
e aceite m de girasol
d Sonnenblumenöl n

1843 supercooled
f surfondu
e sobreenfriado
d unterkühlt

1844 supercooling
f surfusion f
e sobreenfriamiento m
d Unterkühlung f

1845 superheating
f surchauffage f
e sobrecalentamiento m
d Überhitzung f

1846 supersaturated
f sursaturé
e sobresaturado
d übersättigt

* **surface active agent → 1848**

1847 surface tension
f tension f superficielle
e tensión f superficial
d Oberflächenspannung f

1848 surfactant; surface active agent; wetting agent
f agent m tensio-actif; agent m mouillant
e surfactante m; agente m humectante
d Netzmittel n; Oberflächenaktivstoff m

1849 suspension
f suspension f
e suspensión f
d Suspension f

1850 sweat v
f transuder
e exudar; sudar
d durchschwitzen

1851 swede; rutabaga
f navet m de Suède; chou-navet m; rutabaga m
e colinabo m; rutabaga m; nabo m de Suecia
d Steckrübe f; Kohlrübe f

1852 sweet
f doux
e dulce
d süss

* **sweet bay → 1091**

* **sweet pepper → 1363**

1853 sweet potato
f patate f
e batata f
d Süsskartoffel f; Batate f

1854 sweet wort
f moût m adouci
e mosto m dulce
d süsse Würze f

1855 swell
Can of food swollen by production of gas.
f boîte f gonflée
e lata f abombada
d bombierte Dose f

1856 swelling coefficient
f coefficient m de gonflement

   e coeficiente *m* de inflación
   d Quellungskoeffizient *m*

1857 swimmer
   Floating grain of barley.
   f grain *m* flottant; flotteur *m*
   e grano *m* flotante de cebada
   d Schwimmer *m*

1858 swordfish
   Xiphias gladius.
   f espadon *m*
   e pez *m* espada
   d Schwertfisch *m*

1859 symbiosis
   f symbiose *f*
   e simbiosis *f*
   d Symbiose *f*

   * **syndet → 1863**

1860 syneresis
   f synérèse *f*
   e sinéresis *f*
   d Synärese *f*; Ausschwitzen *n*

1861 synergist
   f synergiste *m*
   e sinergisto *m*
   d Synergist *m*

1862 synthetic
   f synthétique
   e sintético
   d synthetisch

1863 synthetic detergent; syndet
   f détergent *m* synthétique
   e detergente *m* sintético
   d synthetisches Reinigungsmittel *n*

   * **synthetic meat → 1902**

1864 syrup
   f sirop *m*
   e jarabe *m*
   d Sirup *m*

table 112

T

* table salt → 1716

1865 tachometer
f tachymètre *m*
e tacómetro *m*
d Tachometer *n*

1866 tachysterol
f tachistéine *f*
e taquisterol *m*
d Tachysterin *n*

1867 tacky
f collant
e pegajoso
d klebrig

1868 tactic
f tactique
e táctico
d taktisch

1869 tag v
f marquer
e marcar
d markieren

1870 tailings
f déchets *mpl* d'orge
e desperdicios *mpl* de cebada
d Gersteabfälle *mpl*

1871 taint v
To cause putrefication and bad smell.
f gâter
e pudrir
d verseuchen

* taint v → 486

1872 takadiastase; koji
f takadiastase *f*; koji *m*
e takadiastasa *f*; koji *m*
d Takadiastase *f*; Koji *n*

1873 talc; talcum
f talc *m*
e talco *m*
d Talk *m*; Talkum *n*

* talcum → 1873

1874 tallow
f suif *m*
e sebo *m*
d Talg *m*

1875 tangerine
Citrus nobilis.
f mandarine *f*
e naranja *f* tangarina; tangarino *m*
d kleine Orange *f*; Mandarine *f*

1876 tannic acid
f acide *m* tannique
e ácido *m* tánico
d Gerbsäure *f*; Tanninsäure *f*

1877 tannin
f tanin *m*; tannin *m*
e tanino *m*
d Tannin *n*

1878 tap v
To draw off liquid.
f retirer
e trasegar
d abzapfen

1879 tap v
f mettre en perce
e instalar un grifo
d anstechen

1880 tapioca
f tapioca *m*
e tapioca *f*
d Tapioka *f*

1881 taraxacum; dandelion
Taraxacum officinale.
f pissenlit *m*; taraxacum *m*
e taraxacón *m*
d Taraxakum *n*; Löwenzahn *m*

1882 tare
f tare *f*
e tara *f*
d Tara *f*

* tare → 1998

1883 tarragon
Artemisia dracunculus.

f estragon *m*
e tarragón *m*; estragón *m*
d Estragon *m*

1884 tartaric acid
f acide *m* tartarique
e ácido *m* tartárico
d Weinsäure *f*; Weinsteinsäure *f*

1885 taste
f goût *m*
e gusto *m*; sabor *m*
d Geschmack *m*

1886 taste buds
f papilles *fpl* gustatives
e papilas *fpl* gustativas
d Geschmacksknospen *fpl*

1887 tasting; gustation
f gustation *f*
e gustación *f*
d Kosten *n*

1888 tautomerism
f tautomérie *f*
e tautomerismo *m*
d Tautomerie *f*

1889 tea
f thé *m*
e té *m*
d Tee *m*

1890 teleost
f téléostéen *m*
e teleosteo *m*
d Knochenfisch *m*

1891 temporary hardness of water
f crudité *f* temporaire de l'eau
e dureza *f* temporal del agua
d vorübergehende Härte des Wassers

1892 tench
Tinca tinca.
f tanche *f*
e tenca *f*
d Schlei *m*

1893 tenderizer
f enzyme *f* attendrisante
e ablandador *m*
d Tenderizer *m*

1894 tenderness
f tendreté *f*
e ternura *f*; blandura *f*
d Zartheit *f*

1895 tenderometer
f tendromètre *m*
e tenderómetro *m*
d Tenderometer *n*

1896 tendon
f tendon *m*
e tendón *m*
d Sehne *f*

1897 terpene
f terpène *m*
e terpeno *m*
d Terpen *n*

1898 test
f épreuve *f*
e prueba *f*
d Probe *f*

1899 testa
f testa *m*; tégument *m*; séminal *m*
e testa *f*
d Samenschale *f*

1900 tetracycline
f tétracycline *f*
e tetraciclina *f*
d Tetracyclin *n*

1901 texture
f texture *f*
e textura *f*
d Konsistenz *f*

**1902 textured vegetable protein;
    synthetic meat**
f protéine *f* végétale texturée; viande
  f synthétique
e proteína *f* vegetal texturizada;
  carne *f* sintética
d struktuiertes Pflanzenprotein *n*;
  struktuiertes Pflanzeneiweiss *n*;
  künstliches Fleisch *n*

1903 thaw *v*
f dégeler
e descongelar
d auftauen; abtauen; tauen

1904 theophylline
f théophylline f
e teofilina f
d Theophyllin n

1905 thermal death point
f température f mortelle
e punto m térmico de muerte
d thermaler Abtötungspunkt m

1906 thermo-couple
f thermocouple m
e termopar m; par m térmico;
  termocupla f
d Thermoelement n

1907 thermodynamics
f thermodynamique f
e termodinámica f
d Thermodynamik f

1908 thermolabile
f thermolabile
e termolábil
d thermolabil

1909 thermolysis
f thermolyse f
e termólisis f
d Thermolyse f

1910 thermometer
f thermomètre m
e termómetro m
d Thermometer n

1911 thermophylic organism
f organisme m thermophile
e organismo m termófilo
d thermophiler Organismus m

1912 thermostat
f thermostat m
e termostato m
d Thermostat n; Temperaturregler m

* **thiamin → 2010**

1913 thickener
f épaississant m
e espesador m
d Verdickungsmittel n

* **thiol → 1205**

1914 thixotrope
f thixotrope m
e tixótropo m
d Thixotrop n

1915 threonine
f thréonine f
e treonina f
d Threonin n

1916 threshold value
f valeur f de seuil; valeur f liminaire
e valor m umbral; valor m liminal
d Schwellenwert m

1917 thyme oil
Oil from *Thymus* sp.
f essence f de thym
e aceite m de tomillo
d Thymianöl n

1918 thyroxine
f thyroxine f
e tiroxina f
d Thyroxin n

1919 tin plate
f fer-blanc m
e hoja f de lata; hojalata f
d Weissblech n; Blech n

* **tocopherol → 2016**

1920 tomato
Fruit of *Lycopersicon esculentum*.
f tomate f
e tomate m
d Tomate f

1921 tonka bean
Dipteryx sp.
f tonka m
e haba f de tonca
d Tonkabohne f

1922 top roller
f cylindre m supérieur
e rodillo m superior
d Oberwalze f

1923 top yeast
f levure f haute
e levadura f alta
d Oberhefe f

1924 toxicity
f toxicité f
e toxicidad f
d Giftigkeit f

1925 toxin
f toxine f
e toxina f
d Toxin n

* **tragacanth gum → 896**

1926 transferase
f transférase f
e transferasa f
d Transferase f

* **transparent → 1380**

1927 transparent packaging
f emballage m transparent
e embalaje m transparente
d Klarsichtpackung f

1928 transpiration
f transpiration f
e transpiración f
d Transpiration f

* **treacle → 1244**

1929 triangle test
f méthode f triangulaire
e prueba f en triadas
d Dreieckstest n

1930 trichinosis
Disease caused by *Trichinella spiralis* worm.
f tricinose f
e triquinosis f
d Trichinose f

1931 trichlorocarbanilide
f trichlorocarbanilide f
e triclorocarbanilida f
d Trichlorkarbanilid n

1932 tripe
f tripes fpl
e tripas fpl
d Kaldaunen fpl; Kutteln fpl;
  Eingeweide npl

1933 triticale
f triticale f
e triticale m
d Tritikale n

1934 truffle
Fruiting body of *Tuber* fungi.
f truffe f
e trufa f
d Trüffel f

1935 trypsin
f trypsine f
e tripsina f
d Trypsin n

1936 tryptophan
f tryptophane m
e triptofano m
d Tryptophan n

1937 tuber
f tubercule f
e tubércula f
d Knolle f

1938 tuberculin
f tuberculine f
e tuberculina f
d Tuberkulin n

1939 tubular boiler
f chaudière f tubulaire
e caldera f tubular
d Wasserrohrkessel m

1940 tubular cooler
f réfrigérant m tubulaire
e enfriadera f tubular; refrigerador
  m tubular
d Rohrenkühler m

1941 tuna
Thunnus sp., *Neothunnus* sp., or
Euthunnus sp.
f thon m
e atún m
d Thunfisch m

1942 tuna oil
Oil from liver of *Thunnus vulgaris*.
f huile f de thon
e aceite m de atún
d Thunfischöl n

1943 tunnel tray dryer
  f tunnel *m* de séchage à plateaux
  e tubo *m* secador en bandejas
  d Trockentunnel *m*

1944 turbid
  f trouble
  e turbio
  d trübe

1945 turbot
  Psetta maxima.
  f turbot *m*
  e rodaballo *m*
  d Steinbutt *m*

1946 turbulent flow
  f courant *m* turbulant
  e flujo *m* turbulento
  d turbulente Strömung *f*

1947 turgor
  f turgescence *f*
  e turgor *m*
  d Turgor *m*; Turgeszenz *f*

* turmeric → 535

1948 turnip
  Top root of *Brassica rapa* or *B. campestris.*
  f navet *m*
  e nabo *m*
  d Kohlrübe *f*; Steckrübe *f*

1949 Twaddell hydrometer
  f hydromètre *m* de Twaddell
  e hidrómetro *m* de Twaddell
  d Twadellsches Hydrometer *n*

1950 two-stage compressor
  f compresseur *m* à deux étages
  e compresor *m* de dos tiempos
  d zweistufiger Kompressor *m*

1951 tyrocidine
  Antibiotic from *Bacillus brevis.*
  f tyrocidine *f*
  e tirocidina *f*
  d Tyrocidin *n*

1952 tyrosine
  f tyrosine *f*
  e tirosina *f*
  d Tyrosin *n*

1953 tyrothricin
  f tyrothricine *f*
  e tirotricina *f*
  d tyrothricin *n*

U

* U.H.T. → 1956

1954 ullage
 f vide m
 e merma f
 d Flüssigkeitsmanko n

1955 ultra-filtration
 f ultrafiltration f
 e ultrafiltración f
 d Ultrafiltration f

1956 ultra-high temperature; U.H.T.
 Refers to sterilization of liquids at
 an ultra-high temperature. See also
 H.T.S.T.
 f ultra-haute-température f
 e temperatura f ultra elevada
 d Ultrahochtemperatur f; U.H.T.

1957 ultrasonics
 f ultrason m
 e ultrasonido m
 d Ultraschall m

1958 ultraviolet
 f ultraviolet
 e ultravioleta
 d ultraviolett

1959 undecalactone
 f undécalactone f
 e undecalactona f
 d Undekalakton n

1960 unsaturated
 f non-saturé
 e insaturado
 d ungesättigt

1961 uperisation
 Sterilization by injecting steam
 under pressure at 150°C. See also
 U.H.T.
 f upérisation f
 e uperización f
 d Uperisierung f

1962 urea
 f urée f

 e urea f
 d Harnstoff m

1963 urea adducts
 Inclusion complexes of urea and,
 usually, an unbranched aliphatic
 hydrocarbon or fatty acid. Used in
 the separation of fatty acids.
 f produits mpl d'insertion avec l'urée
 e aductos mpl de urea
 d Harnstoffaddukte npl

1964 urease
 f uréase f
 e ureasa f
 d Urease f

1965 uric acid
 f acide m urique
 e ácido m úrico
 d Harnsäure f

1966 uridine
 f uridine f
 e uridina f
 d Uridin n

1967 U-tube manometer
 f manomètre m à tube en U
 e manómetro m en U
 d U-Rohr-Manometer n

V

1968 vacuum contact plate process
f séchage *m* à plaques sous vide
e proceso *m* de deshidratación por contacto con platos al vacío
d Vakuumkontaktplattenverfahren *n*

1969 vacuum distillation
f distillation *f* sous vide
e destilación *f* al vacío
d Vakuumdestillation *f*

1970 vacuum drier
Equipment for drying foodstuffs which can be evacuated to give a vacuum to assist dehydration
f séchoir *m* sous vide
e secador *m* de vacío
d Vakuumtrockner *m*

1971 vacuum drying oven
f four *m* à sécher sous vide
e horno *m* de secar al vacío
d Vakuumtrockenofen *m*

1972 vacuum evaporator
f évaporateur *m* sous vide
e evaporador *m* al vacío
d Vakuumeindampfer *m*

1973 vacuum filling
f remplissage *m* sous vide
e llenado *m* al vacío
d Vakuumabfüllung *f*

1974 vacuum filtration
f filtration *f* par le vide
e filtración *f* al vacío
d Vakuumfiltrierung *f*

1975 vacuum gauge
f indicateur *m* de vide
e medidor *m* de vacío
d Unterdruckmesser *m*

1976 vacuum pan
f évaporateur *m* à vide
e evaporador *m* al vacío
d Vakuumpfanne *f*

1977 vacuum pump
f pompe *f* à vide
e bomba *f* de vacío
d Vakuumpumpe *f*

1978 vacuum shelf dryer
f armoire *m* à sécher par le vide
e armario *m* para secar al vacío
d Vakuumtrockenschrank *m*

1979 vacuum still
f alambic *m* sous vide
e alambique *m* al vacío
d Vakuumdestillierapparat *m*

1980 valine
f valine *f*
e valina *f*
d Valin *n*

1981 valve
f soupape *f*
e válvula *f*
d Ventil *n*

1982 vanadium steel
f acier *m* au vanadium
e acero *m* al vanadio
d Vanadinstahl *m*; Vanadiumstahl *m*

1983 vancomycin
Antibiotic produced by *Streptomyces orientalis.*
f vancomycine *f*
e vancomicina *f*
d Vancomycin *n*

1984 vanilla essence
From pods of *Vanilla planifolia.*
f essence *f* de vanille
e esencia *f* de vainilla
d Vanille-Essenz *f*

1985 vanillin
f vanilline *f*
e vainilla *f*
d Vanillin *n*

1986 vaporization
f vaporisation *f*
e vaporización *f*
d Verdampfung *f*

1987 vaporization heat
 f chaleur f de vaporisation
 e calor m de vaporización
 d Verdampfungswärme f

1988 vapour density
 f densité f de vapeur
 e densidad f de vapor
 d Dampfdichte f

1989 vapour pressure
 f tension f de vapeur
 e tensión f del vapor; presión f del
   vapor
 d Dampfdruck m

1990 variable speed drive
 f variateur m de vitesse
 e variador m de velocidad
 d Antrieb m mit variabeler
   Geschwindigkeit; Antrieb m mit
   variabelem Geschwindigkeits-
   bereich

1991 veal
 f veau m
 e ternera f; carne f de ternera
 d Kalbsfleisch n

1992 vegetable black; vegetable charcoal
 f noir m végétal; charbon m végétal
 e negro m vegetal; carbón m vegetal
 d Pflanzenkohle f; Holzkohle f

 * **vegetable charcoal** → 1992

1993 vegetable protein
 f protéine f végétale
 e proteína f vegetal
 d pflanzliches Eiweiss n

1994 venison
 f venaison f
 e carne f montesina; carne f de
   venado
 d Rehwildbret n; Rehfleisch n

1995 vermiculite
 f vermiculite f
 e vermiculita f
 d Vermikulit m

1996 vermin
 f vermine f

 e bicho m
 d Ungeziefer n

1997 vermouth
 f vermouth m
 e vermut m
 d Wermut m

1998 vetch; tare
   Vicia sp.
 f vesce m
 e veza f
 d Wicke f

1999 viable
 f viable
 e viable
 d lebensfähig; lebendig

2000 vibration conveyor
 f transporteur m à vibrations
 e portador m vibratorio de
   transportación
 d Vibrations-Förderer m

2001 vinegar
 f vinaigre m
 e vinagre m
 d Essig m

2002 vinegar generator
 f générateur m de vinaigre
 e generador m de vinagre
 d Essigerzeuger m

2003 viner
   Machine for separating peas from
   pea plants.
 f recolteuse f de pois; moissonneuse
   f à pois
 e segador m hillerador de guisantes
 d Erbsendrescher m; Erbsenerntemaschine f

2004 vinometer; oenometer
 f vinomètre m; oenomètre m
 e enómetro m
 d Weinmesser m

 * **viscometer** → 2005

2005 viscosimeter; viscometer
 f viscosimètre m
 e viscosímetro m

d Viskosimeter *n*; Viskositätsmesser *m*

2006 viscosity
f viscosité *f*
e viscosidad *f*
d Viskosität *f*; Zähigkeit *f*

2007 viscous flow
f écoulement *m* visqueux
e flujo *m* viscoso
d plastisches Fliessen *n*

2008 vitamin
f vitamine *f*
e vitamina *f*
d Vitamin *n*

2009 vitamin A; retinol
f axérophtol *m*; rétinol *m*; vitamine *f* A
e axeroftol *m*; retinol *m*; vitamina *f* A
d Axerophthol *n*; Retinin *n*; Vitamin *n* A

2010 vitamin B₁; thiamin; aneurin
f aneurine *f*; thiamine *f*; vitamine *f* B₁
e aneurina *f*; tiamina *f*; vitamina *f* B₁
d Aneurin *n*; Thiamin *n*; Vitamin *n* B₁

2011 vitamin B₂; riboflavin; lactoflavin
f riboflavine *f*; lactoflavine *f*; vitamine *f* B₂
e riboflavina *f*; lactoflavina *f*; vitamina *f* B₂
d Riboflavin *n*; Laktoflavin *n*; Vitamin *n* B₂

2012 vitamin B₆; pyridoxin; adermin
f pyridoxine *f*; adermine *f*; vitamine *f* B₆
e piridoxina *f*; adermina *f*; vitamina *f* B₆
d Pyridoxin *n*; Adermin *n*; Vitamin *n* B₆

2013 vitamin B₁₂; cyanocobalamin; cobalamin
f cobalamine *f*; cyanocobalamine *f*; vitamine *f* B₁₂

e cobalamina *f*; vitamina *f* B₁₂
d Kobalamin *n*; Vitamin *n* B₁₂

2014 vitamin C; ascorbic acid
f acide *m* ascorbique; vitamine *f* C
e ácido *m* ascórbico; vitamina *f* C
d Askorbinsäure *f*; Vitamin *n* C

2015 vitamin D₂; calciferol
f calciférol *m*; vitamine *f* D₂
e calciferol *m*; vitamina *f* D₂
d Kalziferol *n*; Vitamin *n* D₂

2016 vitamin E; tocopherol
f tocophérol *m*; vitamine *f* E
e tocoferol *m*; vitamina *f* E
d Tokopherol *n*; Vitamin *n* E

2017 vitamin K
f vitamine *f* K
e vitamina *f* K
d Vitamin *n* K

* **vitamin PP** → 1281, 1283

2018 volatile
f volatil
e volátil
d leichtflüchtig

2019 voltmeter
f voltmètre *m*
e voltímetro *m*
d Spannungsmesser *m*; Voltmeter *n*

2020 volume percentage
f pourcentage *m* en volume
e porcentaje *m* en volumen
d Volumenprozentzahl *f*

2021 volumetric analysis
f analyse *f* volumétrique
e análisis *m* volumétrico
d Massanalyse *f*; volumetrische Analyse *f*

2022 votator
Proprietary name of Girdler Corp. for a scraped surface heat exchanger. Used in the manufacture of margarine and shortening.
f votator *m*
e votator *m*

d Votator *m*; Kratzwärmeaustauscher
m

W

2023 walnut
Fruit of *Juglans regia.*
f noix *f*
e nuez *m*
d Walnuss *f*

2024 walnut oil
f huile *f* de noix
e aceite *m* de nuez
d Walnussöl *n*

2025 warfarin
f warfarine *f*
e warfarina *f*; varfarina *f*
d Warfarin *n*

2026 warm air drier
f sécheur *m* à courant d'air chaud
e secador *m* de aire tibio
d Warmlufttrockner *m*

2027 waste product
f déchets *mpl*
e desperdicio *m*; desecho *m*
d Abfallprodukt *n*

2028 water
f eau *f*
e agua *f*
d Wasser *n*

2029 water content
f teneur *f* en eau
e contenido *m* de agua
d Wassergehalt *n*

2030 watercress
Leaves of *Nasturtium officinale.*
f cresson *m* de fontaine
e berro *m*
d Brunnenkresse *f*

2031 water equivalent
f équivalent *m* en eau
e equivalente *m* en agua
d Wasserwert *m*

2032 water-gauge pressure
f pression *f* de colonne d'eau
e presión *f* de columna de agua
d Wasserstandsdruck *m*

* **water glass** → **1729**

2033 water holding capacity
f pouvoir *m* d'absorption de l'eau
e capacidad *f* de retener agua
d Wasserbingungsvermögen *n*

2034 water melon
Citrullus vulgaris.
f melon *m* d'eau
e sandía *f*
d Wassermelone *f*

2035 water of condensation
f eau *f* de condensation
e agua *m* de condensación
d Schwitzwasser *n*

2036 water of crystallization
f eau *f* de cristallisation
e agua *f* de cristalización
d Kristallwasser *n*

2037 waterproof
f imperméable
e impermeable
d wasserdicht; wasserfest

2038 water seal
f joint *m* hydraulique
e sello *m* de agua
d Wasser-Verschluss *m*

2039 wax
f cire *f*
e cera *f*
d Wachs *m*

2040 weed
f mauvaise herbe *f*; plante *f* adventrice
e mala hierba *f*
d Unkraut *n*

2041 weed killer; herbicide
f herbicide *m*
e herbicida *f*
d Unkrautvertilgungsmittel *n*; Herbizid *n*

2042 weight loss
f perte *f* de poids
e pérdida *f* de peso
d Gewichtsverlust *m*

2043 **weight percentage**
 f pourcentage *m* en poids
 e porcentaje *m* en peso
 d Gewichtsprozentzahl *f*

2044 **wet spinning**
 f filage *m* au mouillé
 e hilatura *f* en húmedo
 d Nasspinnen *n*

 * **wetting agent** → 1848

2045 **whale oil**
 Oil from *Cetacea* sp.
 f huile *f* de baleine
 e aceite *m* de ballena
 d Tran *m*; Walfischtran *m*

2046 **wheat**
 Triticum aestivum, also *T. vulgare*,
 T. durum, and *T. compactum*.
 f froment *m*; blé *m*
 e trigo *m*
 d Weizen *m*

2047 **wheat flakes**
 f flocons *mpl* de blé; flocons *mpl* de
 froment
 e hojuelas *fpl* de trigo
 d Weizenflocken *fpl*

2048 **wheat germ oil**
 f huile *f* de germe de blé; huile *f* de
 germe de froment
 e aceite *m* de germen de trigo
 d Weizenkeimöl *n*

 * **wheat meal bread** → 2056

2049 **whelk**
 Buccinum undatum.
 f buccin *m*
 e caracol de mar *m*; buccino *m*
 d Wellhornschnecke *f*

2050 **whey**
 f sérum *m*; lactosérum *m*
 e suero *f*
 d Molke *f*

2051 **whitebait**
 Young of the *Clupea harengus* or
 Sprattus sprattus.
 f blanchaille *f*

 e boquerón *m*
 d Breitling *m*

2052 **whitefish**
 Coregonus sp.
 f lavaret *m*
 e merlán *m*
 d Maräne *f*

2053 **white pepper**
 Husked berries of *Piper nigrum*.
 f poivre *m* blanc
 e pimienta *f* blanca
 d weisser Pfeffer *m*

2054 **whiting**
 Merlangus merlangus.
 f merlan *m*
 e merlán *m*
 d Merlan *m*

2055 **wholemeal bread**
 f pain *m* complet
 e pan *m* integral
 d Vollkornbrot *n*; Schrotbrot *n* mit
 vollem Keimlingsanteil

2056 **whole meal bread; wheat meal
 bread**
 Bread made from coarse whole
 meal.
 f pain *m* complet; pain *m* de farine
 intégrale
 e pan *m* integral
 d Vollkornbrot *n*; Weizenschrotbrot *n*

2057 **whole milk powder**
 f poudre *f* de lait entier
 e polvo *m* de leche entera
 d Vollmilchpulver *n*

2058 **wild oats**
 f avoine *f* folle
 e avena *f* salaje
 d Flugshafer *m*

2059 **wine**
 f vin *m*
 e vino *m*
 d Wein *m*

2060 **wine vinegar**
 f vinaigre *m* de vin
 e vinagre *m* de vino
 d Weinessig *m*

2061 winkle; periwinkle
   Littorina littorea.
   f bigorneau *m*
   e caracol *m* marino
   d Strandschnecke *f*

2062 winnow *v*
   f vanner
   e aventar; ahechar
   d schwingen; wannen; worfeln

2063 wintergreen oil
   Oil from *Gaultheria procumbens.*
   f essence *f* de gaulthérie; essence *f*
   de wintergreen
   e aceite *m* de pirola
   d Wintergrünöl *n*

2064 winterisation
   f winterisation *f*
   e invernización *f*
   d Winterisierung *f*

2065 wood alcohol
   f alcool *m* de bois
   e alcohol *m* de madera
   d Holzgeist *m*

   * **wood sugar** → **2071**

   * **wool fat** → **1081**

2066 worm drive
   f commande *f* par vis sans fin
   e transmisión *f* de tornillo sin fin
   d Schneckenantrieb *m*

2067 wormwood oil; absinth oil
   Oil from *Artemisia absinthium.*
   f essence *f* d'absinthe
   e aceite *m* de ajenjo
   d Wermutöl *n*

2068 wort
   f moût *m*
   e mosto *m*
   d Würze *f*

   * **wortleberry** → **235**

2069 wrapping machine
   f machine *f* à empaqueter;
   empaqueteuse *f*
   e máquina *f* para envolver
   d Verpackungsmaschine *f*

X

2070 xanthophyll
 f xanthophylle *f*
 e xantofila *f*
 d Xanthophyll *n*

2071 xylose; wood sugar
 f xylose *m*; sucre *m* de bois
 e xilosa *f*
 d Xylose *f*; Holzzucker *m*

Y

2072 yam
Dioscorea sp.
f igname *f*
e ñame *m*
d Jamswurzel *f*

2073 yeast
Saccharomycetaceae fam.
f levure *f*
e levadura *f*
d Hefe *f*

2074 yeast extract
f extrait *m* de levure
e extracto *m* de levadura
d Hefe-Extrakt *m*

2075 yeast food
f aliment *m* de la levure
e nutrición *f* de la levadura
d Hefenahrung *f*

2076 yeast pressings
f bière *f* de levure
e cerveza *f* por prensa
d Abpressbier *n*

2077 yeast strain
f race *f* de levure
e raza *f* de levadura
d Heferasse *f*

2078 yield
f rendement *m*
e rendimiento *m*
d Ausbeute *f*

2079 yoghurt; yogurt
Milk cultured with *Lactobacillus bulgaris* or *Streptococcus thermophilus.*
f yahourt *m*; yaourt *m*; yoghourt *m*
e yogurt *m*; yogur *m*
d Joghurt *m*

* yogurt → 2079

2080 Young's modulus
f module *m* d'Young
e módulo *m* de Young
d Youngscher Elastizitätsmodul *m*

Z

2081 zein
 f zéine *f*
 e zeína *f*
 d Zein *n*

2082 zeolite
 f zéolithe *f*
 e zeolita *f*
 d Zeolith *m*

* zwieback → 1584

2083 zwitterion
 f ion *m* amphotérique
 e zwiterrión *m*
 d Zwitterion *n*

2084 zymase
 f zymase *f*
 e zimasa *f*
 d Zymase *f*

2085 zymogen
 f zymogène *m*
 e zimógeno *m*
 d Zymogen *n*

2086 zymometer
 f zymosimètre *m*
 e zimómetro *m*
 d Zymometer *n*; Gärungsmesser *m*

2087 zymotachygraphe
 f zymotachygraphe *m*
 e zimotaquígrafo *m*
 d Zymotachygraph *m*

FRANÇAIS

abattoir 2
abricot 152
absorption 4
acaricide 6
accélérateur 8
accélération de la croissance 887
acétal 9
acétaldéhyde 10
acétate 11
acétate d'amyle 115
acétate d'éthyle 15
acétifiant 17
acétine 18
acétobacter 14
acétoglycéride 19
acétone 20
acétylation 22
acide 26, 1749
acide acétique 12
acide acétique cristallisable 832
acide-aldéhyde 76
acide alginique 86
acide aminé 109
acide arachidonique 154
acide ascorbique 2014
acide aspartique 165
acide benzoïque 230
acide butyrique 337
acide caféique 340
acide cholique 438
acide citrique 448
acide désoxyribonucléique 582
acide érucique 685
acide folique 775
acide formique 790
acide gallique 818
acide gibbérellique 830
acide gluconique 838
acide glutamique 842
acide glycérophosphorique 850
acide glycolique 853
acide gras 719
acide gras essentiel 687
acide hydnocarpique 955
acide hypochloreux 974
acide indolbutyrique 983
acide iso-valérianique 1022
acide lactique 1068
acide laurique 1092
acide linoléique 1118
acide linolénique 1120
acide malique 1161
acide nicotinique 1283
acide nucléique 1301
acide oléique 1321

acide orotique 1336
acide palmitique 1353
acide palmitoléique 1354
acide pantothénique 1360
acide phénylique 1402
acide phytique 1407
acide propionique 1470
acide pyroligneux 1490
acide quinique 1498
acide ribonucléique 1557
acide ricinoléique 1561
acide sorbique 1745
acide stéarique 1804
acide sulfureux 1840
acide tannique 1876
acide tartarique 1884
acide urique 1965
acidifier 30
acidimètre 31
acidimétrie 32
acidolyse 33
aciduler 30
acier au vanadium 1982
acier inoxydable 1785
aconitine 38
actine 39
activer la fermentation 1579
activeur 1466
activité 43
activité optique 1329
actomyosine 45
additif alimentaire 777
adénine 47
adermine 2012
adjonction 46
adsorption 50
aerer 53
aérobie 54
aérosol 56
affiner 539, 1564
aflatoxines 57
agar-agar 58
agave d'Amérique 1690
agent adsorbant 49
agent anti-éclaboussant 149
agent anti-mottant 143
agent dessiccateur 585
agent dispersant 619
agent levant 1510
agent mouillant 1848
agent moussant 771
agent oxydant 1347
agent plastifiant 1424
agent qui retarde le rassissement 150
agent tensio-actif 1848

agglutination 62
agglutinine 63
agitateur 64
agneau 1075
agnelet d'un an 943
agrafeuse 1790
aiglefin 900
aigrefin 900
aiguillat 627
ail 820
airelle 235
airelle rouge 508
air stérile 1812
ajoût 46
alambic 1449
alambic pour la distillation de la bière 223
alambic sous vide 1979
albumen 658
albuminate 70
albumine 69
albumine du sang 263
albuminoïde 71
albumose 72
alcali 90
alcalimètre 92
alcaloïde 93
alcool 73
alcool amylique 116
alcool cétylique 410
alcool de bois 2065
alcool dénaturé 576, 1214
alcool éthylique 692
alcool gras 720
alcool isopropylique 1019
alcool laurique 1093
aldéhyde 75
aldohexose 77
aldol 78
aldose 79
aldostérone 80
aldrine 81
ale 82
alginate 85
alginate de sodium 1709
algue 84
alicyclique 87
aliment 1305
alimentation défectueuse 1162
aliment de la levure 2075
aliphatique 89
alkékenge 357
allantoïne 94
alléthrine 95
allomérique 96

allose 97
alose 1667
alpha-amylase 102
altrose 103
alumine 104
alumine activée 40
alvéographe 105
alvéolage de pain 307
amande 101
amande amère 247
ambre gris 106
améliorant 980
amélioration sanitaire 1611
amer 246
amide 107
amide d'acide 27
amidon 1791
amine 108
amine alipathique 721
amino-acide 109
ammoniac 110
ammonium 111
amour en cage 357
ampholyte 113
amphotère 114
amylase 117
amylase fongique 811
amylographe 119
amyloïde 120
amylopectine 121
amylopsine 122
amylose 123
anaérobie 125
analyse granulométrique 1368
analyse volumétrique 2021
ananas 1414
anchois 127
androgène 128
aneth 609
anéthole 126
aneurine 2010
angle de tranchant 546
anguille 654
anhydre 131
anhydride acétique 13
anhydrite 130
anion 134
anis 135
anisol 137
annatto 138
anode 139
anti-albumose 140
antibiose 141
antibiotique 142
anticatalyseur 144

antienzyme 145
anti-germinant 1781
antihistamine 146
anti-mousse 563
antioxydant 147
antiseptique 148
à odeur de moisi 1262
appareil de Dean et Stark 554
appareil d'hydrogénation 962
appréciation de la qualité 1493
aptitude à former une pâte 630
arabinose 153
arachide 1374
arbre 1768
aréomètre 965
arginine 155
armoire à sécher par le vide 1978
arôme 156
arsenic 158
artichaut 159
ascorbate de sodium 1710
aseptique 160
asperge 164
aspic 166
assaisonnement 1639
asticot 1155
atmosphère 168
atome 169
atome de carbone asymétrique 167
aubergine 173
autocatalyse 174
autoclave 175
autoclave continu 488
autoclave hydrostatique 968
autolyse 176
automation 177
automatisation 177
autoxydation 178
avidine 179
avitaminose 180
avocat 181
avoine 1308
avoine folle 2058
axe 1768
axérophtol 2009
azéotrope 182
azotation 1288
azote 1286

babeurre 333
bacille 183
bactéricide 186
bactérie 191
bactérie coliforme 469
bactérie mésophile 1209

bactérie pathogène 1372
bactérie psychrophile 1479
bactéries acétiques 14
bactériolyse 187
bactériophage 188
bactériostatique 189, 190
bagasse 192
baie de *Dioscoreophyllum cumminsii* 1659
bain 214
balle 411
ballon 369, 758
banane 200
bar 209
barattage 443
baratter 442
barbue 315
barrel 204
barril 1050
base 206
basilic 207
bassin d'évaporation 1604
battre à mousse 53
baudroie 1247
bécher 219
benne à fourche 787
benne transporteuse 491
benzoate de sodium 1711
béribéri 233
bernique 1117
besoins alimentaires 782
besoins nutritifs 782
bêta-amylase 234
betterave à sucre 1833
betterave rouge 226
beurre 332
beurre d'arachide 1375
beurre de cacao 461
bicarbonate de sodium 1712
bidon 350
bière 222
bière de fermentation basse 1074
bière de levure 2076
bière en fût 636
bière prête au débit 748
bigorneau 2061
bile 236
bioluminescence 241
biotine 242
biscotte 1584
biscuit 244
biuret 250
bixine 251
blanc d'oeuf 658

blanchaille 2051
blanchiment 261
blanchiment gras 265
blanchir 258
blé 2046
blé de Turkie 1157
blé dur 913
bleu de méthylène 1216
blé vitreux 913
boeuf 221, 1343
boille 350
boisseau 331
boissons non-alcoholiques 1730
boîte 351
boîte à bourrage 1824
boîte de Pétri 1399
boîte gonflée 1855
boîte sous vapeur 704
bombe calorimétrique 280
bombement de boîtes 270
bonbon 805
bonbons 274
bonde de bouchon 329
botulisme 294
bouchon 328
bouchon-couronne 521
boudin noir 255
boue 1697, 1698
boue d'égouts 1665
bouilleur 1044
bouillie 1698
bouillie bordelaise 285
bouillon 295
boulangerie 194
bouquet 156
bourrache 284
bouvillon 1807
braiser 299
brassage 1185
brasserie 313
brême 311
brevet 1370
brochet 1412
bromate de potassium 1442
bromate de sodium 1713
broméline 320
brosse à son 302
broyeur 616, 1231
broyeur à boulets 198
broyeur à disque 615
broyeur à marteaux 518, 909
broyeur à meules verticales 1359
broyeur de cannes de sucre 1835
broyeur giratoire 899
broyeur pour colloïdes 473

brucine 322
brûler 749
brulûre de congélation 798
brunissement 268
brut 1520
buccin 2049
bulle 324
buse d'atomisation 171

cacheter 1079
cacuéte 1374
café 467
caféine 341
caillé 537
calandre du grain 864
calciférol 2015
calendre 344
calmar 1783
calorie 348
calorimètre de Berthelot 280
canal d'aspiration 808
canelle 446
canne à sucre 1834
canneberge 508
caoutchouc silicone 1684
capelan 358
câpres 359
caproate d'allyle 99
capsicum 400
captan 361
caquer (harengs) 538
caramel 362
caramel moux 805
carboglace 645
carbohydrase 364
carbonate de calcium 345
carbonate de sodium 1714
carboxyméthylcellulose 368
carcinogène 370
cardamome 371
cardine 1198
cari 542
carotène 374
carotte 377
caroube 373
carpe 375
carvi 363
caséine 378
caséine caillée 1543
caséinogène 381
cassave 384
catalase 388
catalyse 390
catalyseur 391
cathépsine 394

cation 395
caustique 397
cave de fermentation 732
cawcher 1059
céleri 402
céleri-rave 401
celluloïde 403
cellulose 404
cendre d'os 281
centigrade 407
céréales 409
céréales pour petit déjeuner 308
cerf 561
cerfeuil 421
cerise 420
cétone 1042
cétose 1043
chaîne de production 1463
chaleur de dissolution 920
chaleur de formation 919
chaleur de vaporisation 1987
chaleur latente 1087
chaleur moléculaire 1245
chaleur spécifique 1758
chambre d'atomisation 1776
champignon 1258
chanvre 924
chapon 360
charançon 864
charbon actif 42
charbon activé 42
charbon de sang 264
charbon d'os 132, 282
charbon végétal 1992
charge 210
châtaigne 422
chat marin 393
chaudière 275, 1800
chaudière tubulaire 1939
chauffage diélectrique 601
chauffage par induction 984
chauffage par injection de vapeur 1801
chauffage rapide 756
chauffer 1624
chaux chlorée 262
chaux hydraulique 957
chemise de vapeur 1802
chevreau 1047
chewing-gum 423
chicle 425
chicorée 670
chien de mer 627
chlorate de sodium 1715
chloration 432
chlordane 430

chlorite de sodium 1717
chlorophylle 433
chlorure d'acide 28
chlorure de chaux 431
chlorure de sodium 1716
chocolat 434, 436
chocolat amer 248
cholestérol 437
choline 439
chou 339
choucroute 1620
choufleur 396
chou frisé 1034
chou marin 1636
chou-navet 1851
choux de Bruxelles 323
chromatine 440
chromatographie 441
chromatographie en phase gazeuse 821
chymotrypsine 444
ciboulette 429
cidre 445
cinnamate de benzyle 232
cinnamate de méthyle 1215
cinnamate d'éthyle 693
cire 2039
cire d'abeilles 225
cire de pétrole 1400
citerne de dégraissage 566
citrate de fer ammoniacal 735
citron 1101
citrouille 1483
civette 429
clarification 450, 562
clarifier 746
classification par air 66
cloche de barbotage 325
clous de girofle 456
clovisse 449
coacervation 457
cobalamine 2013
cochenille 458
coco 462
code de principes (F.A.O.) 464
coefficient d'activité 44
coefficient de gonflement 1856
coenzyme 466
cognac 301
coing 1497
collagène 470
collant 1867
colle 841
colle à base de caséine 379
colle de poisson 1015
colloïdal 472

colloïde 471
colonne d'absorption 5
colophane 474
colorant alimentaire 779
colorimètre de Lovibond 1139
colza 1516
combustion spontanée 1773
commande par vis sans fin 2066
composé aromatique 157
composé d'ammonium quaternaire 1494
composé nitrosé 1291
compresseur à deux étages 1950
concasseur giratoire 899
concentrer 476
concentrer par ébullition 273
concher 477
concombre 532
condensateur Liebig 1112
conditionnement de l'air 67
conditionner 479
conduite de la pâte jusqu'au façonnage 632
confiture 1023
confiture d'oranges 1180
congélateur 797
congélateur discontinu 211
congélation rapide 1496
congélation sous courant d'air 259
congelé à basse température 560
congre 481
conrecoller 1079
conservateur 1457
conservation 1456
conservation par le froid 468
consistance 483
consistant 1814
consistomètre 1553
consommé 484
constituent 485
contamination 487, 1733
contaminer 486
contrôle de la qualité 1492
contrôle organoleptique 1332
convertisseur 1703
coque 459
coqueret 357
coquille St.-Jacques 1626
coriandre 495
"cornflakes" 497
cornue 1548
corrosion 1418
cosse 952
cossette 500
côtelette 545
couche d'aleurone 83

couper en dés 599
courant turbulant 1946
courge à la moelle 1181
courgette 503
couteau 1521
couverture 504
cracker 507
craie 413
crème 511
crème acide 1750
crème cuite 543
crème de tartre 512
crème glacée 975
crème préparée à l'anglaise 454
cresson 515
cresson de fontaine 2030
crevette 1677
cribler 859, 1682
crin 738
cristallisation 531
cristallisation fractionnée 793
cristalliser 530
croustillant 516
croûte 529
croûte du fromage 418
croûton 520
cruche 350
crudité permanente 1392
crudité temporaire de l'eau 1891
cuire au four 1566
cuisson à haute fréquence 1222
cuisson à micro-ondes 1222
curcuma 535
curcumine 536
cuticle 544
cuve à liquide fermenté 224
cuve de fermentation 731, 733
cuve de sédimentation 1662
cuve-matière 1186
cyanocobalamine 2013
cyclamate de sodium 1718
cycle du carbone 366
cyclone 548
cylindre à bagasse 193
cylindres d'alimentation 724
cylindres de broyage 310
cylindres désagrégeurs 310
cylindre supérieur 1922
cynorrhodon 938
cystéine 549
cytochromes 550

daim 561
dame-jeanne 369
datte 552

daurada 1635
débit 573
débitmètre 1574
décantation 555
décanteur 1662
déchets 2027
déchets d'orge 1870
décoction 556
décomposition 557
décongélation 564
décortiqueuse 558
découpoir 245
défault des produits cuits au four 195
défaut d'odeur 1699
défécation 562
défécation au lait de chaux 1116
dégeler 1903
dégivrage 564
dégraissé 1293
dégraisser 565
degré 860
déhuiler 565
déliquescence 572
délisseuse 1676
demande biochimique d'oxygène 239
demi petit fût 750
dénaturation 574, 575
denrée principale 1789
densité 577
densité de vapeur 1988
dépôt 883
dérivé 584
désaminase 553
désémulsionnant 559
déshydratation 568
déshydrater 567
déshydrogénase 570
déshydrogénation 571
désignation spécifique des produits
  alimentaires 780
désintégrateur 616
désodorisant 579
désodorisation 580
désorption 588
désoxy- 581
dessécher 586, 644, 1052
dessiccateur 587
détecteur de métal 1211
détendeur 1459, 1541
détergent 589
détergent synthétique 1863
dextrine 592
dextrogyre 593
dextrose 839
diacétyle 594

dialyse 595
diaphragme 596
diastase 597
dieldrine 600
diététique 603
diffusion 604
digestion 605
digitaline 606
dilatation 608
diluer 610
dimorphe 611
dioxyde de carbone 367
dioxyde de soufre 1839
diphényl 612
disaccharide 614
disperser 618
dispersion macromoléculaire 471
dissociation 620
dissolvant 1741
distillation à la vapeur 1797
distillation flash 754
distillation fractionnée 794
distillation par extraction 714
distillation sous vide 1969
distillerie 621
distributeur 617
diterpène 623
dithione 624
dorada 1635
dose mortelle 1106
dosimètre 1502
doubler 1079
douve 1795
doux 1226, 1852
drêche 1176
drêche de brasserie 312
dulcine 651
dureté 912

eau 2028
eau d'appoint 1158
eau de brassage 314, 1130
eau de condensation 2035
eau de cristallisation 2036
eau de Javel 1025
eau-de-vie de pommes de terre 1448
eau liée 296
eau-mère 1250
eaux d'égout 1663
eaux résiduelles 1663
ébullition 277
écnalote 1668
échange d'ions 1007
échangeur à contrecourant 502
échangeur de chaleur 918

échangeur de chaleur à plaques 1428
échantillon 1606
échantillonnage 1608
échantillonneur 1607
échantillon prélevé au hasard 1514
échauder 1364, 1624
échelle Baumé 218
échelle de Brix 318
échelle Fahrenheit 715
échelle hédonique 921
échelle Réaumur 1524
écorce de chêne 1307
écorce de fruits confit 353
écorce de sapin-ciguë 923
écoulement visqueux 2007
écrémeuse 513, 1656
écrevisse 510
écume 1632
écumer 1694
effervescence 655
efflorescence 267, 656
églefin 900
égout 1666
égrugeoir 1046
éjecteur à vapeur 1798
élasticité de la mie 525
élastine 660
électrode de réference 1533
élévateur à fourche 787
élutriation 662
emballage 1351
emballage transparent 1927
embouteilleuse 287
embryon 664
émissole 627
emmagasinage 1819
empaqueteuse 2069
emporte-pièce 245
émulsifiant 665
émulsificateur 665
émulsion 667
émulsoïde 668
encapsulage 669
encornet 1783
endive 426
endosperme 671
énergie 673
engrais 737, 1175
engrais d'os 283
en marche 1326
enregistreur 1528
enrichi 791
enrichissement 674
ensemencement 1642
ensemencer 993, 1641

enthalpie 675
entraînement 677
entraîneur 676
entropie 678
enveloppe 952
enveloppe d'extracteur 713
enzyme 679
enzyme attendrisante 1893
éosine 680
épais 1814
épaississant 1913
éperlan 1700
épice 1765
épinard 1767
épithélium olfactif 1322
épreuve 1898
épreuve de Gerber 828
épreuve de Gutzeit 898
épreuve de Kreis 1060
épreuve de la catalase 389
épreuve de ninhydrine 1284
épreuve de triage rapide 1629
équivalent en eau 2031
ergostérine 683
ergostérol 683
ergot 684
érythrodextrine 686
espace de tête 917
espadon 1858
esprit de sel 1770
esprit de vin 1771
esprit preuve 1467
essai à la résorcinel 1547
essence d'absinthe 2067
essence d'anis 136
essence de cannelle de Chine 385
essence de cardamome 372
essence de citron 1103
essence de cumin 533
essence de fleurs d'orange 1274
essence de gaulthérie 2063
essence de genièvre 1031
essence de girofle 455
essence de jasmin 1024
essence de lemongrass 1102
essence de mandarine 1172
essence de menthe 1385
essence de moutarde 1261
essence de néroli 1274
essence de romarin 1573
essence de thym 1917
essence de vanille 1984
essence de wintergreen 2063
ester 689
ester acide 29

ester d'acide gras 722
ester de cellulose 405
estérification 690
estragon 1883
esturgeon 1826
étâge-équeutage 1705
état normal 884
éteide de guinée 1319
éther 691
éther acétique 15
éther butylique 336
éthylène 694
étiquetage des produits alimentaires 780
étourdir 1825
étuve à fermentation 1475
étuve de dessiccation 647
eugénol 698
évacuation des eaux résiduelles 1664
évaluation sensorielle 1652
évaporateur à grimpage 453
évaporateur à multiple effet 1254
évaporateur à plaques 1426
évaporateur à simple effet 1687
évaporateur à vide 1976
évaporateur sous vide 1972
évaporation 701
évaporation instantanée 755
exalteur de mousse 1090
examen organoleptique 1332
exhausteur 702
exhausteur d'arôme 763
exothermique 706
extensibilité de gluten 845
extensographe 708
extensomètre 709
extraction 711
extraction à la vapeur 1799
extraction par dissolvant 1742
extraction par partage 1129
extrait de levure 2074
extrait de viande 1194
extrait d'herbes aromatiques 928

fabrication en série 1187
facteurs de Atwater 172
faire bouiller légèrement 1364
faire gonfler 1481
falsification 52
falsification des produits alimentaires 778
farine 766
farine autolevante 1645
farine blanchie 260
farine de broyage 309
farine de maïs 498
farine de pâtisserie 343

farine de qualité 1371
farine d'os 283
farine falsifiée 51
farine fleur 1371
farine panifiable 306
farine pâtissière 343
farinographe 717
farnésol 718
fenouil 726
fenu-grec 727
fer-blanc 1919
ferment 728
fermentation 730
fermentation acétique 16
fermentation aérobie 55
fermentation alcoolique 74
fermentation amylique 118
fermentation bouleuse 278
fermentation panaire 1357
fermenter 729
fermentographe 734
fermeté de la mie 526
fermeture par recouvrement 1083
feuille 774
feuille rétractile 1679
fève 220
fève de cacao 460
fève de marais 319
fibre 738
fibre naturelle 1268
ficine 739
figue 740
filage au mouillé 2044
"filth" 744
filtration accélérée 7
filtration par le vide 1974
filtre 741
filtre à sable 1609
filtre rotatif 1576
filtre Seitz 1644
fines herbes 747
flacon 758
flacon de Kjeldahl 1055
flatulence 759
flatuosité 759
flavone 760
flavoprotéine 761
flet 765
flétan 905
flétan noir 877
flocons de blé 2047
flocons de froment 2047
flocons de maïs 497
flocons d'orge 202
floculation 764

flotteur 1857
fluorescéine 769
fluorescence 770
fluoroacétate de sodium 1719
flux laminaire 1077
flux newtonien 1279
foie 1133
foisonnement 1342
fondant 776
fongicide 812
fongostat 813
force ionique 1009
formaldéhyde-sulfoxylate 788
formaline 789
formation de alvéoles dans la pâte 629
formation de la mie 527
fortifier 792
fosse septique 1657
foudre 383
four 1340
four à sécher sous vide 1971
fournée 210
fourrage grossier 1578
fraise 1822
framboise 1519
fraude 52
friabilité 800
friture 804
fromage 417
fromage de porc 303
fromage fondu 1462
froment 2046
froment vitreux 913
fructose 801
fruit à noyau 1817
fruit climatérique 452
fruit confit 352
fuite 1097
fumage 1702
fumer 538
fumigation 810
furfural 814
fût 204, 383

galactose 816
galantine 817
gallon 819
gâter 1871
gaz ammoniac 110
gaz hilarent 1292
gaz naturel 1269
gel 824
gélatine 825
gel de silice 1683
gelée 1026

gélose inclinée 59
géne 826
générateur de vapeur 1800
générateur de vinaigre 2002
géraniol 827
germe 663
germer 1780
germicide 829
gingembre 831
givre 266
givre gras 265
glace 835, 975
glace carbonique 645
glacer 834
gliadine 836
globuline 837
gluconate de sodium 1720
glucose 839
glume 411
glutamate de sodium 1721
glutamate monosodique 1721
glutamine 843
gluten 844
gluténine 846
glycéride 847
glycérine 848
glycérol 848
glycine 851
glycocolle 851
glycogène 852
glycoside 854
goitre 855
gomme 894
gomme adragante 896
gomme adraganthe 896
gomme arabique 895
gomme de karaya 1036
gomme guar 892
gomme mastic 1189
gossypol 858
goulot d'embouteillage 288
goût 762, 1885
goût défectueux 1318
goyave 893
graduation par densité 578
grain 862
grain de raisin 872
graine de lin 1121
grain flottant 1857
grain plongeur 1688
grains 409
graisse de copra 463
graisse de laine 1081
graisse de rognon 1831
graisse de rôti 641

graisse durcie 911
graisse hydrogénée 911
gramicidine 866
gramme-équivalent 865
gram-négatif 868
gram-positif 869
grenada 1439
grenadille 870
grenadine 879
griller 881
grondin 897
groseille à maquereau 857
groseilles 540
groseille verte 857
groupe acétoxyle 21
groupe acétyle 24
gruau d'avoine 882
grumeler (se) 342
guanine 889
guano 890
guanosine 891
gustation 1887

hachoir 1235
halite 907
hareng 929
hareng salé et fumé 1054
haricot 915
haricot d'Espagne 1583
hématine 901
hématoxyline 902
hémicellulose 922
hémoglobine 903
héparine 925
heptachlore 926
herbe 927
herbicide 2041
hespéridine 930
hétérocyclique 931
hexachlorobenzène 933
hexachlorocyclohexane 932
hexachlorure de benzène 229
hexose 935
histamine 939
histidine 940
homard 1136
homogénéisation 944
hormone 947
hotte 808
houblon 946
huile d'arachide 1376
huile de baleine 1764, 2045
huile de coco 463
huile de colza 1517
huile de coton 501

huile de foie de flétan 906
huile de foie de morue 465
huile de foie de requin 1670
huile de fusel 815
huile de germe de blé 2048
huile de germe de froment 2048
huile de lin 1122
huile de muscade 1150
huile de noix 2024
huile de palme 1356
huile de palmiste 1355
huile de poisson 753
huile de ricin 386
huile de soja 1754
huile de spic 1766
huile de thon 1942
huile de tournesol 1842
huile d'eucalyptus 697
huile d'olive 1323
huile essentielle 688
huile hydrogénée 960
huile lubrifiante 875
huile sésame 1661
huile siccative 646
huile sulfonée 1838
huile volatile 688
huître 1349
humectant 949
humidité 950
humidité relative 1539
humidité relative d'équilibre 682
humus 951
hyaluronidase 953
hydatide 954
hydratation 956
hydrate de carbone 365
hydrateur 1184
hydrazide maléique 1160
hydrazone 958
hydrocellulose 959
hydrogénation 961
hydrogène sulfuré 963
hydrolysat de caséine 380
hydrolyse 964
hydromètre 965
hydromètre de Twaddell 1949
hydrophile 966
hydrophobe 967
hydroxyanisol butylé 334
hydroxyde de potassium 1443
hydroxymercurichlorophénol 969
hydroxymercuricrésol 970
hydroxytoluène butylé 335
hygiène 971
hygromètre 972

hygroscopique 973

igname 2072
immunité 978
imperméable 2037
imprégner 979
impuretés 626
inconsommable 986
indicateur 982
indicateur de vide 1975
indicateur d'extension 709
indicateur d'oxydo-réduction 1346
indice d'acétyle 25
indice d'acide 37
indice de réfraction 1536
indice d'iode 1006
indice d'oxydation 1395
industrie des conserves 356
inerte 987
infestation par les prédateurs 1398
infuser 988
infusion 989
ingrédient 990
inhibiteur 991
inhibiteur de croissance 885
initiateur 992
innocuité 1592
inoculer 993
inodore 1314
inoffensif 1591
inosine 994
inositol 995
insecticide 996
inspection des viandes 1195
instantanéiser 997
instrumentation 998
instrumentation rhéologique 1551
insuline 999
interestérification 1000
intoxication alimentaire 781
inuline 1002
inversion 1003
invertase 1004
ion amphotérique 2083
ionisation 1010
ionone 1011
ipécacuana 1012
irradiation 1013, 1507
isoeugénol 1017
isoler 1655
isoleucine 1018
isomère optique 1330
isosafrol 1020
isothiocyanate 1021
iso-thiocyanate d'allyle 100

issues 1316

jambon 908
jambon fumé 1701
jarret 941
jaune d'oeuf 659
jaune lieu 1433
joint 1637
joint hydraulique 2038
joule 1029
jus 1030
jus de décongélation 640
jus de fruit 802
jute 1033

kaolin 1035
kari 542
kebâb 1038
kératine 1040
kérosène 1041
kieselgur 1049
koji 1872
kumquat 534

labile 1061
lacrymogène 1062
lactalbumine 1064
lactame 1065
lactase 1066
lactate 1067
lactobutyromètre 1069
lactoflavine 2011
lactone 1070
lactose 1071
lactosérum 2050
laisser reposer la pâte 1474
lait 1228
laitance 1234
lait chocolaté 436
lait concentré 699
lait concentré sucré 478
lait de beurre 333
laite 1234
lait écrémé 1695
lait emprésuré 1032
lait entier 806
lait entier concentré 700
laiteux 1230
lait malté 1166
lait sec 638
laitue 1107
laitue de mer 1095
lamelle 1076
lamelle couvre-objet 505
laminée 1078

laminer 1079
lancéolé 1080
langouste 509
langoustine 1451
lanoléine 1081
lanoline 1081
lanostérol 1082
lapin 1500
laque 1063
lard 184
latex 1088
laurier 1091
lauryl-sulfate de sodium 1723
lavaret 2052
lavende 1094
laveuse de bouteilles 289
lécithine 1099
légumineuse 1482
lentille 1105
lessivage 1096
lessive 1143
lessive résiduaire 1763
leucine 1108
levain 203, 1098, 1417, 1751, 1793
levée 1565
levée de la pâte par agents chimiques 419
lève-palette 787
lévogyre 1072
lévulose 801
levure 2073
levure basse 292
levure chimique 197
levure de bière 203
levure haute 1923
levure sèche 639
liaisons doubles conjuguées 482
liaison transversale 519
liant 237
libérer 1109
lichen 1110
liège 496
lièvre 914
lignine 1114
limande 551, 1104
limon 1115
lin 1121
linoléine 1119
linters 1123
lipase 1125
lipolyse 1126
lipoxydase 1127
lipoxygenase 1127
liquéfaction 1128
liqueur de Fehling 725
liseron 238

liseron des champs 238
litre 1132
loi de Raoult 1515
lot 210
lotte de mer 1247
lotte de rivière 330
lubie 1155
lumen 1141
lutéine 1142
lyophilisation 796
lysine 1144
lysosome 1145
lysozime 1146

macaroni 1147
macédoine 1149
macérer 1151
mâcher 1188
machine à empaqueter 2069
machine à enrober de chocolat 435
machine à remplir les bouteilles 287
machine à rincer les bouteilles 289
machine rectiligne à laver des bidons 1821
macis 1148
macromolécule 1153
macroscopique 1154
maille 1207
maïs 1157
maische 1183
malathion 1159
malaxage 1058
malaxer 1057, 1237
malaxeur 1570
malnutrition 1162
malt 1163
maltase 1165
malter 1164
malterie 1167
maltose 1169
malt torréfié 253
malt touraillé 1053
malt vert 878
mandarine 1171, 1875
manomètre 1174
manomètre à tube en U 1967
maquereau 1152
maquette 1241
marc 1176
margarine 1177
marinade 1178
mariner 1752
marjolaine 1179
marmite 1044
marmite à pression 1458

marquer 1869
marron 422
massepain 1182
mastiquer 1188
matière carbonisée 415
matière cellulosique 522
matière étrangère 786
matière gras 1675
matière plastique 1423
maturation 60, 1190
maturer 539, 1564
maturité de la pâte 633
matzo 1191
mauvaise herbe 2040
mauvais goût 1318
mayonnaise 1192
mélange 1239
mélanger 1237
mélangeur 1238
mélangeur à cylindres 1570
mélangeur à tonneau 205
mélangeur en discontinu 212
mélanine 1199
mélasse 1244
mêler 1237
melica 1232
mélique 1232
mélisse 199
mélitose 1200
mellorine 1201
melon 1202
melon d'eau 2034
membrane 596
menthe 1236
menthol 1203
menthone 1204
mercaptan 1205
méringue 1206
merlan 2054
merlu 904
merluche 904
merlus 904
métabisulfite de potassium 1444
métabolisme 1210
métal alcalin 91
métallique 1212
méthionine 1213
méthode de Kjeldahl 1056
méthode triangulaire 1929
méthylstyrolène 1218
mettre en bouteilles 286
mettre en perce 1879
meule verticale 653
meunerie 1233
micelle 1219

micron 1220
microscopique 1221
mie 524
miel 945
migration 1225
mijoter 1685
mil 1232
mildiou 1227
millet 1232
minoterie 1233
mise en boîtes 355
mitonner 1685
mobilité 1251
mode d'emploi 613
modéle 1241
module d'Young 2080
moisissure 1252
moisson 916
moissonneuse à pois 2003
moissonneuse-batteuse 475
moka 1240
molasses noires 257
molécule-gramme 867
monoglycéride 1248
monomoléculaire 1249
monostéarate de glycérine 849
morceau de sucre 1836
morue sèche 1816
motilité 1251
mou 1113
moule 1259
moulin 1231
moulin à galets 198
mousse d'Irlande 376
mousse perlée 376
moût 1260, 2068
moût adouci 1854
moutarde des champs 416
moutarde sauvage 416
mouton 1263
mulet 880
mûre 1253
mûre de Boysen 297
mûre de ronce 252
mûre sauvage 252
mûrir 1564
muscle 1257
mycélion 1264
mycélium 1264
mycotoxine 1265
myoglobine 1266
myrtille 235

narcotique 1267
nauséabond 1270

navet 1948
navet de Suède 1851
nectarine 1271
nèfle 1138, 1197
nettoyage in situ 451
neurine 1276
neutraliser 1278
neutre 1277
niacinamide 1281
niacine 1283
nicotinamide 1281
nicotine 1282
nisine 1285
nitrate de potassium 1445
nitrate de sodium 1724
nitre 1445
nitrite de potassium 1446
nitrite de sodium 1725
nitrogénase 1287
nitrogène 1286
nitrosamine 1290
nocif 1300
noir animal 132, 282
noir d'os 282
noir végétal 1992
noix 1303, 2023
noix d'Amérique 304
noix d'anacarde 382
noix de cajou 382
noix du Brésil 304
noix muscade 1304
nombre de saponification 1613
non-gras 1293
non-miscible 977
non-saturé 1960
norleucine 1295
normal 1297
norme 1296
notatine 1299
nouilles 1294
nucléoprotéine 1302

oculaire 1310
odeur 1313
odorant 1311
odoriférant 1311
odorimétrie 1312
oenomètre 2004
oestrogène 1315
oléate de diglycol 607
oléfine 1320
omble 414
omble chevalier 414
ombre 874
onion 1325

opacimètre 1273
opalescence 1327
opaque 1328
opération discontinue 213
orange 1331
organe sensible 1650
organisme thermophile 1911
orge 201
orge de brasserie 1168
orienter 1333
orifice 1334
ormeau 1
ornithine 1335
osmose 1337
osséine 1338
ovalbumine 1339
"overrun" 1342
oxide nitreux 1292
oxydase 1344
oxydation 1345
oxyde de mésityle 1208
oxyde d'éthylène 695
oxytétracycline 1348
ozone 1350

pain 305
pain complet 2055, 2056
pain de farine intégrale 2056
pain fait avec du bicarbonate de soude
    1708
palmier 1352
palourde 449
pamplemousse 873
panais 1367
pancréatine 1358
panier 208
panne 1085
panse 1582
pantothénate de calcium 346
papaïne 1361
papaye 1362
papier-filtre 742
papier-filtre sans cendres 163
papier parcheminé 1365
papilles gustatives 1886
par hasard 1513
pasteurisation 1369
pasteurisation H.T.S.T. 937
patate 1853
pâte 215
pâte à frire 216
pâte à mâcher 423
pâte d'arachide 1375
patelle 1117
pâtes alimentaires 88

pâtisserie 194
pauvre en calories 1140
pécan 1378
pectine 1379
pellucide 1380
pénétromètre 1381
pénicilline 1382
pentose 1383
pepsine 1386
peptisation 1387
peptone 1388
perborate de sodium 1726
perception sensorielle 1653
perche 1389
percolation 1390
péricarpe 1391
période d'induction 985
perméabilité 1393
peroxydase 1394
peroxyde d'acétylbenzoyle 23
peroxyde de benzoyle 231
persil 1366
persulfate de sodium 1727
persulphate d'ammoniaque 112
perte à la cuisine 196
perte au stockage 1678
perte de poids 2042
perte par rayonnement 1503
pesticide 1397
petit lait 1695
petit pois 1373
pétrissage 631, 1058
pétrissage intensifié 936
pétrissage rapide 936
pétrisser 1057
pétrole lampant 1041
phénol 1402
phosphate de calcium 347
phosphatide 1404
phospholipide 1405
photosynthèse 1406
phytochimique 1408
phytocolle 844
phytol 1409
phytostérol 1410
piment 98, 1363
pipette 1415
pipette graduée 861
piquer 625
piqûre 1418
pissenlit 1881
pistache 1416
plancton 1420
plante adventrice 2040
plantes fourragères 785

plasma 1422
plie 1419
pocher 1431
poids atomique 170
poids spécifique 1757
point d'achèvement 672
point d'ébullition 279
point de congélation 799
point de cristallisation 863
point de granulation 863
point de remollissement 1731
point de rosée 591
point d'inflammabilité 757
point isoélectrique 1016
poire 1377
poiré 1396
poireau 1100
pois 1373
pois chiche 424
poivre 1384
poivre blanc 2053
poivre de Cayenne 400
poivre d'Espagne 400
poivre d'Inde 400
poivre noir 254
poivron 1363
polarimètre 1432
polyéthylène 1434
polymorphisme 1435
polyose 1436
polyphosphate 1437
polypropylène 1438
pomme 151
pomme de terre 1447
pompe à air 68
pompe aspirante 1830
pompe à vide 1977
pompe centrepète 408
pompe de circulation 447
porosité de pain 307
porphyrine 1440
pot 350
potable 1441
potasse caustique 398, 1443
poudre à blanchir 262, 431
poudre de lait entier 2057
poudre d'os 283
poudre levante chimique 197
poulpe 1309
pourcentage en poids 2043
pourcentage en volume 2020
pourpier 1485
pousse 1565
poutassou 271
pouvoir d'absorption de l'eau 2033

pouvoir d'amertume 249
pouvoir de formation des gaz 822
pouvoir diastasique 598
préchauffeur 1454
précipité 1452
prémélange 1455
préséchoir 1453
presse à filtrer 743
presse continue 490
presse de cisaillement 1672
presse hélicoïdale 1631
presse mécanique 1196
pression de colonne d'eau 2032
pression de vapeur 1803
présure 1542, 1544
prisme Nicol 1280
procédé 1461
procédé de Campden 349
procédé Keyes 1045
procédé Steffens 1808
productivité 1464
produire de la vapeur 1508
produit d'addition 46
produit de tête 751
produit filtré 745
produit fumigatoire 809
produits alimentaires 783
produits d'insertion avec l'urée 1963
produit secondaire 338
produit sucré 480
profondeur de la cannelure 583
proline 1465
pro-oxydant 1468
propanol 1469
propionate d'amyle 124
propionate de sodium 1728
protéase 1471
protéine 1472
protéine animale spécifique 133
protéine brute 523
protéine monocellulaire 1686
protéine végétale 1993
protéine végétale texturée 1902
protoplasme 1473
prune 1429
pruneau 1476
prune de reine-claude 876
pseudo-acide 1477
pseudo-base 1478
ptomaïne 1480
purée de fruits 803
purine 1484
putréfaction 1486
putréfier (se) 1487
putride 1488

pyréthrine 1489
pyridoxine 2012
pyrolyse 1491
pyrophosphate sodique de fer 1722

qualité hygiénique 1610
quartier de lard 1701
quercétine 1495
quinine 1499

race de levure 2077
rachitisme 1562
racloir 1628
radical acide 34
radical libre 795
radioactif 1504
radioactivité 1505
radis 1506
raffinerie 1534
raffinose 1200
raie 1692
raifort 948
raisin 872
raisins de Corinthe 541
raisin sec 1509
raisin sec de Smyrne 1841
raisin sec muscatel 1255
ralentissement 716
rance 1511
rancidité 1512
rancissement 1512
rancissure 1512
raréfaction 1518
rassissement 1786
rate 1772
ration journalière 1527
rayonnement 1501
réactif de Fischer 752
réactif de Karl Fischer 1037
réactif de Nessler 1275
réaction 1522
réaction de Baudouin 217
réaction de Maillard 1156
réaction en chaîne 412
réaction irréversible 1014
réactivation 1523
récepteur sensoriel 1654
réchauffeur à plaques 1427
réchauffeur hélicoïdal 1769
récipient 1525
recolteuse de pois 2003
recoupe 1223
recoupettes 1224
rectification 1529
récupération du solvant 1743

recyclage 1526
redevance 1581
redresseur 1530
réduction 1532, 1549
réduire par ébullition 273
reflux 1535
réfrigérant 1537
réfrigérant à plaques 1425
réfrigérant tubulaire 1940
réfrigération 1538
réfrigération par déshydration 569
réfrigération par saumure 317
réfrigérer 427
refroidir 427
refroidissement 1538
refroidissement par atomisation 1777
refroidissement par saumure 317
refroidisseur-plongeur 981
réglementation légale 1794
réglisse 1111
rejet 1674
remplissage aseptique 161
remplissage sous vide 1973
remplisseuse de bouteilles 287
rendement 2078
rendement en pâte 634
rendement en volume 1135
rénine 1544
reposer 479
requin 1669
residu 291
résilience 1545
résilience de la mie 525
résine 1546
résine à échanges d'ions 1008
résine de guaïac 888
résistance au cisaillement 1671
restauration 392
réticulation 519
rétinol 2009
retirer 1878
rétrécissement 1678
rétrogradation 1786
revêtir 1073
réviser 1341
rhéologie 1552
rhéopexie 1554
rhodopsine 1555
rhubarbe 1556
riboflavine 2011
ribose 1558
ricine 1560
rigidité cadavérique 1563
riz 1559
robinet à pointeau 1272

robinet d'arrêt 1818
rognon 1048
rogue 1568
romarin 1572
ronce-framboise 1137
rotation moléculaire 1246
roténone 1577
rôtir 1566
rouge de méthyle 1217
rouget-barbet 1531
rouille 1585, 1704
rouille noire 256
rouleau alimenteur 723
roussir 1627
roux 1580
rumen 1582
rutabaga 1851

saccharimètre 1587, 1589
saccharine 1588
saccharose 1590
safran 1594
safran des Indes 535
sagou 1596
saindoux 1085
Saint Pierre 1028
salade de chou 1696
salé 1605
saler 538
salicoque 1677
salin 1598
salissure 1733
salive 1599
salmonelle 1601
salpêtre 1445
salpêtre du Chili 1724
salsifis 1602
sandre 1413
sans couture 1638
sans soudure 1638
saponification 1612
saponine 1614
sarcosine 1615
sardine 1616
sarriette 1623
sassaparille 1617
saturation 1619
sauce au soja 1755
sauce vinaigrette 1597
saucisse 1621
saucisson 1621
sauge 1595
saumatre 298
saumon 1600
saumure 316

saumurer 1411
saunerie 1604
sauter 1622
saveur 762
savon 1707
savon mou 1732
savonner 1089
scatol 1693
schéma de fabrication 767
scorbut 1633
scutellum 1634
séchage à plaques sous vide 1968
séchage de mousse 772
séchage de mousse sous vide 773
séchage en continu 489
séchage par atomisation 1778
sécher 644, 1052
sécheur à courant d'air chaud 2026
séchoir 587, 1051
séchoir à cylindres 1569
séchoir à deux cylindres 628
séchoir à gaz 1430
séchoir à lit fluidisé 768
séchoir à tambour 642
séchoir de Birs 243
séchoir rotatif 1575
séchoir sous vide 1970
séchoir-tunnel 650
sédiment 1640
seiche 547
seigle 1586
sel 1603
sel acide 35
sel de cuisine 1716
sel de fonte 666
sel de Glauber 833
sel d'Epsom 681
sel de Seignette 1567
sel émulsifiant 666
sel tampon 326
semi-conservé 1647
séminal 1899
semi-perméable 1646
semoule 1648
semoule de blé dur 652
sénescence 1649
sénévol 1261
sensibilité 1651
séparateur électrostatique 661
séparateur magnétique à tambour 643
séparation par air 66
séparer 1655
séquestration 1658
sérine 1660
sérum 2050

shoddy 1673
siccatif 1680
silicate de sodium 1729
sillon 514
siphonner 1689
sirop 1864
sirop de glucose 840
sirop de maïs 499
sirop de sucre 856
sisal 1690
sitostérol 1691
soja 1753
sol 1734
sole 1086, 1737
solubilité 1738
solution 1740
solution acide 36
solution de Benedict 228
solution de Dragendorff 635
solution molaire 1243
solution normale 1298, 1787
solution saturée 1618
solution tampon 327
solvant 1741
solvant d'extraction 710
son 300
sons 300
sorbet 1744
sorbitol 1746
sorbose 1747
sorgho 1748
soude 1714
soude caustique 399
soudure 1736
soudure à recouvrement 1084
soudure de boîtes métalliques 1735
soufflante 269
souillure 1733
souillures 744
soupape 1981
soupape de retenue 1324
soupape de sûreté 1593
soupape d'évacuation d'air 65
sous-produit 338
soutireuse à bouteilles 287
soya 1753
spécificité 1759
spécimen 1606
spectre 1762
sporulation 1774
sprat 1775
squalène 1782
stabilisateur 1784
staphylocoque 1788
stéarine 1805

stéréo-isomère 1809
stéréospécifique 1810
stérile 1811
stérilisation force 10 293
stériliser 1813
stimulateur de croissance 886
stimulus 1815
stockage sous atmosphère controllée 823
stockfisch 1816
stout 1820
streptomycine 1823
sublimation 1827
substance dissoute 1739
substance étrangère 786
subtiline 1829
suc 1030
succédané 1828
succédané d'oeuf 657
sucre 1832
sucre brut 321
sucre colonial 1421
sucre cristallisé 871
sucre de betteraves 227
sucre de bois 2071
sucre de canne 354
sucre de fruit 801
sucre de lait 1071
sucre de malt 1169
sucre de saturne 1837
sucre en poudre 387
sucre glace 976
sucre inverti 1005
sucre mélis 1134
sucre roux 321
sucrose 1590
suif 1874
suintement 1390
suinter 1643
sulfate ferreux 736
surchauffage 1845
surfondu 1843
surfusion 1844
sursaturé 1846
suspension 1849
symbiose 1859
synérèse 1860
synergiste 1861
synthétique 1862

tacaud 1450
tachistéine 1866
tachymètre 1865
tactique 1868
takadiastase 1872
talc 1873

tamis 1681
tamiser 859, 1682
tanche 1892
tanin 1877
tank de soutirage 290
tannin 1877
tapioca 1880
taraxacum 1881
tare 1882
tartrate de potassium 512
tartre 276, 1625
tas de malt 1170
tautomérie 1888
taux de cendres 162
taux d'extraction 712
tégument 1899
téléostéen 1890
température absolue 3
température critique 517
température mortelle 1905
tendon 1896
tendreté 1894
tendromètre 1895
teneur en amidon 1792
teneur en cendres 162
teneur en eau 2029
teneur en humidité 1242
tension de vapeur 1803, 1989
tension interfaciale 1001
tension superficielle 1847
terpène 1897
terre à foulon 807
terre à porcelaine 1035
terre d'infusoires 1049
testa 1899
test de la phosphatase 1403
têtes 751
tétracycline 1900
tétraphosphate d'hexaéthyle 934
texture 1901
texture de lait 1229
texture de la mie 528
texturomètre 1672
thé 1889
théophylline 1904
thermocouple 1906
thermodynamique 1907
thermolabile 1908
thermolyse 1909
thermomètre 1910
thermostat 1912
thiamine 2010
thioalcool 1205
thixotrope 1914
thon 1941

thréonine 1915
thyroxine 1918
tiré au tonneau 637
tocophérol 2016
tomate 1920
tonka 1921
tonneau 383
topinambour 1027
touraille 1051
tour d'absorption 5
tour d'atomisation 1779
tour de séchage 649
tournesol 1131
tourteau 506
tourteau dégraissé 707
toute-épice 98
toxicité 1924
toxine 1925
traces de prédatures 744
traitement 1461
traitement des boues activées 41
traitement préalable 1460
transférase 1926
transparent 1380
transpiration 1928
transporteur 491
transporteur à courroies 492
transporteur à vibrations 2000
transporteur à vis sans fin 1630
transuder 1850
trempe 1183
tremper 1706
trempfer 1806
trichlore d'azote 1289
trichlorocarbanilide 1931
tricinose 1930
tripaille 1317
tripe 428
tripes 1932
triphosphate d'adénosine 48
triticale 1933
trouble 1944
trou de visite 1173
trou d'homme 1173
truffe 1934
trypsine 1935
tryptophane 1936
tubercule 1937
tuberculine 1938
tunnel de réfrigération 494
tunnel de séchage à plateaux 1943
turbo-séparation 66
turbot 1945
turgescence 1947
tuyau perforé 1756

tyrocidine 1951
tyrosine 1952
tyrothricine 1953

ultrafiltration 1955
ultra-haute-température 1956
ultrason 1957
ultraviolet 1958
undécalactone 1959
unité Angström 129
upérisation 1961
uréase 1964
urée 1962
uridine 1966

valeur alimentaire 784
valeur biologique 240
valeur de l'acidité 37
valeur de Lintner 1124
valeur de seuil 1916
valeur diène 602
valeur liminaire 1916
valeur nutritionnelle 1306
valeur pH 1401
valeur rH 1550
valine 1980
vancomycine 1983
vanilline 1985
vanilline d'éthyle 696
vanne de détente 1541
vanner 2062
vapeur 1796
vapeur d'échappement 705
vaporisation 1986
varec 1039
variateur de vitesse 1990
vase 219
vase clos de propagation des bactéries
    185
vase Dewar 590
veau 1991
venaison 1994
ventilateur 703
ventiler 53
ver 1155
vermiculite 1995
vermine 1996
vermouth 1997
verre soluble 1729
vesce 1998
viable 1999
viande 1193
viande synthétique 1902
vide 1954
vieillissement 61, 1649

vin 2059
vinaigre 2001
vinaigre de vin 2060
vinasse de distillerie 622
vin blanc du Rhin 942
vin doux 1260
vin muscat 1256
vinomètre 2004
viscosimètre 2005
viscosité 1571, 2006
viscosité relative 1540
viscosité spécifique 1760
vitamine 2008
vitamine A 2009
vitamine B_1 2010
vitamine B_2 2011
vitamine B_6 2012
vitamine B_{12} 2013
vitamine C 2014
vitamine D_2 2015
vitamine E 2016
vitamine K 2017
vitamine PP 1281, 1283
vitesse d'accroissement de la viscosité 272
voie de production 1463
volant 910
volatil 2018
voltmètre 2019
volume des alvéoles 406
volume spécifique 1761
votator 2022

warfarine 2025
winterisation 2064

xanthophylle 2070
xylose 2071

yahourt 2079
yaourt 2079
yoghourt 2079

zéine 2081
zéolithe 2082
zeste confit 353
zone de refroidissement 493
zone de séchage 648
zymase 2084
zymogène 2085
zymosimètre 2086
zymotachygraphe 2087

ESPAÑOL

abadejo 1433
abertura 1334
ablandador 1893
abombamiento de latas 270
abono fertilizante 1175
absorción 4
acaricida 6
acedo 1749
aceite de ajenjo 2067
aceite de ajonjolí 1661
aceite de anís 136
aceite de atún 1942
aceite de ballena 2045
aceite de cacahuete 1376
aceite de cardamomo 372
aceite de casia 385
aceite de castor 386
aceite de coco 463
aceite de colza 1517
aceite de comino 533
aceite de enebro 1031
aceite de esperma 1764
aceite de eucalipto 697
aceite de fusel 815
aceite de germen de trigo 2048
aceite de girasol 1842
aceite de habas de soja 1754
aceite de higado de bacalao 465
aceite de higado de mero 906
aceite de hígado de tiburón 1670
aceite de jazmín 1024
aceite de linaza 1122
aceite de macis 1150
aceite de maní 1376
aceite de menta 1385
aceite de mostaza 1261
aceite de neroli 1274
aceite de nuez 2024
aceite de nuez de palma 1355
aceite de oliva 1323
aceite de palma 1356
aceite de pescado 753
aceite de pirola 2063
aceite de ricino 386
aceite de romero 1573
aceite de semillas de algodón 501
aceite de tomillo 1917
aceite esencial 688
aceite hidrogenado 960
aceite lubricante 875
aceite secante 646
aceite sulfonado 1838
aceite volátil 688
acelerador 8
acelerante 8

acero al vanadio 1982
acero inoxidable 1785
acetal 9
acetaldehido 10
acetato 11
acetato de amilo 115
acetato de etilo 15
acetificante 17
acetilación 22
acetina 18
acetoglicérido 19
acetona 20
acidificar 30
acidimetría 32
acidímetro 31
ácido 26, 1749
ácido acético 12
ácido acético glacial 832
ácido aldehídico 76
ácido algínico 86
ácido araquidónico 154
ácido ascórbico 2014
ácido aspártico 165
ácido benzoico 230
ácido butírico 337
ácido cafeico 340
ácido carbólico 1402
ácido cítrico 448
ácido cólico 438
ácido desoxirribonucléico 582
ácido erucico 685
ácido esteárico 1804
ácido fítico 1407
ácido fólico 775
ácido fórmico 790
ácido gálico 818
ácido giberélico 830
ácido glicerofosfórico 850
ácido glicólico 853
ácido glucónico 838
ácido glutámico 842
ácido graso 719
ácido graso esencial 687
ácido hidnocárpico 955
ácido hipocloroso 974
ácido indolbutírico 983
ácido isovalérico 1022
ácido láctico 1068
ácido láurico 1092
ácido linoléico 1118
ácido linolénico 1120
acidólisis 33
ácido málico 1161
ácido nicotínico 1283
ácido nucléico 1301

ácido oléico 1321
ácido orótico 1336
ácido palmítico 1353
ácido palmitoléico 1354
ácido pantoténico 1360
ácido piroleñoso 1490
ácido propiónico 1470
ácido quínico 1498
ácido ribonucléico 1557
ácido ricinoléico 1561
ácido sórbico 1745
ácido sulfuroso 1840
ácido tánico 1876
ácido tartárico 1884
ácido úrico 1965
acidular 30
aclarar 746
acondicionamiento del aire 67
acondicionar 479
aconitina 38
actina 39
activador 1466
activar la fermentación 1579
actividad 43
actividad diastática 598
actividad óptica 1329
actomiosina 45
achicoria 426
achiote 138
adenina 47
adermina 2012
aditivo 46
aditivo alimenticio 777
adsorbente 49
adsorción 50
aductos de urea 1963
adulteración 52
adulteración de alimentos 778
aeración de la masa 629
aerobio 54
aerosol 56
aflatoxinas 57
afrecho 300
agar-agar 58
agar inclinado 59
ageno 1289
agente antisalpicador 149
agente arrastrante 676
agente de mejoración de espuma 1090
agente de oxidación 1347
agente dispersante 619
agente espumador 771
agente humectante 1848
agitación 443
agitador 64

aglomerante 237
aglutinación 62
aglutinante 237
aglutinina 63
agrio 1749
agrumarse 342
agua 2028
agua adicional 1158
aguacate 181
agua de cocimiento 314, 1130
agua de condensación 2035
agua de cristalización 2036
agua de Javel 1025
agua de relleno 1158
agua enlazada 296
agua madre 1250
aguardiente de patatas 1448
aguas cloacales 1663
agujero de hombre 1173
agujero del tapón 329
agujero de visita 1173
ahechadura 411
ahechar 2062
ahumado 1702
aire esterilizado 1812
aislar 1655
ajedrea 1623
ajo 820
alambique 1449
alambique al vacío 1979
alambique de cerveza 223
alantoína 94
al azar 1513
albahaca 207
albañal 1666
albaricoque 152
albumen 658
albúmina 69
albúmina de huevo 1339
albúmina de sangre 263
albuminado 70
albuminoide 71
albumosa 72
alcabarras 359
alcachofa 159
álcali 90
alcalímetro 92
alcaloide 93
alcohol 73
alcohol amílico 116
alcohol cetílico 410
alcohol de madera 2065
alcohol desnaturalizado 576
alcohol etílico 692
alcohol graso 720

alcohol isopropílico 1019
alcohol láurico 1093
alcohol metilado 1214
aldehido 75
aldohexosa 77
aldol 78
aldosa 79
aldosterona 80
aldrina 81
ale 82
aletrina 95
alfa-amilasa 102
alfrecho 1224
alga 84
algaroba 373
alginato 85
alginato sódico 1709
alholva 727
alicíclico 87
alifático 89
alimentos 783
aliño 1639
almacenamiento 1819
almacenamiento a baja temperatura 468
almacenamiento bajo atmósfera
   controlada 823
almáciga 1189
almeja 449, 1259
almendra 101
almendra amarga 247
almidón 1791
alomérico 96
alosa 97, 1667
alquequenje 357
altabaquillo 238
alta temperatura por corto tiempo 937
altrosa 103
alúmina 104
alúmina activada 40
alveógrafo 105
amargo 246
amasadura 1058
amasadura de la masa 631
amasar 1057, 1237
ámbar gris 106
amida 107
amida de ácido 27
amilasa 117
amilasa de hongos 811
amilógrafo 119
amiloide 120
amilopectina 121
amilopsina 122
amilosa 123
amina 108

amina alifática 721
aminoácido 109
amonia 110
amoníaco 110
amonio 111
análisis del tamaño de partículas 1368
análisis volumétrico 2021
ananás 1414
anato 138
anchoa 127
andrógeno 128
anetol 126
aneurina 2010
anfólito 113
anfótero 114
angelote 1247
Angström 129
anguila 654
ángulo de cortadura 546
anhídrido acético 13
anhídrita 130
anhidro 131
anillo sellador 1637
anión 134
anís 135
anisol 137
ánodo 139
antialbumosa 140
antibiosis 141
antibiótico 142
anticatalizador 144
antienzima 145
antiespumante 563
antigerminante 1781
antiglutinante 143
antihistamina 146
antioxidante 147
antiséptico 148
aparato de Dean y Stark 554
apio 402
apio napiforme 401
aquaturma 1027
arabinosa 153
arandano 235
arándano 508
arcacil 159
arcilla 1035
arenque 929
arenque ahumado 1054
arenque pequeño 1775
areómetro 965
arginina 155
armario para secar al vacío 1978
aroma 156, 1313
arrastre 677

arroz 1559
arsénico 158
asar 1481, 1566
asar a la parilla 881
ascalonia 1668
ascorbato sódico 1710
aséptico 160
aspirador accionado por vapor 1798
atmósfera 168
átomo 169
átomo de carbono asimétrico 167
atún 1941
aturdir 1825
autocatálisis 174
autoclave 175
autoclave hidrostático 968
autólisis 176
automatización 177
autoxidación 178
avena 1308
avena salaje 2058
aventar 2062
avidina 179
avitaminosis 180
avocado 181
axeroftol 2009
azafrán 1594
azúcar 1832
azúcar blanco 1421
azúcar colonial 1421
azúcar de caña 354
azúcar de nevar 976
azúcar de pilón 1134
azúcar de plomo 1837
azúcar de remolacha 227
azúcar en polvo 387
azúcar granulado 871
azúcar invertido 1005
azúcar moreno 321
azul de metileno 1216

bacalao seco 1816
bacilo 183
bacteria 191
bacteria coliforme 469
bacteria mesófila 1209
bacteria patógena 1372
bacteria psicrofílica 1479
bacterias acéticas 14
bactericida 186
bacteriófago 188
bacteriólisis 187
bacteriostático 190
bacteriostato 189
bagazo 192, 1176

bajo contenido calorífico 1140
banana 200
baño 214
baño desengrasante 566
barbada 551
barbo 393
barbo de mar 1531
barrel 204
barril 204, 383
barrilito 1050
barrilito medio 750
base 206
batata 1853
batido 443
batir 477
batir a espuma 53
batir la leche 442
baya de *Dioscoreophyllum cumminsii* 1659
bazo 1772
benzoato sódico 1711
berenjena 173
beriberi 233
berro 515, 2030
berza 339
berza marina 1636
besugo 900, 1635
beta-amilasa 234
bicarbonato sódico 1712
bicho 1996
bilis 236
bioluminescencia 241
biotina 242
biscocho 244
biuret 250
bixin 251
bizcocho 1584
blandura 1894
blanquear 258
blanqueo 261
bocio 855
bodega de fermentación 732
bofes 1113
bomba aspirante 1830
bomba centrípeta 408
bomba circulante 447
bomba de aire 68
bomba de vacío 1977
bombón 805
boquerón 2051
borra de algodón 1123
borraja 284
borrego 943
botulismo 294
braceaje 1185

bretón 1034
bretones 323
bromato potásico 1442
bromato sódico 1713
bromelina 320
brote 1674
brucina 322
bucarda 459
buccino 2049
buey 1343
buey joven 1807
burbuja 324

cabrito 1047
cacahuete 1374
café 467, 1240
cafeina 341
caja de escape 704
calabacera 1483
calabaza 1483
calabaza succhini 503
calamar 1783
calandria 344
calciferol 2015
cal clorada 262
caldera 275
caldera tubular 1939
caldereta 1044
caldo 295, 484
caldo bordelés 285
caldo de Burdeos 285
calentador de platos 1427
calentador helicoidal 1769
calentamiento dieléctrico 601
calentamiento por inducción 984
calentamiento por injección de vapor
    1801
calentamiento rápido 756
cal hidráulica 957
calificar 859
calor de formación 919
calor de solución 920
calor de vaporización 1987
calor específico 1758
caloría 348
calorímetro de combustión 280
calor latente 1087
calor molecular 1245
cámara de atomización 1776
cámara de fermentación 1475
camisa de vapor 1802
campana de gasos 808
canela 446
cangrejo 506
cangrejo de río 510

caña de azúcar 1834
cáñamo 924
caolín 1035
capacidad de retener agua 2033
capacidad para formar gas 822
capacidad para formar masas
    630
capa de aleurona 83
capa de empaquetadura 1824
capelin 358
capón 360
caproato de alilo 99
capsula de Petri 1399
captano 361
caracol de mar 459, 2049
caracol marino 2061
caramelo 362
caramelos 274
carbohidrasa 364
carbohidrato 365
carbón activado 42
carbón animal 132, 282, 415
carbonato cálcico 345
carbonato sódico 1714
carbón de huesos 282, 415
carbón de sangre 264
carbón vegetal 1992
carboximetilcelulosa 368
carcinógeno 370
cardamomo 371
carne 1193
carne de ternera 1991
carne de vaca 221
carne de venado 1994
carne montesina 1994
carnero 1263
carne sintética 1902
caroteno 374
carpa 375
cáscara 952
caseína 378
caseína al cuajo 1543
caseinógeno 381
casquete de burbujeo 325
castaña 422
casual 1513
catador 1607
catadura 1608
catalasa 388
catálisis 390
catalizador 391
catepsina 394
catión 395
cáustico 397
cazabe 384

cebada 201
cebada de maltear 1168
cebolla 1325
cebolleta 429
celuloide 403
celulosa 404
ceniza de huesos 281
centeno 1586
centígrado 407
cera 2039
cera de abejas 225
cera del petróleo 1400
cereal 862
cereales 308, 409
cereza 420
cervecería 313
cerveza 222
cerveza de barril 636
cerveza de fermentación baja 1074
cerveza de sifón 636
cerveza lista para consumo 748
cerveza negra 1820
cerveza por prensa 2076
cetona 1042
cetosa 1043
ciclamato sódico 1718
ciclo del carbono 366
ciervo 561
cilindro de alimentación 723
cilindros de alimentación 724
cinamato de bencilo 232
cinamato de etilo 693
cinamato de metilo 1215
cinturón portador 492
ciruela 1429
ciruela pasa 1476
ciruela verdal 876
cisteína 549
citocromos 550
citrato férrico-amónico 735
clara de huevo 658
clarificación 450, 562
clarificación con lechada de cal 1116
clarificar 746
clasificar 859
claudia 876
clavillos 456
clavos de especia 456
cloaca 1666
cloración 432
clorato sódico 1715
clordán 430
clorito sódico 1717
clorofila 433
cloruro de ácido 28

cloruro de cal 431
cloruro sódico 1716
coacervación 457
cobalamina 2013
cocimiento botulínico 293
cocinado por microondas 1222
coco 462
cochinilla 458
código de principios (F.A.O.) 464
coeficiente de actividad 44
coeficiente de inflación 1856
coenzima 466
cohombro 532
col 339
cola 841
cola a basa de caseína 379
cola de pescado 1015
colágeno 470
colapez 1015
coles de Bruselas 323
colesterol 437
coliflor 396
colina 439
colinabo 1851
colmino 363
colofonia 474
coloidal 472
coloide 471
colorante alimenticio 779
colza 1516
combustión espontánea 1773
compilación de leges (F.A.O.) 464
compresor de dos tiempos 1950
compuesto amónico cuaternario 1494
compuesto aromático 157
compuesto nitroso 1291
concentrar 476
concentrar por ebullición 273
concha 529
conchar 477
condensador de Liebig 1112
condimento 1639, 1765
conducto de ventilación 808
conejo 1500
confite 353
confitería 480
congelado a baja temperatura 560
congelador 797
congelador discontinuo 211
congelamiento por convección forzada 259
congelamiento rápido 1496
congestionamiento 288
congrio 481
conservación 1456

consistencia 483
consistencia de leche 1229
consistente 1814
consommé 484
constituyente 485
consumo recomendado 1527
contador 1528
contaminación 487, 1733
contaminar 486
contenido de agua 2029
contenido de humedad 1242
contenido en almidón 1792
contenido en cenizas 162
control de cualidad 1492
coñac 301
copa 219
copos de maíz 497
corcho 496
cordero 1075
cornezuelo 684
correguela 238
correhuela 238
corrupción 557
cortador de bizcochos 245
cortador de galletas 245
cortar en cubos 599
corteza 529
corteza de abeto 923
corteza de queso 418
corteza de roble 1307
cosecha 916
costura de latas 1735
cotufa 1027
crema 511
crema agria 1750
crema de cacahuete 1375
cremor tártaro 512
cresa 1155
crescer 1474
crespo 516
criba 1681
cribar 1682
cristalización 531
cristalización fraccionada 793
cristalizar 530
cromatina 440
cromatografía 441
cromatografía de gases 821
crudo 1520
cuajada 537, 1032
cuajo 1542
cualidad sanitaria 1610
cuba de fermentación 731
cuba de mosto 1186
cuba mezcladora 1184

cuba para líquidos fermentados 224
cubierta 504
cubo de pan tostado 520
cubre objeto 505
cucúrbita ovífera 1181
culantro 495
curar 538, 539
cúrcuma 535
curcumina 536
curry 542
cutícula 544

chalote 1668
chamuscar 1627
chícharo 424
chirivia 1367
chocolate 434
chocolate amargo 248
chocolate de leche 436
chorizo 1621
chucrut 1620
chuleta 545

damajuana 369
dátil 552
decantación 555
decocción 556
defecto de horneado 195
deixar 1474
delicuecencia 572
demanda bioquímica de oxígeno 239
densidad 577
densidad de vapor 1988
depósito 883
depósito desengrasante 566
depósito para la propagación de bacterias
   185
derecho 1581
derivado 584
desaminasa 553
descenso 716
descomposición 557
descongelación 564
descongelar 1903
descortezadora mecánica 558
descripción de alimentos 780
desecador 585, 587
desecar 586, 644, 1052
desecho 2027
desemulsificador 559
desgrasar 565
deshidratación 568
deshidratar 567
deshidrocongelamiento 569
deshidrogenación 571

deshidrogenasa 570
desintegrador 616
desmenuzador 1676
desnaturalización 574, 575
desodorante 579
desodorización 580
desodorizante 579
desorción 588
desoxi- 581
desperdicio 2027
desperdicios 1316
desperdicios de cebada 1870
destilación al vacío 1969
destilación en corriente de vapor 754
destilación extractiva 714
destilación fraccionada 794
destilación por vapor 1797
destilería 621
detector de metal 1211
detergente 589
detergente sintético 1863
dextrina 592
dextrógiro 593
dextrorrotatorio 593
dextrosa 839
diacetilo 594
diáfano 1380
diafragma 596
diagrama de flujo 767
diálisis 595
diastasa 597
dieldrina 600
dietético 603
difenilo 612
difusión 604
digestión 605
digitalina 606
dilatación 608
diluir 610
dimórfico 611
dióxido de azufre 1839
dióxido de carbono 367
disacárico 614
disgregador 616
disminución 716
disociación 620
dispensador 617
dispersar 618
dispersión macromolecular 471
diterpeno 623
dición 624
dosímetro 1502
dosis letal 1106
duela 1795
dulce 1852

dulcería 480
dulcina 651
dureza 912
dureza permanente 1392
dureza temporal del agua 1891

ebullición 277
efervescencia 655
eflorescencia 656
eje 1768
elasticidad de la miga 525
elastina 660
electrodo de referencia 1533
elevadora de horquilla 787
elutriación 662
embalaje 1351
embalaje transparente 1927
embeber 1706
embotellar 286
embrión 664
embutido 1621
empanado 216
emulsificador 665, 666
emulsión 667
emulsoide 668
encapsulación 669
encogimiento 1678
endive 670
endosperma 671
eneldo 609
energía 673
enfriadera tubular 1940
enfriador de platos 1425
enfriador por inmersión 981
enfriamiento con soluciones salinas 317
enfriamiento por atomización 1777
enfriar 427
engrapadora 1790
enlaces dobles conjugados 482
enlatado 355
en marcha 1326
enmohecido 1262
enómetro 2004
enradera 238
enrarecimiento 1518
enriquecimiento 674
ensalada 1149
ensalada de col 1696
ensalada de frutas 1149
ensordecer 1825
entalpía 675
entraga 573
entropía 678
envasado aséptico 161
envasadora de botellas 287

envejecimiento 61, 1649
envenenamiento alimenticio 781
envoltura de aparato de extracción 713
enzima 679
eosina 680
epitelio olfacterio 1322
equivalente en agua 2031
equivalente-gramo 865
ergosterol 683
eritrodextrina 686
escabechar 1411
escabeche 1178
escala Baumé 218
escala de Brix 318
escala de Reaumur 1524
escala Fahrenheit 715
escala hedónica 921
escaldar 1624
escalfar 1431
escaloña 1668
escatol 1693
escombro 1152
escorbuto 1633
esencia de clavillos 455
esencia de espliego 1766
esencia de lemongras 1102
esencia de limón 1103
esencia de mandarina 1172
esencia de vainilla 1984
espacio vacío 917
espárrago 164
especia 1765
especificidad 1759
especifidad 1759
espectro 1762
esperlán 1700
espesador 1913
espinaca 1767
espíritu de sal 1770
espíritu de vino 1771
espliego 166, 1094
espuma de impurezas 1632
espumante 771
espumar 1694
esqualeno 1782
estabilizador 1784
estado fundamental 884
estafilococo 1788
estanque de evaporación 1604
estearina 1805
éster 689
éster ácido 29
éster de celulosa 405
estereoespecífico 1810
estereoisómero 1809

éster graso 722
esterificación 690
estéril 1811
esterilizar 1813
estimulación del crecimiento 887
estimulador del crecimiento 886
estímulo 1815
estocafis 1816
estofar 299
estragón 1883
estreptomicina 1823
estrógeno 1315
estufa 1340
estufa de secado 647
esturión 1826
éter 691
éter acético 15
éter butílico 336
etileno 694
eugenol 698
evacuación de aguas cloacales 1664
evaluación de cualidad 1493
evaluación sensorial 1652
evaporación 701
evaporación instantanea 755
evaporadora de película ascendiente 453
evaporador al vacío 1972, 1976
evaporador de efecto múltiple 1254
evaporador de platos 1426
evaporador de un solo paso 1687
examen organoléptico 1332
exhaustador 702
exotérmico 706
extensibilidad del gluten 845
extensógrafo 708
extensómetro 709
extracción 711
extracción por partición 1129
extracción por solvente 1742
extracción por vapor 1799
extracto de carne 1194
extracto de hierbas 928
extracto de levadura 2074
exudado 640
exudar 1850

fabricación en serie 1187
fabro 1028
factores de Atwater 172
factor protéico animal 133
faneca 1450
fanega 331
fango 1697
fango cloacal 1665
farinógrafo 717

farnesol 718
fenogreco 727
fenol 1402
fermentación 730
fermentación acética 16
fermentación aeróbica 55
fermentación alcohólica 74
fermentación amílica 118
fermentación de la masa 1357
fermentación tumultuosa 278
fermentado químico 419
fermentar 729
fermento 728, 1510
fermentógrafo 734
fertilizante 737
fibra 738
fibra cruda 522
fibra natural 1268
ficina 739
fijación del nitrógeno 1288
filtración acelerada 7
filtración al vacío 1974
filtro 741
filtro de arena 1609
filtro de Seitz 1644
filtro rotatorio 1576
firmeza de miga 526
fitol 1409
fitoquímico 1408
fitosterol 1410
flan 543
flatulencia 759
flavona 760
flavoproteína 761
floculación 764
flujo laminar 1077
flujo Newtoniano 1279
flujo turbulento 1946
flujo viscoso 2007
fluoresceína 769
fluorescencia 770
fluoroacetato sódico 1719
formación de esporas 1774
formación de miga 527
formaldehido-sulfoxilato 788
formalina 789
forraje 785, 1578
fortificado 791
fortificar 792
fortuito 1513
fosfátido 1404
fosfato cálcico 347
fosfolípido 1405
fotosíntesis 1406
fragancia 156

frambueza 1519
frasco 758
frasco de Kjeldahl 1055
frasco Dewar 590
freir 1622
fresa 1822
fresco de barril 637
friabilidad 800
frito 804
fritura 804
fructosa 801
fruta azucarada 352
fruta climatérica 452
fruta de hueso 1817
fruta del pimiento de Jamaica 98
fruto del rosal 938
fuerza iónica 1009
fumigación 810
fumigante 809
fundente 776
fungicida 812
fungistato 813
furfural 814

galactosa 816
galantina 817
galón 819
galleta 244
galleta de soda 507
gamba 1451
gámbaro 1677
garbanzo 424, 1373
garrafa 369
gas hilarante 1292
gas natural 1269
gel 824
gelatina 825, 1026
gel de sílice 1683
gen 826
gene 826
generador de vapor 1800
generador de vinagre 2002
geraniol 827
germén 663
germicida 829
germinar 1780
ginabra 831
giste 203
glasé 835
glasear 834
gliadina 836
glicérido 847
glicerina 848
glicerol 848
glicina 851

glicocola 851
glicógeno 852
glicósido 854
globulina 837
gluconato sódico 1720
glucosa 839
glutamato monosódico 1721
glutamato sódico 1721
glutamina 843
gluten 844
glutenina 846
goma 894
goma arábica 895
goma de adraganto 896
goma de guayaco 888
goma de karaya 1036
goma de tragacanto 896
goma guar 892
goma para mascar 423
goma silicónica 1684
gorgojo 864
gosipol 858
grado 860
grado alcohólico 1467
gramicidina 866
gram-negativo 868
gram-positivo 869
granada 1439
granadilla 870
granadina 879
grano 862
grano de avena 882
grano de cervecero 312
grano flotante de cebada 1857
grano pesado 1688
granos 409
grasa de asado 641
grasa de riñón 1831
grasa endurecida 911
grasa hidrogenada 911
grieta 1097
grifo 1818
groselas 540
grosella espinosa 857
grupo acetilo 24
grupo acetoxilo 21
guanina 889
guano 890
guanosina 891
guayaba 893
guisante 1373
gustación 1887
gusto 762, 1885

haba 220, 319

haba de soja 1753
haba de tonca 1921
halita 907
harina 766
harina adulterada 51
harina autolevantadora 1645
harina blanqueada 260
harina de huesos 283
harina de maíz 498
harina de pastelería 343
harina gruesa 309
harina para pan 306
harina patente 1371
helado 975
helar 427
hemaglobina 903
hematina 901
hematoxilina 902
hemicelulosa 922
heparina 925
heptacloro 926
herbicida 2041
hermejo 1580
hervir 1624
hervir a fuego lento 1685
hervir parcialmente 1364
hesperidina 930
heterocíclico 931
hexaclorobenceno 933
hexaclorociclohexano 932
hexacloruro de benceno 229
hexosa 935
hez 1098
hialuronidasa 953
hidátide 954
hidracida del ácido maléico 1160
hidratación 956
hidrato de carbono 365
hidrazona 958
hidrocelulosa 959
hidrófilo 966
hidrófobo 967
hidrogenación 961
hidrolisado de caseína 380
hidrólisis 964
hidrómetro 965
hidrómetro de Twaddell 1949
hidroxianisol butilado 334
hidróxido potásico 1443
hidroximercuriclorofenol 969
hidroximercuricresol 970
hidroxitolueno butilado 335
hielo seco 645
hierba 927
hierbas finas 747

hígado 1133
higiene 971
higo 740
higrómetro 972
higroscópico 973
hilatura en húmedo 2044
hinojo 726
histamina 939
histidina 940
hoja de lata 1919
hojalata 1919
hojuelas de cebada 202
hojuelas de maíz 497
hojuelas de trigo 2047
homogenización 944
hongo 1252, 1258
hormona 947
horno 1340
horno continuo 488
horno de secar al vacío 1971
hueva 1568
humectante 949
humedad 950
humedad en equilibrio 682
humedad relativa 1539
humus 951

impermeable 2037
impregnar 979
impurezas 626
incomestible 986
inconsútil 1638
incrustación 1625
incrustación de calderas 276
indicador 982
indicador de oxidación-reducción 1346
índice de acetilo 25
indice de acidez 37
índice de refracción 1536
índice de yodo 1006
industria conservera 356
inerte 987
inestable 1061
infestación por pestes 1398
infiltración 1390
infiltrarse 1643
infusión 989
ingrediente 990
inhibidor 991
inhibidor del crecimiento 885
iniciador 992, 1793
inmiscible 977
inmunidad 978
inocular 993
inodoro 1314

inosina 994
inositol 995
insaturado 1960
insecticida 996
inspección de carne 1195
instalar un grifo 1879
instantaneizar 997
instrucciones 613
instrumentación 998
instrumentación reológica 1551
insulina 999
intercambiador de calor 918
intercambiador de calor por
  contracorriente 502
intercambio de iones 1007
interesterificación 1000
inulina 1002
invernización 2064
inversión 1003
invertasa 1004
ionización 1010
ionona 1011
ipecacuana 1012
irradiación 1013
isoeugenol 1017
isoleucina 1018
isómero óptico 1330
isosafrol 1020
isotiocianato 1021
isotiocianato de alilo 100

jabón 1707
jabón blando 1732
jacqueca 1198
jamón 908
jarabe 1864
jarabe de azúcar 856
jarabe de glucosa 840
jarabe de maíz 499
jarro 350
jibia 547
jiste 203
joule 1029
judía escarlata 1583
judía verde 915
judía verde trepadora 1583
jugo 640, 1030

kebab 1038
keroseno 1041
kieselgur 1049
koji 1872
kosher 1059
kumquat 534

lábil 1061
laca 1063
lacrimógeno 1062
lactalbúmina 1064
lactama 1065
lactasa 1066
lactato 1067
lácteo 1230
lactobutirómetro 1069
lactoflavina 2011
lactona 1070
lactosa 1071
lámina 774, 1076
laminado 1078
lámina encogible 1679
laminar 1079
laminilla 505, 1076
lana de desecho 1673
lanceolado 1080
langosta 509
langosta de mar 1136
lanolina 1081
lanosterol 1082
lapa 1117
lardo 184
lardo ahumado 1701
lata 351
lata abombada 1855
látex 1088
laurel 1091
laurilsulfato sódico 1723
lavadora de botellas 289
lavador continuo de latas 1821
lavanda 1094
lecitina 1099
lecha 1234
lechada 1698
lechaza 1234
leche 1228
leche completa 806
leche completa evaporada 700
leche condensada azucarada 478
leche descremada 1695
leche desecada 638
leche evaporada 699
leche malteada 1166
leche separada 1695
lechoza 1362
lechozo 1230
lechuga 1107
legumbre 1482
lejía 1143
lenguado 765, 1086, 1104, 1737
lenteja 1105
leucina 1108

levadura 2073
levadura alta 1923
levadura baja 292
levadura desecada 639
levadura de siembra 1417
levógiro 1072
levorrotatorio 1072
levulosa 801
ley de Raoult 1515
liberar 1109
licor 1130
licuefacción 1128
liebre 914
lignina 1114
lija 627
lima 1115
limón 1101
limpieza en al sitio 451
linaza 1121
línea de producción 1463
linoleína 1119
linteres 1123
liofilización 796
lipasa 1125
lipólisis 1126
lipoxidasa 1127
lipoxigenasa 1127
liquen 1110
líquido filtrado 745
lisina 1144
lisosoma 1145
lisozima 1146
litro 1132
lixiviación 1096
lobina 209
lote 210
lozania 266, 268
lucio 1412
lumen 1141
lúpulo 946
lustre 265
luteína 1142

llave 1818
llenado al vacío 1973
llenadora de botellas 287
llicle 425

macarrones 1147
macerar 1151
macia 1148
macromolécula 1153
macroscópico 1154
machacador de azúcar 1835
maduración 60, 1190

maduración de la masa 633
madurar 1564
mahonesa 1192
maíz 1157
mala hierba 2040
malatión 1159
malnutrición 1162
mal olor 1699
malo sabor 1318
malta 1163
malta colorante 253
maltasa 1165
malta tostada 1053
malta verde 878
maltear 1164
maltería 1167
maltosa 1169
malla 1207
maní 1374
manómetro 1174
manómetro en U 1967
manteca 1085, 1675
manteca de cacao 461
mantequilla 332
mantequilla de maní 1375
manzana 151
maqueta 1241
máquina para envolver 2069
máquina para lavar botellas 289
máquina para revestir de chocolate 435
máquina picadora de carne 1235
marcar 1869
margarina 1177
marinar 1752
marisco 1259
marjorana 1179
marmita 1044
masa 215
masa fermentada 1751
mascar 1188
masticar 1188
matadero 2
materia extraña 786
matraz 758
matzo 1191
mayonesa 1192
mazapán 1182
medidor de vacío 1975
mejorador 980
mejoramiento sanitario 1611
mejorana 1179
melanina 1199
melaza 1244
melazas de mieles pobres 257
melisa 199

melitosa 1200
melón 1202
melorina 1201
membrana 596
membrillo 1497
menta 1236
mentol 1203
mentona 1204
menudillos 1317
mercaptano 1205
merengue 1206
merlán 271, 2052, 2054
merlango 904
merluza 904
merma 1954
mermelada 1023, 1180
mero 315, 905
mero negro 877
metabisulfito potásico 1444
metabolismo 1210
metal alcalino 91
metálico 1212
metilestireno 1218
metionina 1213
método 1461
método de Kjeldahl 1056
mezcla 1239
mezcla azeotrópica 182
mezclado a alta velocidad 936
mezclador 1238
mezclador de tambor giratorio 205
mezclador para tratamiento por lotes 212
mezclar 1237
micela 1219
micelio 1264
micotoxina 1265
micrón 1220
microorganismo anaeróbico 125
microscópico 1221
miel 945
miga 524
migración 1225
mijo 1232
mildiu 1227
mioglobina 1266
mírtilo 235
mixturar 1237
moca 1240
módulo de Young 2080
moho 1252
molécula-gramo 867
moledora de cilindros 1570
molienda 1233
molino 1231
molino a disco 615

molino batidor de martillos 518
molino de bolas 198
molino de rodillas lisas 1703
molino de rodillos 1359
molino para coloides 473
molinos 310
mondadura 1705
monoestearato de glicerina 849
monoglicérido 1248
monomolecular 1249
montacarga 787
mora 1137, 1253
morcilla 255, 1621
moscatel 1255
mostaza 416
mosto 1183, 1260, 2068
mosto dulce 1854
motilidad 1251
muela vertical 653
muestra 1606
muestra al azar 1514
muestrador 1607
mújil 880
mujol 1531
músculo 1257
musgo irlandés 376
mustela 330
mustela de río 1450

nabo 1948
nabo de Suecia 1851
naranja 1331
naranja mandarina 1171
naranja tangarina 1875
narcótico 1267
nariz atomizadora 171
nata 511
nata agria 1750
nata gruesa 454
natillas 543
nauseabundo 1270
navaja 1521
nectarina 1271
nefelómetro 1273
negro vegetal 1992
neurina 1276
neutralizar 1278
neutro 1277
niacina 1283
niacinamida 1281
Nicol 1280
nicotina 1282
nicotinamida 1281
niel 236

nisina 1285
níspola 1138, 1197
nitrato de Chile 1724
nitrato potásico 1445
nitrato sódico 1724
nitrito potásico 1446
nitrito sódico 1725
nitrogenasa 1287
nitrógeno 1286
nitrosamina 1290
nocivo 1300
no graso 1293
norleucina 1295
norma 1296
normal 1297
notatina 1299
no tóxicidad 1592
no tóxico 1591
nucleoproteína 1302
nuez 1303, 2023
nuez del Brasil 304
nuez del nogal americano 1378
nuez de merey 382
nuez moscada 1304
número de saponificación 1613
nutrición de la levadura 2075
nutrimento 1305

ñame 2072

ocular 1310
odorante 1311
odorífero 1311
odorimetría 1312
oleato de diglicol 607
olefina 1320
olor 1313
olla a presión 1458
omaso 1582
opaco 1328
opalescencia 1327
operación por lotes 213
orden estatutoria 1794
oreja marina 1
organismo termófilo 1911
orientar 1333
orificio 1334
ornitina 1335
orozuz 1111
orujo 1176
oscurecimiento no enzimático 1156
oseína 1338
ósmosis 1337
ostra 1349

ova 1095
oveja 1263
ovoalbúmina 1339
oxidación 1345
oxidante 1347
oxidasa 1344
óxido de etileno 695
óxido de mesitilo 1208
óxido nitroso 1292
oxitetraciclina 1348
ozono 1350

palma 1352
palmera 1352
palmera de aceite 1319
pan 305
panadería 194
pancreatina 1358
pan de soda 1708
pan integral 2055, 2056
pantotenato cálcico 346
panza 1582
papaína 1361
papaya 1362
papel de filtro 742
papel de filtro sin cenizas 163
papel vitela 1365
papera 855
papilas gustativas 1886
parte para enfriar 493
par térmico 1906
partida 210
pasa 1509
pasas de Corinto 541
pasita 1841
pasta 1294
pastas alimenticias 88
pasteurización 1369
pataca 1027
patata 1447
patente 1370
pectina 1379
pechina 1626
pegajosidad 1571
pegajoso 1867
peine 449
pelúcido 1380
pelusilla 267
penetrómetro 1381
penicilina 1382
pentosa 1383
pepino 532
pepsina 1386
peptización 1387
peptona 1388

pera 1377
perborato sódico 1726
perca 209, 1389
percepción sensorial 1653
percolación 1390
pérdida al hornear 196
pérdida de peso 2042
pérdida por radiación 1503
perejil 1366
pericarpio 1391
perifollo 421
período de inducción 985
permeabilidad 1393
peroxidasa 1394
peróxido de acetilbenzoilo 23
peróxido de benzoilo 231
persulfato amónico 112
persulfato sódico 1727
pesa-ácidos 31
pescadilla 1433
peso atómico 170
peso específico 1757
pesticida 1397
petróleo de lámpara 1041
pez espada 1858
picado 1418
picar 625
pila de malta 1170
pimienta 1384
pimienta blanca 2053
pimienta de Cayena 400
pimienta dulce 1363
pimienta negra 254
pinchos 1038
piña 1414
pipeta 1415
pipeta graduada 861
piretrina 1489
piridoxina 2012
pirofosfato sódico de hierro 1722
pirólisis 1491
pistacho 1416
plancton 1420
plasma 1422
plástico 1423
plastificante 1424
plátano 200
platija 1419
pliegue 514
poder de amargor 249
podrido 1488
polarímetro 1432
polietileno 1434
polifosfato 1437
polimorfismo 1435

poliosa 1436
polipropileno 1438
polvo blanqueador 262
polvo de hornear 197
polvo de leche entera 2057
polvo para blanquear 431
poner en infusión 988
porcentage en volumen 2020
porcentaje de extracción 712
porcentaje en peso 2043
porfirina 1440
portador 491
portador vibratorio de transportación
  2000
potable 1441
potasa cáustica 398
potencia del fermento 1565
potenciador de sabor 763
pozo séptico 1657
precalentador 1454
precipitado 1452
premezclado 1455
premezclador 1184
prensa continua 490
prensa de esfuerzo 1672
prensa helicoidal 1631
prensa mecánica 1196
prensa para filtrar 743
presecador 1453
preservación 1456
preservativo 150, 1457
presión de columna de agua 2032
presión del vapor 1989
presión de vapor 1803
procedimiento 1461
proceso 1461
proceso de Campden 349
proceso de deshidratación por contacto
  con platos al vacío 1968
proceso de hacer la masa 632
proceso Keyes 1045
proceso Steffens 1808
producir espuma 1089
producir vapor 1508
productividad 1464
producto de cabeza 751
producto principal 1789
producto secundario 338
profundidad del canal 583
prolina 1465
prooxidante 1468
propanol 1469
propionato de amilo 124
propionato sódico 1728
proteasa 1471

proteína 1472
proteína cruda 523
proteína unicelular 1686
proteína vegetal 1993
proteína vegetal texturizada 1902
protoplasma 1473
provisión 392
prueba 1606, 1898
prueba de catalasa 389
prueba de fosfatasa 1403
prueba de Gerber 828
prueba de Gutzeit 898
prueba de Kreis 1060
prueba de ninhidrina 1284
prueba de resorcinol 1547
prueba en triadas 1929
prueba rápida 1629
prueba sensorial 1652
pseudoácido 1477
pseudobase 1478
ptomaína 1480
pudrir 1871
puerro 1100
pulido de salvado 302
pulpa de frutas 803
pulpo 1309
punto de congelación 799
punto de cristalización 863
punto de ebullición 279
punto de inflamabilidad 757
punto de rocío 591
punto de valoración 672
punto final 672
punto isoeléctrico 1016
punto térmico de muerte 1905
purina 1484
putrefacción 1486
putreficar 1487
pútrido 1488

quebrantadora giratoria 899
quelpo 1039
quemadura por frío 798
quemar 749
queratina 1040
quercetina 1495
queso 417
queso de cerdo 303
queso procesado 1462
quimotripsina 444
quinina 1499

rábano 1506
rábano silvestre 948
radiación 1501

radiactividad 1505
radiactivo 1504
radical ácido 34
radical libre 795
radurización 1507
rafinosa 1200
rancidez 1512
ráncido 1511
raquitismo 1562
rarefacción 1518
rascador 1628
raya 1692
raza de levadura 2077
reacción 1522
reacción de Baudouin 217
reacción en cadena 412
reacción irreversible 1014
reactivación 1523, 1549
reactivo de Fischer 752
reactivo de Karl Fischer 1037
reactivo de Nessler 1275
rebanda de remolacha en forma de V 500
receptor sensorial 1654
recipiente 1525
recirculación 1526
rectificación 1529
rectificador 1530
recuperación de solvente 1743
reducción 1532
refinería 1534
reflujo 1535
reforzamiento 674
refrescos 1730
refrigeración 1538
refrigerador tubular 1940
refrigerante 1537
regalía 1581
regaliz 1111
registrador 1528
rejilla 208
remojar 1806
remolacha 226
remolacha azucarera 1833
rendimiento 2078
rendimiento de la masa 634
renina 1544
reología 1552
reómetro 1553
reopexia 1554
requerimientos alimenticios 782
requesón 537, 1032
residuo 291
residuo de destilación 622
resiliencia 1545
resina 1546

resina intercambiadora de iones 1008
resistencia al desgarro 1671
reticulación 519
retinol 2009
retorta 1548
retrogradación 1786
revestir 1073
revisar 1341
rezumar 1643
riboflavina 2011
ribosa 1558
ricina 1560
rigor mortis 1563
riñón 1048
rizado 516
róbalo 900
rodaballo 1945
rodillo para bagazo 193
rodillo superior 1922
rodopsina 1555
rojo de metilo 1217
romero 1572
rotación molecular 1246
rotámetro 1574
rotenona 1577
roya negra 256
ruibarbo 1556
rust 1585
rutabaga 1851

sabor 762, 1885
sacarímetro 1587
sacarina 1588
sacarómetro 1589
sacarosa 1590
sagú 1596
sain 1085
sal 1603
sal ácida 35
salado 1605
salchicha 1621
salchichón 1621
sal de Epsom 681
sal de Glauber 833
sal de mesa 1716
sal de Rochelle 1567
sal emulsificante 666
salina 1604
salino 1598
salitre 1445
salitre de Chile 1724
saliva 1599
salmastro 298
salmón 1600
salmonela 1601

salmuera 316
salsa de ensalada 1597
salsa de soja 1755
salsifí 1602
sal tampón 326
salvado 300, 1223, 1224
salvia 1595
sandía 2034
saponificación 1612
saponina 1614
sarcosina 1615
sardina 1616
sardineta 1775
sargo 311
saturación 1619
sauerkraut 1620
sazón 1639
scutellum 1634
sebo 1874
secadero 587, 1051
secado a espuma 772
secado a espuma al vacío 773
secado continuo 489
secado por atomización 1778
secador a cama fluidizada 768
secador de aire tibio 2026
secador de Birs 243
secador de cilindros 1569
secador de doble tambor 628
secador de vacío 1970
secador neumático 1430
secador rotativo 642
secador rotatorio 1575
secante 1680
secar 644, 1052
secativo 1680
secuestración 1658
seguridad 1592
sedimento 883, 1640
segador 475
segador hillerador de guisantes 2003
seguro 1591
sellado por superposición de solapas 1083
sello de agua 2038
sembrar 1641
semilla de cacao 460
semipermeable 1646
semipreservado 1647
sémola 1648
sémola de trigo duro 652
sensitividad 1651
sensor 1650
separación de partículas en corriente de
  aire 66
separación por densidad 578

separador 1656
separador ciclónico 548
separador de crema 513
separador electrostático 661
separador magnético tipo tambor 643
separer 1655
sepia 547
serina 1660
seta 1258
sidra 445
siembra 1642
sifonar 1689
silicato sódico 1729
siluro 393
silvestre 416
simbiosis 1859
sinéresis 1860
sinergisto 1861
sintético 1862
sisal 1690
sitosterol 1691
sobrecalentamiento 1845
sobrecrecimiento 1342
sobreenfriado 1843
sobreenfriamiento 1844
sobresaturado 1846
soja 1753
sol 1734
soldadura 1736
soldadura a solape 1084
soldadura de recubrimiento 1084
solubilidad 1738
solución 1740
solución ácida 36
solución de Benedict 228
solución de Dragendorff 635
solución de Fehling 725
solución molar 1243
solución normal 1298, 1787
solución saturada 1618
solución tampón 327
soluto 1739
solvente 1741
solvente de extracción 710
sollo 1413
soplante 269
sorbete 1744
sorbita 1746
sorbitol 1746
sorbosa 1747
sorgo 1748
sosa 1714
sosa cáustica 399
suave 1226
sublimación 1827

subproducto 338
substituto 1828
substituto del huevo 657
subtilina 1829
succedáneo 1828
suciedad 744
sucrosa 1590
sudar 1850
suero 333, 2050
sulfato de cálcio anhidro 130
sulfato ferroso 736
sulfuro de hidrógeno 963
sultana 1841
surfactante 1848
suspensión 1849

tacómetro 1865
táctico 1868
takadiastasa 1872
talco 1873
tamíz 1681
tamizar 1682
tanda 210
tangarino 1875
tanino 1877
tanque a presión 290
tanque de fermentación 733
tanque de sedimentación 1662
tanque hidrogenador 962
tapa de botillas de gaseosas 521
tapioca 1880
tapón 328
taquisterol 1866
tara 1882
taraxacón 1881
tarragón 1883
tartrato potásico 512
tautomerismo 1888
té 1889
teleosteo 1890
temperatura absoluta 3
temperatura crítica 517
temperatura de reblandecimiento 1731
temperatura ultra elevada 1956
tenca 1892
tenderómetro 1895
tendón 1896
tensión del vapor 1989
tensión interfacial 1001
tensión superficial 1847
teofilina 1904
termocupla 1906
termodinámica 1907
termointercambiador 918

termointercambiador de platos 1428
termolábil 1908
termólisis 1909
termómetro 1910
termopar 1906
termopermutador 918
termostato 1912
ternera 1991
ternura 1894
terpeno 1897
terrón de azúcar 1836
testa 1899
tetraciclina 1900
tetrafosfato de hexaetilo 934
textura 1901
textura de miga 528
textura de pan 307
tiamina 2010
tiburón 1669
tierra decolorante 807
tierra de diatomas 1049
tina de mezcla 1186
tintómetro de Lovibond 1139
tirocidina 1951
tirosina 1952
tirotricina 1953
tiroxina 1918
tixótropo 1914
tiza 413
tizón 1704
tobillo 941
tocino 184
tocino ahumado 1701
tocoferol 2016
tomate 1920
tornasol 1131
tornillo sin fin 1630
toronja 873
torre de absorción 5
torre de atomización 1779
torre de secado 649
torta residua 707
tostado 516
tostador 1051
tostar 1566
toxicidad 1924
toxina 1925
transferasa 1926
transmisión de tornillo sin fin 2066
transparente 1380
transpiración 1928
trasegar 1878
tratamiento de fangos 41
tratamiento preliminar 1460
treonina 1915

triclorocarbanilida 1931
tricloruro de nitrógeno 1289
trifosfato de adenosina 48
trigla 897
trigo 2046
trigo duro 913
tripa 428
tripas 1932
tripsina 1935
triptofano 1936
triquinosis 1930
triticale 1933
triturador 1046, 1676
triturador de martillos 909
trufa 1934
tubércula 1937
tuberculina 1938
tubo rociador 1756
tubo secador en bandejas 1943
tunel de enfriamiento 494
tunel de secado 650
turbio 1944
turgor 1947

ultrafiltración 1955
ultrasonido 1957
ultravioleta 1958
umbla 874
umbra 414
undecalactona 1959
uperización 1961
urea 1962
ureasa 1964
uridina 1966
ustílago 1704
uva 872

váina 952
vainilla 1985
vainillina de etilo 696
valina 1980
valor alimenticio 784
valor biológico 240
valor de dienos 602
valor de Lintner 1124
valor de peróxidos 1395
valor liminal 1916
valor nutritivo 1306
valor pH 1401
valor rH 1550
valor umbral 1916
válvula 1981
válvula de aguja 1272
válvula de escape del aire 65
válvula de retención 1324

válvula de seguridad 1541, 1593
válvula reductora de presión 1459
vancomicina 1983
vapor 1796
vapor de escape 705
vaporización 1986
varfarina 2025
variador de velocidad 1990
vaso 350
velocidad de aumento de viscosidad 272
vello 267
venera 1626
ventilador inhalador 703
ventilar 53
verdolaga 1485
vermiculita 1995
vermut 1997
veza 1998
viable 1999
vidrio soluble 1729
vinagre 2001
vinagre de vino 2060
vinagreta 1178, 1597
vinaza 1763
vino 2059
vino blanco del Rhin 942
vino de peras 1396
vino moscatel 1256
viscosidad 1571, 2006
viscosidad específica 1760
viscosidad relativa 1540
viscosímetro 2005
vitamina 2008
vitamina A 2009
vitamina B_1 2010
vitamina B_2 2011
vitamina B_6 2012
vitamina B_{12} 2013
vitamina C 2014
vitamina D_2 2015
vitamina E 2016
vitamina K 2017
vitamina PP 1281, 1283
volante 910
volátil 2018
voltímetro 2019
volumen de alveolos 406
volumen de celdas 406
volumen del pan 1135
volumen específico 1761
votator 2022

warfarina 2025

xantofila 2070

xilosa 2071

yema de huevo 659
yogur 2079
yogurt 2079
yute 1033

zanahoria 377
zarza 252
zarzamora 252
zarzamora de Boysen 297
zarzaparilla 1617
zeína 2081
zeolita 2082
zimasa 2084
zimógeno 2085
zimómetro 2086
zimotaquígrafo 2087
zona de secado 648
zumo 1030
zumo de frutas 802
zurrón 411
zwiterrión 2083

DEUTSCH

Aal 654
Abbau 557
Abdampf 705
Abdampfbecken 1604
Abfälle 1316
abfallender Geschmack 1318
Abfallprodukt 2027
abfüllen 286
abhebern 1689
abimpfen 993
abklären 746
Abklarung 450
Abkömmling 584
abkühlen 427
Abkühlungszone 493
Ablassventil 1593
Ablauge 1763
Abpressbier 2076
Absatz 1640
Absaugventilator 702
Abschaum 1632
abschäumen 1694
Absetzbecken 1662
absolute Temperatur 3
Absonderung 1658
Absorption 4
Absorptionsturm 5
Absperrhahn 1818
Abstreifer 1628
Absud 556
abtauen 1903
Abwasser 1663
Abwasserbeseitigung 1664
Abwasserkanal 1666
Abwasserschlamm 1665
abzapfen 1878
Abzug 808
Acetal 9
Acetaldehyd 10
Acetat 11
Acetin 18
Acetobakterien 14
Acetoglyzerid 19
Aceton 20
Acetoxylgruppe 21
Acetylbenzoylperoxyd 23
Acetylgruppe 24
Acetylierung 22
Acetylzahl 25
Acidimetrie 32
Acidolyse 33
Ackersenf 416
Ackerwinde 238
Additiv 46
Adenin 47

Adenosintriphosphat 48
Adermin 2012
Adsorption 50
Adsorptionsmittel 49
Aerobe 54
aerobe Gärung 55
Aerobier 54
Aerosol 56
Aflatoxine 57
Agar-agar 58
Agarschrägfläche 59
Agglutination 62
Agglutinin 63
Akarizid 6
Akonitin 38
Aktin 39
aktivierter Kohlenstoff 42
aktivierte Tonerde 40
Aktivierungsmittel 1466
Aktivität 43
Aktivitätskoeffizient 44
Aktivkohle 42
Aktomyosin 45
Albumen 658
Albumin 69
Albuminat 70
Albuminoid 71
Albumose 72
Aldehyd 75
Aldehydsäure 76
Aldohexose 77
Aldol 78
Aldose 79
Aldosteron 80
Aldrin 81
Ale 82
Aleuronschicht 83
Alge 84
Alginat 85
Alginsäure 86
aliphatisch 89
aliphatisches Amin 721
alizyklisch 87
Alkali 90
Alkalimetall 91
Alkalimeter 92
Alkaloid 93
Alkohol 73
alkoholfreie Getränke 1730
Alkoholgärung 74
Allantoin 94
Allethrin 95
allomerisch 96
Allose 97
Allyl-isothiocyanat 100

Allylkaproat 99
Alpha-Amylase 102
Alse 1667
Altbackenwerden 1786
Altern 1649
Älterung 61, 1649
Alterung 1190
Altrose 103
Alveograph 105
Ameisensäure 790
Amid 107
Amin 108
Amino-Karbonyl-Bräunung
1156
Aminosäure 109
Ammoniak 110
Ammonium 111
Ammoniumperchlorat 112
Ampholyte 113
amphoter 114
Amylacetat 115
Amylalkohol 116
Amylalkoholgärung 118
Amylase 117
Amylograph 119
Amyloid 120
Amylopektin 121
Amylopsin 122
Amylose 123
Amylpropionat 124
Anaerobe 125
Ananas 1414
Anchovis 127
Androgen 128
Anethol 126
Aneurin 2010
Anfeuchter 949
angereichert 791
Angströmeinheit 129
Anhydrit 130
Anion 134
Anis 135
Anisöl 136
Anisol 137
Annatto-Farbstoff 138
Anode 139
Anreicherung 674
ansäuern 30
anstechen 1879
Anstellhefe 1417
Antialbumose 140
Antibiose 141
Antibiotikum 142
Antienzym 145
Antihistaminstoff 146

Antikatalysator 144
Antioxydant 147
Antioxydationsmittel 147
Antiseptikum 148
Antrieb mit variabelem Geschwindigkeits-
bereich 1990
Antrieb mit variabeler Geschwindigkeit
1990
Apfel 151
Apfelmost 445
Apfelsäure 1161
Aprikose 152
Arabinose 153
Arachidonsäure 154
Arachisöl 1376
Arbeitsstrasse 1463
Areometer 965
Arginin 155
Aroma 156
aromatische Verbindung 157
Arsen 158
Artischocke 159
Asche 874
Aschengehalt 162
aschfreies Filterpapier 163
aseptisch 160
aseptisches Abfüllen 161
Askorbinsäure 2014
Asparaginsäure 165
Aspik 166
asymmetrisches Kohlenstoffatom 167
Äther 691
ätherisches Öl 688
Äthylacetat 15
Äthylalkohol 692
Äthylcinnamat 693
Äthylen 694
Äthylenoxyd 695
Äthylvanillin 696
Atmosphäre 168
Atom 169
Atomgewicht 170
Attrappe 1241
Atwaterfaktoren 172
ätzend 397
Ätzkali 398, 1443
Ätznatron 399
Aubergine 173
Aufbrausen 655
aufgehen lassen 1474
aufgelöster Stoff 1739
aufgiessen 988
Aufguss 989
Auflösungswärme 920
Aufschlag 1342

Aufspaltung 620
Auftauen 564
auftauen 1903
Augenlinse 1310
Ausbackverlust 196
Ausbeute 712, 2078
Ausblühung 267
ausbrühen 1624
ausdarren 1052
Ausdehnung 608
Ausflockung 764
Ausgabeapparat 617
auskochen 1624
auslaugen 988
Auslaugen 1096
Auslaughülse 713
Ausmahlungsgrad 712
ausschneiden 1655
Ausschwitzen 1860
Auster 1349
austrocknen 586
Auswaschung 662
Autokatalyse 174
Autoklav 175
Autolyse 176
Automation 177
Automatisierung 177
Autoxydation 178
Avidin 179
Avitaminose 180
Avokato-Birne 181
Axerophthol 2009
Azeotrop 182

Bacillus 183
Backen 804
Bäckerei 194
Backfett 1675
Backofen 1340
Backpulver 197
Backtriebmittel 1510
Bad 214
Bagasse 192
Bagassenwalze 193
Bakterie 191
Bakterienfortpflanzungsbehälter 185
Bakteriolyse 187
Bakteriophag 188
Bakteriostat 189
bakteriostatisch 190
Bakterizid 186
Ballon 369
Banane 200
Barrel 204
Barsch 1389

Base 206
Basilikum 207
Batate 1027, 1853
Baudouin-Reaktion 217
Baumé-Skala 218
Baumodell 1241
Baumöl 1122
Baumwollsamenöl 501
Becherglas 219
Beere des *Dioscoreophyllum cumminsii*
    1659
befreien 1109
Begasung 810
beimpfen 993
Beimpfen 1642
Beinschwarz 132
Belebtschlammprozess 41
belüften 53
Benedikt-Lösung 228
Benetzungsmittel 949
Benzoesäure 230
Benzolhexachlorid 229
Benzoylperoxyd 231
Benzylcinnamat 232
Bereicherung 674
Beriberi 233
Beschleuniger 8, 1466
beschleunigte Filtrierung 7
Bestandteil 485, 990
Bestrahlung 1013
Beta-Amylase 234
betäuben 1825
Betäubungsmittel 1267
Beweglichkeit 1251
Bezugselektrode 1533
Bienenwachs 225
Bier 222
Bierbottich 224
Bierdestillierapparat 223
Biertreber 312
Bier vom Fass 636
Bildungswärme 919
Bindemittel 237
biochemischer Sauerstoffverbrauch 239
biologische Wertigkeit 240
Biolumineszenz 241
Biotin 242
Birne 1377
Birnenwein 1396
Birs Trockenturm 243
Biscuit 244
bitter 246
Bittermandel 247
Bittersalz 681
Bitterschokolade 248

Bitterwert 249
Biuret 250
Bixin 251
Blähung 759
blanchieren 258
Blase 324
Blasenglocke 325
Blasenwurm 954
Blättchen 1076
blauer Wittling 271
Blech 1919
Blechdose 351
bleibende Härte 1392
bleibende Wärme 1087
Bleichen 261
Bleichkalk 262, 431
Bleichpulver 262, 431
Bleizucker 1837
Blieschen 551
Blumenkohl 396
Blutalbumin 263
Blüte 267
Blutschwarz 264
Blutwurst 255
Bockshornkraut 727
Bodensatz 1640
Bohne 220
Bohnenkraut 1623
Bombage von Dosen 270
bombierte Dose 1855
Bonbons 274
Bordeaux-Brühe 285
Borretsch 284
Botulinum-Kochung 293
Botulismus 294
Bouillon 295
Brachsen 311
brackig 298
Branntwein 301
Brassen 311
Braten 804
braten 1566, 1622
Bratenfett 641
Brauerei 313
Braugerste 1168
Bräunung 268
Bräunungsreaktion 1156
Brauwasser 314, 1130
Brechungsexponent 1536
Brechwurzel 1012
Brei 1698
Breitling 2051
Brennerei 621
Brix-Skala 318
brodeln 1685

Brombeere 252
Bromelin 320
Brot 305
Brotgärung 1357
Brotmehl 306
Brot mit Natriumbikarbonat gemacht 1708
Brotteiggärung 1357
Brüchigkeit 800
Brucin 322
Brühe 295
brühen 1364
Brunnenkresse 2030
Büchse 351
Butter 332
Buttermilch 333
buttern 442
Buttern 443
Buttersäure 337
Butyläther 336
Butylhydroxyanisol 334
Butylhydroxytoluol 335

campdensches Verfahren 349
Captan 361
Caschewnuss 382
Cayennepfeffer 400
Celsiusskala 407
Champignon 1258
Charge 210
chemische Lockerung des Teiges 419
Chiclegummi 425
Chilesalpeter 1724
Chinasäure 1498
Chinin 1499
Chiordan 430
Chlorierung 432
Chlorkalk 262, 431
Chlorophyll 433
Cholesterin 437
Cholin 439
Chromatin 440
Chromatographie 441
Chymosin 1544
Chymotrypsin 444
Coffein 341
"Cornflakes" 497
Couverture 504
Curry 542

Dampf 1796
Dampfdichte 1988
Dampfdruck 1803, 1989
Dampfdrucktopf 1458
Dampf erzeugen 1508

Dampferzeuger 1800
Dampfextraktion 1799
Dampfinjektionserhitzung 1801
Dampfmantel 1802
Dampfstrahlapparat 1798
Darre 1051
darren 1052
Darrmalz 1053
Dattel 552
Daube 1795
Dean und Stark Apparat 554
Deckgläschen 505
dehydrierung 568
Dehydrierung 571
Dehydrogenase 570
Dekantierung 555
denaturierter Alkohol 576
denaturierter Spiritus 1214
Denaturierung 574
Derivat 584
Desaminase 553
Deshydrogefrieren 569
Desodoriermittel 579
Desodorisierung 580
Desorption 588
Desoxy- 581
Desoxyribonukleinsäure 582
Destillationsapparat 1449
Destillationskolben 1548
Detergens 589
Dewar-Gefäss 590
Dextrin 592
Dextrose 839
Diacetyl 594
Dialyse 595
Diaphragma 596
Diastase 597
diastatische Kraft 598
diätetisch 603
Diatomenerde 1049
Dichte 577
Dichtesortierung 578
Dichtungsring 1637
Dickmilch 1032
Dieldrin 600
dielektrische Erwärmung 601
Dienzahl 602
Diffusion 604
Digitalin 606
Diglykololeat 607
Dilatation 608
Dill 609
dimorph 611
Diphenyl 612
Disaccharid 614

discontinuierlicher Chargenfreezer 211
dispergieren 618
Dispergiermittel 619
Dissoziation 620
Diterpen 623
Dithion 624
Dornhai 627
dörren 538, 644
Dorschlebertran 465
Dosimesser 1502
Dosimeter 1502
Dragendorffsche Lösung 635
Drehfilter 1576
Dreieckstest 1929
Druckmesser 1174
Druckreduzierventil 1459
Drucktank 290
Duft 156
Dulcin 651
Düngemittel 737
Dünger 1175
durcharbeiten 1057
Durchlässigkeit 1393
durchschwitzen 1850
durchsichtig 1380
Durchsickern 1390
durchsickern 1643
Durumweizen 913
Durumweizengriess 652

Eau de Javelle 1025
echte Kastanie 422
Efferveszenz 655
Effloreszenz 656
Eichenrinde 1307
Eidotter 659
Eieralbumin 1339
Ei-Ersatz 657
Eigelb 659
Eiklar 658
eindampfen 273
Eindosen 355
Eingeweide 1932
einjähriges Schaf 943
Einrichtung zum Trocknen durch
   Fluidisieren 768
einsähen 1641
Einsähen 1642
einsalzen 538
einstechen 625
Einstufen-Eindampfer 1687
einweichen 1151, 1706
Einzellerprotein 1686
Eisenammoniumcitrat 735
Eisessig 832

Eiskrem 975
Eiweiss 658, 1472
ekelhaft 1270
Elastin 660
Embryo 664
Empfindlichkeit 1651
empfohlene Aufnahme 1527
Emulgator 665
Emulsion 667
Emulsoid 668
Endivie 670
Endosperm 671
Endpunkt 672
Energie 673
englische Krankheit 1562
englischer Rahm 454
englische Sahne 454
Engpass 288
Entemulgator 559
Entfettungstank 566
Entfeuchter 587
Entfrostung 564
Enthalpie 675
Entholzungsmaschine 558
Entlüftungsventil 65
entölen 565
entrahmte Milch 1695
Entrahmungszentrifuge 513
Entropie 678
entwässern 567
Enzym 679
Eosin 680
Epsomsalz 681
Erbse 1373
Erbsendrescher 2003
Erbsenerntemaschine 2003
Erdbeere 1822
Erdgas 1269
Erdnuss 1374
Erdnussbutter 1375
Erdnussmasse 1375
Erdnussöl 1376
Ergosterin 683
Ernte 916
Ersatz 1828
Erschüttern 443
Ertragsfähigkeit 1464
Erucasäure 685
Erweichungspunkt 1731
Erythrodextrin 686
essentielle Fettsäure 687
Essig 2001
Essigäther 15
Essigerzeuger 2002
Essigsäure 12

Essigsäureanhydrid 13
Essigsäuregärung 16
Ester 689
Estragon 1883
Eugenol 698
Eukalyptusöl 697
evaporierte Milch 699
evaporierte Vollmilch 700
Exhaustierbad 704
Exhaustor 702
exotherm 706
Expansionverdampfung 755
Exsiccator 587
Extensograph 708
Extensometer 709
Extraktion 711
Extraktionshülse 713
Extraktionsmittel 710
Extraktivdestillation 714

Fabrikationsschema 767
Fadenziehen 1571
Fahrenheit-Skala 715
falsche Ernährung 1162
Fälschung 52
Farbmalz 253
Farinograph 717
Farin-Zucker 321
Farnesol 718
Faser 738
Fass 204, 383
Fässchen 1050
Faulbrand 1704
Fäulnis 1486
Faulraum 1657
Fehlerernährung 1162
fehlerhafter Geschmak 1318
Fehlingsche Lösung 725
Feige 740
Fenchel 726
Ferment 728
Fermentation 730
fermentieren 729
Fermentograph 734
Ferriammoniumcitrat 735
Ferrosulfat 736
fertiges Bier 748
Fertigmehl 1645
Fettalkohol 720
Fettester 722
fettfrei 1293
Fettreif 265
Fettsäure 719
Fettspaltung 1126
Feuchtigkeit 950

Feuchtigkeitsgehalt 1242
Feuerbohne 1583
Fiber 738
Ficin 739
Filter 741
Filterpapier 742
Filterpresse 743
"Filth" 744
Filtrat 745
Fischerisches Reagens 752
Fischleim 1015
Fischöl 753
Flammpunkt 757
Flasche 758
Flaschenfüllmaschine 287
Flaschenspülmaschine 289
Flavon 760
Flavoprotein 761
Flechte 1110
Fleisch 1193
Fleischbeschau 1195
Fleischbohne 915
Fleischbrühe 484
Fleischextrakt 1194
Fleischwolf 1235
Fliesskunde 1552
Fliesslehre 1552
Flockenbildung 764
Flugshafer 2058
Flunder 765
Fluoreszein 769
Fluoreszenz 770
Flüssig-Flüssig-Extraktion 1129
Flüssigkeitsextraktion 1742
Flüssigkeitsmanko 1954
Flüssigwerden 572
Flusskrebs 510
Folie 774, 1078
Folinsäure 775
Fondant 776
Förderanlage 491
Förderband 492
Förderleistung 573
Förderschnecke 1630
Formaldehydsulfoxylat 788
Formalin 789
fraktionierte Destillation 794
Franzosendorsch 1450
freies Radikal 795
Fremdkörper 626
Fremdstoff 786
frisch vom Fass 637
Fruchthülse 1391
Fruchtmark 803
Fruchtsaft 802

Fruchtschnaps 301
Fruchtzucker 801
Frühstücksnahrung aus Weizen, Mais
    usw. 308
Fruktose 801
Fühler 1650
Fullererde 807
Fungistat 813
Fungizid 812
Furche 514
Furfural 814
Fuselöl 815
Futterpflanzen 785

Gabelstapler 787
Galaktose 816
Galle 236
Gallensäure 438
Gallone 819
Gallussäure 818
Gärbottich 731
gären 729
Gärkeller 732
Garnele 1677
Gärschrank 1475
Gärtank 733
Gärung 730
Gärung beleben 1579
Gärungsmesser 2086
Gasbildungsvermögen 822
Gaschromatographie 821
Gaslagerung 823
Gastrockner 1430
gebackener Brotwürfel 520
Gebäckfehler 195
Gebläse 269
gebleichtes Mehl 260
Gebrauchsanweisung 613
gebundenes Wasser 296
gedörrte Pflaume 1476
Gefrieranlage 797
Gefrierbrand 798
Gefrierpunkt 799
Gefriertrocknung 796
gefrostet 560
Gefüge der Milch 1229
Gegenstromwärmeaustauscher 502
gehärtetes Fett 911
gehärtetes Öl 960
Gel 824
Geläger 883
Gelatine 825
Gelee 1026
Gelöstes 1739
Gemisch 1239

gemischte Kräuter 747
Gen 826
Geraniol 827
geräucherter Schinken 1701
Gerberprobe 828
Gerbsäure 1876
Gerste 201
Gersteabfälle 1870
Gerstenflocken 202
Geruch 1313
geruchlos 1314
Geruchsfehler 1699
Geruchsmessung 1312
Geruchsorgan-Epithel 1322
gesättigte Lösung 1618
geschlagener Teig 216
geschlossene Reinigung 451
Geschmack 762, 1885
Geschmackfehler 1318
Geschmacksknospen 1886
Geschmackverstärker 763
Geschmackversteigerer 763
geschwefeltes Öl 1838
Geschwindigkeit des Anwachsens der
   Viskosität 272
gesetzliche Verordnung 1794
Gesundheitspflege 971
Getreidearten 409
Getreidekorn 862
Getreideschildchen 1634
Gewichtsprozentzahl 2043
Gewichtsverlust 2042
Gewichtsverlust beim Backen 196
gewickeltes Kalbsfleisch in Gelee 817
Gewürz 1639, 1765
Gewürz-Myrte 98
Gewürznelken 456
gezuckerte Kondensvollmilch 478
Gibberellinsäure 830
Giftigkeit 1924
glasieren 834
Glasur 835
Glattbutt 315
Glatthai 627
Glattwalzenstuhl 1703
Glaubersalz 833
Gleichgewichtsdestillation 754
Gleichgewichtsfeuchte 682
Gleichrichter 1530
Gliadin 836
Globulin 837
Glockenmühle 899
Glukonsäure 838
Glukose 839
Glutamin 843

Glutaminsäure 842
Gluten 844
Glutenin 846
Glutin 844
Glykogen 852
Glykokoll 851
Glykolsäure 853
Glykosid 854
Glyzerid 847
Glyzerin 848
Glyzerinmonostearat 849
Glyzerinphosphorsäure 850
Glyzin 851
Gossypol 858
Gramicidin 866
Grammäquivalent 865
Grammolekul 867
gram-negativ 868
gram-positiv 869
Granatapfel 1439
Granulierpunkt 863
Grasöl 1102
grauer Amber 106
Greiferpumpe 408
Grenadine 879
Grenzflächenspannung 1001
Griess 1648
Griesskleie 1224
grillen 881
Grundsatzbestimmungen (F.A.O.) 464
Grundzustand 884
Grünkohl 1034
Grünmalz 878
Guajabe 893
Guajakharz 888
Guanin 889
Guano 890
Guanosin 891
Guarangummi 892
Gummi 894
Gummiarabikum 895
Gummi-Mastiche 1189
Gurke 532
Güte 860
Gutzeitprobe 898
Gutzeittest 898

Hafer 1308
Hafergrütze 882
Haferwurz 1602
Hagebutte 938
Hai 1669
Haifischtran 1670
halbdurchlässig 1646
halbes Fässchen 750

halb-konserviert 1647
halbsalzig 298
Halit 907
haltbar machen 538
Hämatin 901
Hämatoxylin 902
Hammelfleisch 1263
Hammermühle 909
Hämoglobin 903
Handrad 910
Hanf 924
Harnsäure 1965
Harnstoff 1962
Harnstoffaddukte 1963
Härte 912
Härtemesser 1381
Hartkeks 507
Härtungskessel 962
Hartweizen 913
Harz 1546
Hase 914
Haupterzeugnis 1789
Hauptprodukt 1789
Hecht 1412
Hechtdorsch 904
hedonische Skala 921
Hefe 1098, 2073
Hefe-Extrakt 2074
Hefenahrung 2075
Heferasse 2077
Heftmaschine 1790
Heidelbeere 235
Heilbutt 905
Heilbuttlebertran 906
Heilwurz 1617
Heizrohr 344
helles Weizenmehl 1371
Hemizellulose 922
Hemlockrinde 923
Heparin 925
Heptachlor 926
herbe Schokolade 248
Herbizid 2041
Hering 929
Herstellungsverfahren 1461
Herzmuschel 459
Hesperidin 930
heterozyklisch 931
Hexaäthyltetraphosphat 934
Hexaclorbenzol 933
Hexaclorzyklohexan 932
Hexose 935
Hickorynuss 1378
Himbeere 1519
Himbeere-Brombeere-Kreuzung 297, 1137

Hirse 1232
Histamin 939
Histidin 940
Holzessigsäure 1490
Holzfaserstoff 1114
Holzgeist 2065
Holzkohle 1992
Holzzucker 2071
Homogenisierung 944
Honig 945
Hopfen 946
Hormon 947
Hornstoff 1040
H.T.S.T. Erhitzung 937
Hubstapler 787
Huhn in Gelee 817
Hülse 952
Hülsenfrüchte 1482
Hummel 1136
Humus 951
Hyaluronidase 953
Hydnokarpussäure 955
Hydration 956
Hydrazon 958
Hydrierung 961
Hydrolyse 964
Hydrometer 965
hydrophil 966
hydrophob 967
hydrostatischer Autoklav 968
Hydroxymerkurichlorophenol 969
Hydroxymerkurikresol 970
Hydrozellulose 959
Hygenik 971
Hygiene 971
hygienische Qualität 1610
hygienische Qualitätsverbesserung 1611
Hygrometer 972
hygroskopisch 973

Immunität 978
impfen 993
Impfen 1642
imprägnieren 979
in Betrieb 1326
Indikator 982
Indolbuttersäure 983
Induktionsperiode 985
induktive Heizung 984
inert 987
Infusion 989
Infusorienerde 1049
Ingwer 831
Inhibitor 991
Initiator 992

Innereien 1317
Inosin 994
Inositol 995
Insektenbekämpfungsmittel 996
Insektizid 996
instantisieren 997
Instrumentierung 998
Insulin 999
Intensivkneten 936
Inulin 1002
Inversion 1003
Invertase 1004
Invertzucker 1005
in Würfel schneiden 599
Ionenaustausch 1007
Ionenaustauschharz 1008
Ionenspaltung 1010
Ionenstärke 1009
Ionisation 1010
Ionisierung 1010
Ipekakuanha 1012
irlandisches Moos 376
Irradiation 1013
irreversible Reaktion 1014
isoelektrischer Punkt 1016
Isoeugenol 1017
Isoleucin 1018
Isopropylalkohol 1019
Isosafrol 1020
Isothiocyanat 1021
Isovaleriansäure 1022

Jamswurzel 2072
japanische Mispel 1138
Jasminöl 1024
Javellesche Lauge 1025
Jodzahl 1006
Joghurt 2079
Johannisbeeren 540
Johannisbrot 373
Jonon 1011
Joule 1029
Judenkirsche 357
junger Ochse 1807
Jute 1033

Kaffee 467
Kaffeesäure 340
Kaisergranat 1451
Kaiserhummer 1451
Kakaobohne 460
Kakaobutter 461
Kakaomilch 436
Kalbsfleisch 1991
Kaldaune 428

Kaldaunen 1932
Kalisalpeter 1445
Kaliumbromat 1442
Kaliumhydroxyd 1443
Kaliummetabisulfit 1444
Kaliumnitrat 1445
Kaliumnitrit 1446
Kaliumtartrat 512
Kalmar 1783
Kalorie 348
kalorienarm 1140
kalorimetrische Bombe 280
Kalziferol 2015
Kalziumkarbonat 345
Kalziumpantothenat 346
Kalziumphosphat 347
Kamm-Muschel 1626
Kandisfrucht 352, 353
Kaninchen 1500
Kanne 350
Kanneneintauch-Kühler
   981
Kanzerogen 370
Kaolin 1035
Kapaun 360
Kapern 359
Kapsikum 400
Karamell 362
Karayagummi 1036
Karbohydrase 364
Karbolsäure 1402
Karboxymethylzellulose 368
Kardamom 371
Kardamomöl 372
karieren 599
Karl Fischer Reagens 1037
Karotin 374
Karotte 377
Karpfen 375
Karrageen 376
Karstenit 130
Kartoffel 1447
Kartoffelspiritus 1448
Karub 373
Karube 373
kaschieren 1079
Kaschunuss 382
Käse 417
Käsebruch 537
Kasein 378
Kaseinhydrolysat 380
Kaseinleim 379
Kaseinogen 381
Käserinde 418
Kassawa 384

Kassiaöl 385
Katalase 388
Katalaseprobe 389
Katalysator 391
Katalyse 390
Katfisch 393
Kathepsin 394
Kation 395
kauen 1188
Kaugummi   423
Kautchukmilch 1088
Kebab 1038
Keim 663
keimen 1780
keimfrei 1811
Keimhemmungsmittel 1781
Keimling 663
Keimtötungsmittel 829
Keks 244
Keksausstecher 245
Kelp 1039
Keratin 1040
Kerbel 421
Kernfrucht 1817
Kerosin 1041
Kessel 275, 1044
Kesselstein 1625
Kesselsteinablagerung 276
Keton 1042
Ketose 1043
Kettenreaktion 412
Keyesches Verfahren 1045
Kichererbse 424
Kieselgur 1049
Kirsche 420
Kjeldahlkolben 1055
Kjeldahlsche Methode 1056
Klarbecken 1662
Klarsichtpackung 1927
Klarung 450
Klärung 562
Kleberdehnbarkeit 845
klebrig 1867
Klebstoff 841
Kleie 300
Kleiebürste 302
kleine Orange 1875
Kleister 841
klimakterische Frucht 452
Klimatisierung 67
klumpen (sich) 342
kneten 1057
Kneten 1058
Kneten des Teiges 631
Knoblauch 820

Knochenasche 281
Knochenfisch 1890
Knochenkohle 132, 282
Knochenmehl 283
Knochenschwarz 282
Knockengallerte 1338
Knolle 1937
Knollensellerie   401
Knurrhahn 897
knusperig 516
Koazervation 457
Kobalamin 2013
Kochen 277
kochende Gärung 278
Kochkessel 1044
Kochsalz 1716
Koenzym 466
Koferment 466
Koffein 341
Kognak 301
Kohl 339
Kohlendioxyd 367
Kohlenhydrat 365
kohlensaurer Kalk 345
Kohlenstoffzyklus 366
Kohlrübe 1851, 1948
Kohlsalat 1696
Koji 1872
Kokosfett 463
Kokosnuss 462
Kokosnussöl 463
Kolben 758
Kolibakterie 469
Kollagen 470
Kollergang 1359
Kollermühle 1359
Kolloid 471
kolloidal 472
Kolloidmühle 473
Kolonialzucker 1421
Kolophonium 474
konchieren 477
Kondensmilch 699
konditionieren 479
Konfekt 480
Konfitüre 1023
konjugierte Doppelverbindungen   482
Konservenindustrie 356
konservieren 538
Konservierung 1456
Konservierungsmittel 1457
Konsistenz 483, 1901
Konsistenzmesser 1553
Kontamination 487
kontaminieren 486

kontinuierliche Presse 490
kontinuierlicher Autoklav 488
kontinuierliche Trocknung 489
konzentrieren 476
Kopfraum 917
Kopfsalat 1107
Korb 208
Korbflasche 369
Koriander 495
Korinthen 541
Kork 496
Korn 862
Kornkäfer 864
Kornkrebs 864
Korrosion 1418
Koschenillefarbstoff 458
koscher 1059
Kosten 1887
Kotelett 545
Krabbe 506, 1677
Krake 1309
Kratzwärmeaustauscher 2022
Kraut 339, 927
Kräuter-Extrakt 928
krebserzeugende Substanz 370
Kreide 413
Kreiselbrecher 899
Kreisprobe 1060
Krem 543
Kresse 515
Kristallisation 531
kristallisieren 530
Kristallwasser 2036
Kristallzucker 871
kritische Temperatur 517
Kronkorken 521
Kronsbeere 508
Kropf 855
Krume 524
Krumenbildung 527
Krumenelastizität 525
Krumenfestigkeit 526
Krummenbeschaffenheit 307, 528
Kruste 529
Kuchenmehl 343
Kugelmühle 198
kühlen 427
Kühllagerung 468
Kühlmittel 1537
Kühltunnel 494
Kühlung 1538
Kuminöl 533
Kümmel 363
Kumquat 534
Kunstdünger 737

künstliches Fleisch 1902
Kunststoff 1423
Kürbis 1483
Kurkuma 535
Kurkumin 536
Kutikula 544
Kutteln 428, 1932

Lab 1542
Labferment 1544
labil 1061
Labkasein 1543
Lachgas 1292
Lachs 1600
Lack 1063
Lackmus 1131
Lagerbier 1074
Lagerung 1819
Lakritze 1111
Laktalbumin 1064
Laktam 1065
Laktase 1066
Laktat 1067
Laktobutyrometer 1069
Laktoflavin 2011
Lakton 1070
Laktose 1071
Lamelle 1076
laminare Strömung 1077
Laminate 1078
Lamm 1075
Langskannenwaschmaschine 1821
Languste 509
Lanolin 1081
Lanosterin 1082
lanzenförmig 1080
latente Wärme 1087
Latex 1088
Lattich 1107
Lauch 1100
Läufer 653
Lauge 1143
Laugenmesser 92
Laugung 1096
Laurinsäure 1092
Laurylalkohol 1093
Lavendel 1094
Lävulose 801
lebendig 1999
lebensfähig 1999
Lebensmittel 783
Lebensmittelfarbe 779
Lebensmittelkennzeichnung 780
Lebensmittelverfälschung 778

Lebensmittelzusatz 777
Leber 1133
Lecithin 1099
Leck 1097
Leichenstarre 1563
leichtflüchtig 2018
Leim 841
Leinöl 1122
Leinsaat 1121
Leinsamen 1121
Lemongrasöl 1102
Leuchtpetroleum 1041
Leuzin 1108
Liebigkühler 1112
Lignin 1114
Limande 1104
Limone 1115
linksdrehend 1072
Linolein 1119
Linolensäure 1120
Linolsäure 1118
Linse 1105
Linters 1123
Lintnerwert 1124
Lipase 1125
Lipolyse 1126
Lipoxydase 1127
Lipoxygenase 1127
Liter 1132
Lizenzabgabe 1581
Lochfrass 1418
Lodde 358
Lorbeer 1091
Löslichkeit 1738
Lösung 1740
Lösungsmittel 1741
Lösungsmittelwiedergewinnung 1743
Lösungswärme 920
Löten 1736
Lötnaht bei Dosen 1735
Lovibond-Kolorimeter 1139
Löwenzahn 1881
Lüfter 703
Luftgefrieren 259
Luftpumpe 68
Lumen 1141
Lumpenwolle 1673
Lungen 1113
Lutein 1142
Lyophilisieren 796
Lysin 1144
Lysosom 1145
Lysozym 1146

Made 1155

Magermilch 1695
magnetischer Trommelscheider 643
Mähdrescher 475
Mahlen 1233
Mahlkleie 300
Maifisch 1667
Mais 1157
Maischbottich 1186
Maische 1183
Maischen 1185
Maischepfanne 1184
Maisflocken 497
Maismehl 498
Majoran 1179
Makkaroni 1147
Makrele 1152
Makromolekül 1153
makromolekulare Lösung 471
makroskopisch 1154
Malathion 1159
Maleinsäurehydrazid 1160
Maltase 1165
Maltose 1169
Malz 1163
mälzen 1164
Malzerei 1167
Malzhaufen 1170
Malzmilch 1166
Malztreber 1176
Malzzucker 1169
Mandarine 1171, 1875
Mandarinenöl 1172
Mandel 101
Maniokwurzel 384
Mannloch 1173
Manometer 1174
Maräne 2052
Margarin 1177
Margarine 1177
Marinade 1178
marinieren 1752
markieren 1869
Markkürbis 1181
Marmelade 1023
Marone 422
Marzipan 1182
Masche 1207
Maschine zum Bürsten der Kleie 302
Massanalyse 2021
Massenproduktion 1187
Mastix 1189
Matze 1191
Maulbeere 1253
Mayonnaise 1192
mazedoine 1149

Mazisöl 1150
mechanische Presse 1196
Meeraal 481
Meerasche 880
Meerbarbe 1531
Meerbarsch 209
Meerbrassen 1635
Meerhecht 904
Meerlattich 1095
Meerrettich 948
Meerscheide 1521
Mehl 766
Mehlschwitze 1580
Mehltau 1227
Mehl von den Schrotpassagen 309
Mehrfachverdampfapparat 1254
Melanin 1199
Melasse 1244
Melis 1134
Melisse 199
Meliszucker 1134
Melitose 1200
Mellorine 1201
Melone 1202
Membran 596
Menthol 1203
Menthon 1204
Meringe 1206
Merkaptan 1205
Merlan 2054
Mesityloxyd 1208
mesophile Bakterie 1209
Messpipette 861
Metalldetektor 1211
metallisch 1212
Methionin 1213
Methylcinnamat 1215
Methylenblau 1216
Methylrot 1217
Methylstyrol 1218
Miesmuschel 1259
Migration 1225
Mikron 1220
mikroskopisch 1221
Mikrowellenkochen 1222
Milch 1228, 1234
milchig 1230
Milchkakao 436
Milchsaft 1088
Milchsäure 1068
milchsaures Salz 1067
Milchzucker 1071
mild 1226
Milz 1772
Minze 1236

mischen 1237
Mischer 1238
Mischung 1239
Mischwalzwerk 1570
Mispel 1197
Mitschleppen 677
Mitschleppmittel 676
Mittel gegen Altbackenwerden 150
Mittel gegen das Spritzen 149
Mittelmehl 1223
Mizelle 1219
Möhre 377
Mohrenhirse 1748
Mohrrübe 377
Mokka 1240
Mol 867
molare Lösung 1243
Molekulardrehung 1246
Molekularwärme 1245
Molke 2050
Monoglyzerid 1248
monomolekular 1249
Mononatriumglutamat 1721
Moosbeere 508
Most 1260
muffig 1262
Mühle 1231
Mündung 1334
Muskatblüte 1148
Muskatblütenöl 1150
Muskatellerwein 1256
Muskatnuss 1304
Muskatrosine 1255
Muskel 1257
Muskelzucker 995
Muster 1606
Mutterkorn 684
Mutterlaufge 1250
Mykotoxin 1265
Myoglobin 1266
Myzelium 1264

Nachreife 60
Nadelventil 1272
Nährgewebe 671
Nährstoff 1305
Nahrungsbedarf 782
Nahrungsmittel 783
Nahrungsmittelvergiftung 781
Nährwert 784, 1306
nahtlos 1638
Napfschnecke 1117
nasse Scheidung 1116
Nasspinnen 2044
Natriumalginat 1709

Natriumaskorbat 1710
Natriumbenzoat 1711
Natriumbikarbonat 1712
Natriumbromat 1713
Natriumchlorat 1715
Natriumchlorid 1716
Natriumchlorit 1717
Natriumeisenpyrophosphat 1722
Natriumfluoracetat 1719
Natriumglukonat 1720
Natriumglutamat 1721
Natriumkarbonat 1714
Natriumlaurylsulfat 1723
Natriumnitrat 1724
Natriumnitrit 1725
Natriumperborat 1726
Natriumpersulfat 1727
Natriumpropionat 1728
Natriumsilikat 1729
Natriumzyklamat 1718
Naturfaser 1268
Nebenprodukt 338
Nektarine 1271
Nelkenöl 455
Nelkenpfeffer 98
Neroliöl 1274
Nesslersches Reagens 1275
Netzmittel 1848
Neurin 1276
neutral 1277
neutralisieren 1278
Newtonsche Strömung 1279
Niazin 1283
Niazinamid 1281
nicht-garkochen 1364
Nicolsches Prisma 1280
Niederschlag 1452
Niere 1048
Nierenfett 1831
Nierentalg 1831
Nikotin 1282 ·
Nikotinamid 1281
Nikotinsäure 1283
Ninhydrinprobe 1284
Ninhydrinreaktion 1284
Nisin 1285
Nitrogenase 1287
Nitrosamin 1290
Nitrosoverbindung 1291
Norleucin 1295
Norm 1296
normal 1297
Normallösung 1298, 1787
Normalweingeist 1467
Notatin 1299

Nudeln 1294
Nukleinsäure 1301
Nukleoprotein 1302
Nuss 1303

Oberflächenaktivstoff 1848
Oberflächenspannung 1847
Oberhefe 1923
Oberwalze 1922
Ochse 1343
Ofen 1340
Öffnung 1334
Okular 1310
okulieren 993
Olefin 1320
Olivenöl 1323
Ölpalme 1319
Ölsäure 1321
Opaleszenz 1327
optische Aktivität 1329
optisches Isomer 1330
Orange 1331
Orangenkonfitüre 1180
Orangenmarmelade 1180
orientieren 1333
Ornithin 1335
Orotsäure 1336
Osmose 1337
Östrogen 1315
Ovalbumin 1339
"Overrun" 1342
Oxydase 1344
Oxydation 1345
oxydationsförderndes Mittel 1468
Oxydationsmittel 1347
Oxydations-Reduktionsindikator 1346
Oxydationszahl 1395
Oxytetracyclin 1348
Ozon 1350

Packung 1351
Palme 1352
Palmitinsäure 1353
Palmitoleinsäure 1354
Palmkernöl 1355
Palmöl 1356
Pampelmuse 873
Pankreatin 1358
Pansen 1582
Pantothensäure 1360
Papain 1361
Papaya 1362
Paprika 1363
Paranuss 304
Partie 210

Passionsfrucht 870
Pasteurisierung 1369
Pastinak 1367
Pastinake 1367
Patent 1370
pathogene Bakterie 1372
Pektin 1379
Penetrationsmesser 1381
Penicillin 1382
Pentose 1383
Pepsin 1386
Peptisieren 1387
Pepton 1388
Pergamentpapier 1365
Perikarp 1391
Perlmoos 376
Permeabilität 1393
Peroxydase 1394
Pestizid 1397
Petersfisch 1028
Petersilie 1366
Petrischale 1399
Petroleumwachs 1400
Pfeffer 1384
Pfefferminzöl 1385
pflanzenchemisch 1408
Pflanzenkohle 1992
pflanzliches Eiweiss 1993
Pflaume 1429
pH-Wert 1401
Phenol 1402
Phosphatasetest 1403
Phosphatid 1404
Phospholipid 1405
Photosynthese 1406
phytinsäure 1407
phytochemisch 1408
Phytol 1409
Phytosterin 1410
Pilz 1258
Pilzamylase 811
Pipette 1415
Pistazie 1416
Plankton 1420
Plasma 1422
Plastifiziermittel 1424
plastisches Fliessen 2007
Plattenhitzer 1427
Plattenkühler 1425
Plattenverdampfer 1426
Plattenwärmeaustauscher 1428
Plätzchen 244
pochieren 1431
pökeln 538, 1411
Polarisationsmesser 1432

Pollack 1433
Polyäthylen 1434
Polymorphismus 1435
Polyose 1436
Polyphosphat 1437
Polypropylen 1438
Porenvolumen 406
Porphyrin 1440
Porree 1100
Portulak 1485
Porzellanerde 1035
Praline 805
Preiselbeere 508
Presskopf 303
Presskuchen 707
Probe 1606, 1898
Probenahme 1608
Probenehmer 1607
Probieren 1608
Prolin 1465
Promoter 1466
Prooxydans 1468
Propanol 1469
Propionsäure 1470
Protease 1471
Protein 1472
Protoplasma 1473
Prunkbohne 1583
Pseudobase 1478
Pseudosäure 1477
psychrophile Bakterie 1479
Ptomain 1480
Puderzucker 387, 976
puffen 1481
Pufferlösung 327
Puffersubstanz 326
Purin 1484
Pyrethrin 1489
Pyridoxin 2012
Pyrolyse 1491

Qualität 860
Qualitätsbeurteilung 1493
Qualitätskontrolle 1492
Quappe 330
quaternäre Ammoniumverbindung 1494
Quellungskoeffizient 1856
Quercetin 1495
Quitte 1497

Rachitis 1562
radioaktiv 1504
Radioaktivität 1505
Radurisation 1507

Raffinerie 1534
Raffinose 1200
Rahm 511
ranzig 1511
Ranzigkeit 1512
Raoultsches Gesetz 1515
Raps 1516
Rapsöl 1517
Räucherhering 1054
Räuchermittel 809
räuchern 538
Räuchern 1702
Raufutter 1578
Rauschgift 1267
Reaktion 1522
Reaktionseinleiter 992
Reaktivierung 1523
Reaumur-Skala 1524
rechtsdrehend 593
Reduktion 1532
Refraktionszahl 1536
Registrierapparat 1528
Reh 561
Rehfleisch 1994
Rehwildbret 1994
Reif 266
reifen 539, 1564
Reifen 1190
Reine-Claude 876
Reinigungsmittel 589
Reis 1559
Reiz 1815
Reizmittel 1815
Rektifikation 1529
relative Feuchtigkeit 1539
relative Viskosität 1540
Rennin 1544
Resorcinprobe 1547
Restmelasse 257
Retinin 2009
Retorte 1548·
Retrogradation 1786
Rettich 1506
rh-Wert 1550
Rhabarber 1556
Rheinwein 942
Rheologie 1552
rheologische Instrumentierung
    1551
Rheometer 1553
Rheopexie 1554
Rhodopsin 1555
Riboflavin 2011
Ribonukleinsäure 1557
Ribose 1558

Riche 1692
riechend 1311
Riffeltiefe 583
Rigor mortis 1563
Rindfleisch 221
Rizin 1560
Rizinolsäure 1561
Rizinusöl 386
Rochellesalz 1567
Rogen 1568
Roggen 1586
roh 1520
Rohfaser 522
Rohprotein 523
Rohrenkühler 1940
Rohrzucker 354
Rohzucker 321
rösch 516
Rosenkohl 323
Rosine 1509
Rosmarin 1572
Rosmarinöl 1573
Rost 1585
rösten 881
rosten 1566
rostfreier Stahl 1785
Röstmalz 253
Rotadurchflussmesser 1574
Rotenon 1577
rote Rübe 226
Rübenzucker 227
Rüböl 1517
Rückfluss 1535
Rückprallelastizität 1545
Rückstand 291
Rückstrom 1535
Rückströmventil 1324
Rührwerk 64
Runkelrübe 226

Saccharimeter 1587
Saccharin 1588
Saccharometer 1589
Saccharose 1590
Safran 1594
Saft 1030
Sago 1596
Sahne 511
Sahneeis 975
Saibling 414
Salatsosse 1192, 1597
Salbei 1595
Saline 1604
Salmonella 1601
Salpeter 1445

Salz 1603
salzhaltig 1598
salzig 1598, 1605
Salzlake 316
Salzlösung 316
Salzsäure 1770
Samenschale 1899
Sammelbehälter 1525
Sander 1413
Sandfilter 1609
Sandklaffmuschel 449
Sandzunge 1086
Saponin 1614
Sardelle 127
Sardine 1616
Sarkosin 1615
Sassaparille 1617
Sättigung 1619
Satzbetrieb 213
Satzmischer 212
Saubohne 319
sauer 1749
Sauerkraut 1620
Sauerrahm 1750
Sauerteig 1098, 1751
Saugpumpe 1830
Säure 26
Säureamid 27
Säurechlorid 28
Säurelösung 36
Säuremesser 31
Säureradikal 34
saurer Ester 29
saures Salz 35
Säurewecker 1793
Säurezahl 37
schädlich 1300
Schädlingsbekämpfungsmittel 1397
Schädlingsfrass 1398
Schaffleisch 1263
Schälmaschine 558
Schalotte 1668
Schankbier 636
Scharbe 551
schäumen 1089
Schaummittel 771
Schaum schlagen 53
Schaumsprühtrocknung 773
Schaumtrocknung 772
Schaumverbesserer 1090
Schaumzerstörungsmittel 563
Scheefsnut 1198
Scheffel 331
Scheibenmühle 615
Schellfisch 900

schematischer Arbeitsplan 767
Scherbet 1744
Scherpresse 1672
Scheuerfestigkeit 1671
Schildchen 1634
Schiller 1327
Schimmel 1252
Schimmelpilz 1252
Schimmelvernichtungsmittel 812
Schinken 908
Schlachtabfälle 1317
Schlachthaus 2
Schlagkreuzmühle 518
Schlamm 1697, 1698
Schlämmung 662
Schlei 1892
Schleimzucker 801
Schlempe 622
Schmelzkäse 1462
Schmelzsalz 666
Schmieröl 875
Schmierseife 1732
schmoren 299
schmorren 1566
Schneckenantrieb 2066
Schneckenpresse 1631
Schneidewinkel 546
Schnellerhitzung 756
Schnellgefrieren 1496
Schnellkneten 936
Schnellsäurer 17
Schnelltest zum Aussieben 1629
Schnippeln 1705
Schnittlauch 429
Schnitzel 545
Schokolade 434
Schokoladen-Überziehmaschine 435
Scholle 1419
Schöpfenfleisch 1263
Schössling 1674
Schrotbrot mit vollem Keimlingsanteil
    2055
Schrote 952
Schrotmehl 309
Schrotwalzen 310
Schrumpffolie 1679
Schwarzer Heilbutt 877
schwarzer Kornwurm 864
schwarzer Pfeffer 254
Schwarzrost 256
Schwefeldioxyd 1839
schwefelige Säure 1840
Schwefelwasserstoff 963
Schweine-Schmalz 1085
Schwellenwert 1916

Schwertfisch 1858
Schwimmer 1857
schwingen 2062
Schwitzwasser 2035
Schwund 1678
Seehecht 904
Seekohl 1636
Seeohr 1
Seeteufel 1247
Seewolf 393
Seezunge 1737
Sehne 1896
Seife 1707
Seitzfilter 1644
Selbstverbrennung 1773
Sellerie 402
Senföl 1261
Senkwaage 965
sensorische Prüfung 1652
sensorischer Rezeptor 1654
sensorische Wahrnehmung 1653
Separator 1656
Sequestration 1658
Serin 1660
Sesamöl 1661
Shoddywolle 1673
Sicherheitsventil 1593
Sieb 1681
sieben 1682
Sieden 277
Siedepunkt 279
Sikkativ 1680
Silikagel 1683
Silikonkautschuk 1684
Sinker 1688
Sinnenprüfung 1332
Sinneswahrnehmung 1653
Sirup 1864
Sisalhanf 1690
Sitosterin 1691
Skatol 1693
Skorbut 1633
Soda 1714
Sojabohne 1753
Sojabohnenöl 1754
Sojasosse 1755
Sol 1734
Sole 316
Solekühlung 317
Sonnenblumenöl 1842
Sorbett 1744
sorbinsäure 1745
Sorbit 1746
Sorbose 1747
Sorghum 1748

Sorte 860
sortieren 859
spanischer Pfeffer 400
Spannungsmesser 2019
Spargel 164
Speck 184
Speckbohne 915
Speichel 1599
Speiseeis 975
Speisewalze 723
Speisewalzen 724
Spektrum 1762
Spelze 411
Spermöl 1764
spezifisches Gewicht 1757
spezifisches Volumen 1761
spezifische Viskosität 1760
spezifische Wärme 1758
Spezifität 1759
Spiköl 1766
Spinat 1767
Spindel 1768
Spiralhitzer 1769
Sporenbildung 1774
Spreu 411
spröd 516
Sprotte 1775
Sprunggelenk 941
Spundloch 329
Squalen 1782
Stabilisator 1784
Stachelbeere 857
Staphylokokkus 1788
Starkbier 1820
Stärke 1791
Stärkegehalt 1792
Stärkesirup 499, 840
Staubzucker 387, 976
Stearin 1805
Stearinsäure 1804
Steckrübe 1851, 1948
Steffensches Verfahren 1808
steif 1814
Steinbutt 1945
Steinobst 1817
Steinsalz 907
Stellhefe 203
Stereoisomer 1809
stereospezifisch 1810
steril 1811
sterile Luft 1812
sterilisieren 1813
Stichprobe 1514
Stickoxydul 1292
Stickstoff 1286

Stickstoffbindung 1288
Stickstofftrichlorid 1289
Stimulans 1815
Stint 1700
stippen 625
Stockfisch 1816
Stoffwechsel 1210
Stopfbüchse 1824
Stör 1826
Strahlung 1501
Strahlungsverlust 1503
Strandschnecke 2061
Streptomycin 1823
struktuiertes Pflanzeneiweiss 1902
struktuiertes Pflanzenprotein 1902
Sublimation 1827
Subtilin 1829
Sukini 503
Sukkade 353
Sukrose 1590
Sultanine 1841
Sülze aus Schweinefleisch 303
Sulze (bei Fleisch) 1026
Suspension 1849
süss 1852
süsse Würze 1854
Süssholz 1111
Süsskartoffel 1853
Süssware 480
Symbiose 1859
Synärese 1860
Synergist 1861
synthetisch 1862
synthetisches Reinigungsmittel 1863

Tachometer 1865
Tachysterin 1866
Takadiastase 1872
taktisch 1868
Talg 1874
Talk 1873
Talkum 1873
Tannin 1877
Tanninsäure 1876
Tapioka 1880
Tara 1882
Taraxakum 1881
tauen 1903
Taupunkt 591
Tautomerie 1888
Tee 1889
Teig 215
Teigausbeute 634
Teigbildungsvermögen 630
Teigführung 632

Teigkneten 631
Teiglockerung 629, 1565
Teiglockerungsmittel 197
Teigreife 633
Teigwaren 88
Teilchengrössenbestimmung 1368
Temperaturregler 1912
Tenderizer 1893
Tenderometer 1895
Terpen 1897
Tetracyclin 1900
Theophyllin 1904
thermaler Abtötungspunkt 1905
Thermodynamik 1907
Thermoelement 1906
thermolabil 1908
Thermolyse 1909
Thermometer 1910
thermophiler Organismus 1911
Thermostat 1912
Thiamin 2010
Thioalkohol 1205
Thixotrop 1914
Threonin 1915
Thunfisch 1941
Thunfischöl 1942
Thymianöl 1917
Thyroxin 1918
tiefgefroren 560
tierischer Eiweissfaktor 133
Tierproteinfaktor 133
Tintenfisch 547
tödliche Dosis 1106
Tokopherol 2016
Tomate 1920
Tonerde 104
Tonkabohne 1921
Topinambur 1027
Toxin 1925
Tragantgummi 896
träge 987
Tran 2045
tränenerregend 1062
Transferase 1926
Transpiration 1928
Traube 872
Traubenzucker 839
Treber 1176
trenken 1706
trennen 1655
Trester 1176
Trichinose 1930
Trichlorkarbanilid 1931
Trieb 1565
trinkbar 1441

Tritikale 1933
Trockenabteil 648
Trockeneis 645
Trockenhefe 639
Trockenkasten 647
Trockenmilch 638
Trockenmittel 1680
Trockenofen 647, 1340
Trockenschrank 647
Trockentunnel 650, 1943
Trockenturm 649
trocknen 538, 567, 644
trocknendes Öl 646
Trockner 1051
Trocknungsmittel 585
Trommelfilter 1576
Trommelmischer 205
Trommeltrockner 642, 1575
Tropfsaft 640
trübe 1944
Trübungsmesser 1273
Trüffel 1934
Trypsin 1935
Tryptophan 1936
Tuberkulin 1938
turbulente Strömung 1946
Turgeszenz 1947
Turgor 1947
Twadellsches Hydrometer 1949
Tyrocidin 1951
Tyrosin 1952
tyrothricin 1953

Überdruckventil 1541
Überhitzung 1845
überholen 1341
Überlappsiegeln 1083
Überlappungsschweissung 1084
übersättigt 1846
U.H.T. 1956
Ultrafiltration 1955
Ultrahochtemperatur 1956
Ultraschall 1957
ultraviolett 1958
Umesterung 1000
Umkehrung 1003
Umkristallisation 793
Umlauf 1526
ummanteln 1073
Umsetzung 1225
Umwalzpumpe 447
unbedenklich 1591
Unbedenklichkeit 1592
Undekalakton 1959

undurchsichtig 1328
ungeniessbar 986
ungesättigt 1960
Ungeziefer 1996
Unkraut 2040
Unkrautvertilgungsmittel 2041
unmischbar 977
unterchlorige Säure 974
Unterchlorsäure 974
Unterdruckmesser 1975
Unterernährung 1162
untergärige Hefe 292
unterkühlt 1843
Unterkühlung 1844
Uperisierung 1961
Urease 1964
Uridin 1966
U-Rohr-Manometer 1967

Vakuumabfüllung 1973
Vakuumdestillation 1969
Vakuumdestillierapparat 1979
Vakuumeindampfer 1972
Vakuumfiltrierung 1974
Vakuumkontaktplattenverfahren 1968
Vakuumpfanne 1976
Vakuumpumpe 1977
Vakuumtrockenofen 1971
Vakuumtrockenschrank 1978
Vakuumtrockner 1970
Valin 1980
Vanadinstahl 1982
Vanadiumstahl 1982
Vancomycin 1983
Vanille-Essenz 1984
Vanillin 1985
Ventil 1981
Verbesserungsmittel 980
Verdampfer mit aufsteigendem Film 453
Verdampfrohr 344
Verdampfung 701, 1986
Verdampfungswärme 1987
Verdauung 605
Verdickungsmittel 1913
verdorben 986
verdünnen 610
Verdünnung 1518
Veresterung 690
verfälschtes Mehl 51
verfaulen 1487
verfault 1488
verfeuern 749
Verflüssigung 572, 1128
Vergallung 575

Verkapselung 669
verkochen 273
verkohltes Material 415
vermengen 1237
Vermikulit 1995
vermodern 1487
Vernetzung 519
Verpackungsmaschine 2069
Verpflegung 392
Verschmutzung 1733
Verseifung 1612
Verseifungszahl 1613
versengen 1627
verseuchen 1871
verstärken 792
Verteiler 617
Verunreinigung 487, 1733
Vibrations-Förderer 2000
Vielgestältigkeit 1435
Viskosimeter 2005
Viskosität 1571, 2006
Viskositätsmesser 2005
Vitamin 2008
Vitamin A 2009
Vitamin B_1 2010
Vitamin B_2 2011
Vitamin B_6 2012
Vitamin B_{12} 2013
Vitamin C 2014
Vitamin D_2 2015
Vitamin E 2016
Vitamin K 2017
Vitamin PP 1281, 1283
Vollkornbrot 2055, 2056
Vollmilch 806
Vollmilchpulver 2057
Voltmeter 2019
Volumenausbeute 1135
Volumenprozentzahl 2020
volumetrische Analyse 2021
Vorbehandlung 1460
Vordermagen 1582
Vorlauf 751
Vormischung 1455
Vorprodukt 751
Vorrichtung zur elektrostatischen
    Trennung 661
Vortrockner 1453
vorübergehende Härte des Wassers 1891
Vorwärmer 1454
Votator 2022

Wachholderöl 1031
Wachs 2039

Wachstumsbeschleunigung 887
Wachstumsförderung 887
Wachstumshemmungsfaktor 885
Walfischtran 2045
Walnuss 2023
Walnussöl 2024
Walzenmühle 1570
Walzentrockner 1569
Wanderung 1225
wannen 2062
Warfarin 2025
Wärmeaustauscher 918
Warmlufttrockner 2026
Wasser 2028
wasseraufnehmend 973
Wasserbingungsvermögen 2033
Wasserdampfdestillation 1797
wasserdicht 2037
Wasserentziehung 568
wasserfest 2037
wasserfrei 131
wasserfreier Gips 130
Wassergehalt 2029
Wasserglas 1729
Wasserkalk 957
Wassermelone 2034
Wasserrohrkessel 1939
Wasserstandsdruck 2032
Wasserstoffanlagerung 961
Wasser-Verschluss 2038
Wasserwert 2031
weichen 1806
weicher Bonbon 805
Wein 2059
Weinbeere 872
Weinessig 2060
Weingeist 1771
Weinmesser 2004
Weinsäure 1884
weinsaures Kalium 512
Weinstein 512
Weinsteinrahm 512
Weinsteinsäure 1884
Weintraube 872
Weissblech 1919
weisser Pfeffer 2053
Weisszucker 1421
Weizen 2046
Weizenflocken 2047
Weizenkeimöl 2048
Weizenschrotbrot 2056
Wellhornschnecke 2049
Wermut 1997
Wermutöl 2067
Wicke 1998

widerlich 1270
Wiederbelebung 1549
Winde 238
Windsichtung 66
Wintergrünöl 2063
Winterisierung 2064
Wolf 1235
Wollfett 1081
worfeln 2062
Wuchsstoff 886
würfeln 599
Wurst 1621
Wurstvergiftung 294
Würze 156, 1639, 2068

Xanthophyll 2070
Xylose 2071

Youngscher Elastizitätsmodul 2080

Zähigkeit 2006
Zander 1413
Zapfen 328
Zapfenloch 329
Zartheit 1894
Zein 2081
Zellfarbstoffe 550
Zellstoff 404
Zelluloid 403
Zellulose 404
Zelluloseester 405
Zentripetalpumpe 408
Zeolith 2082
Zerfaserer 1676
zerkleinern 1188
Zerkleinerungsmaschine 616, 1046, 1676
Zerlegung 557
Zerstäuberrohr 1756
Zerstäubungsdüse 171
Zerstäubungskühlung 1777
Zerstäubungsraum 1776
Zerstäubungstrocknung 1778
Zerstäubungsturm 1779
Zetylalkohol 410
Zeug 203
Zichorie 426
Zicklein 1047
Ziegenhamm 1047
Zimt 446
Zitronat 353
Zitrone 1101
Zitronengrasöl 1102
Zitronenöl 1103
Zitronensäure 448
Zucker 1832

Zuckeralkohol 1746
Zuckerbildungsvermögen 598
Zuckerguss 835
Zuckerrohr 1834
Zuckerrohrquetsche 1835
Zuckerrübe 1833
Zuckerrübenschnitzel 500
Zuckersirup 856
Zuckerwerk 480
Zuckerwürfel 1836
Zuckerwurzel 1367
zufällig 1513
Zurückgehen 716
Zusammenbacken verhütendes Mittel 143
zusammenrühren 1237
Zusatzmittel 46
Zusatzstoff 46
Zusatzwasser 1158
Zutat 990
zweistufiger Kompressor 1950
Zweiwalzentrockner 628
Zwergpomeranze 534
Zwetsche 1429
Zwetschge 1429
Zwieback 1584
Zwiebel 1325
Zwitterion 2083
Zyklonenscheider 548
Zymase 2084
Zymogen 2085
Zymometer 2086
Zymotachygraph 2087
Zystein 549
Zytochrome 550

LATINUM

Abramis 311
Achrus sapota 425
Acipenser 1826
Aconitum napellus 38
Agave sisalana 1690
Allium ascalonicum 1668
Allium cepa 1325
Allium porrum 1100
Allium schoenoprasum 429
Alosa sapidissima 1667
Anacardium occidentale 382
Ananas comosus 1414
Anarhicas lupus 393
Anethum graveolens 609
Anguilla anguilla 654
Anthriscus cerefolium 421
Apium graveolens 402
Apium graveolens rapaceum 401
Arachis hypogaea 1374
Armoracia lapathifolia 948
Artemisia absinthium 2067
Artemisia dracunculus 1883
Asparagus officinalis 164
Aspergillus flavus 57
Aspergillus orizae 811
Astacus fluvialis 510
Astragalus 896
Avena sativa 1308

Bacillus brevis 1951
Bacillus subtilis 1829
Bacterium acetii 14
Basidiomycetes 1585, 1704
Bertholletia excelsa 304
Beta vulgaris 226, 1833
Bixa orellana 251
Borago officinalis 284
Brassica campestris 1948
Brassica napus 1516
Brassica oleracea 339
Brassica oleracea capitata 396
Brassica oleracea gemmifera 323
Brassica rapa 1948
Buccinum undatum 2049

Cambarus affinis 510
Cancer paguras 506
Capparis spinosa 359
Capsicum annuum 1363
Capsicum frutescens 400
Cardium edule 459
Carica papaya 1362
Carum carvi 363
Carya illinoensis 1378
Cassia 385

Castanea 422
Caulopsetta scaphus 315
Cephaelis ipecacuanha 1012
Ceratonia siliqua 373
Cetacea 2045
Chichorium intybus 426
Chondrus crispus 376
Cicer arietinum 424
Cichorium endivia 670
Cinchona 1499
Cinnamomum 446
Citrullus vulgaris 2034
Citrus aurantifolia 1115
Citrus aurantium 534, 1274
Citrus limon 1101
Citrus nobilis 1875
Citrus paradisi 873
Citrus reticulata 1171
Citrus sinensis 1331
Claviceps purpurea 684
Clostridium botulinum 294
Clupea harengus 929, 2051
Coccus cacti 458
Cocos nucifera 462
Coffea arabica 467
Coffea robusta 467
Conger conger 481
Corchorus 1033
Coriandrum sativum 495
Crambe maritima 1636
Crangon 1677
Crassostrea 1349
Crocus longa 536
Cucumis 532
Cucumis sativus 532
Cucurbita 1181, 1483
Cucurbiticea 1202
Cuminum cyminum 533
Curcuma longa 535
Cydonia oblonga 1497
Cynara scolymus 159
Cyprinus carpio 375

Dahlia 1002
Daucus carota 377
Digitalis purpurea 606
Dioscorea 2072
Dioscoreophyllum cumminsii 1659
Dipteryx 1921

Elaeis guineensis 1319
Elaesis guineensis 1355
Elettaria cardamomum 371
Engraulis encrasicholus 127
Epimotis gibbosus 765

Eriobotrya japonica 1138
Erysiphe graminis 1227
Escherichia coli 469
Esox lucius 1412
Eucalyptus 697
Eugenia caryophyllus 456
Euthunnus 1941

Ficus 740
Ficus carica 740
Foeniculum vulgare 726
Fragasia 1822
Fucus 1039

Gadus 465
Gaultheria procumbens 2063
Glycine 1753
Glycyrrhiza glabra 1111
Gossypium 501

Haliotis 1
Helianthus annuus 1842
Helianthus tuberosus 1002, 1027
Hevea brasiliensis 1088
Hippoglossus 905
Homarus 1136
Hordeum vulgare 201
Humulus lupulus 946

Jasminum grandiflorum 1024
Juglans regia 2023
Juniperus communis 1031

Lactobacillus bulgaris 2079
Lactuca sativa 1107
Laminaria 1039
Laurus nobilis 1091
Lavandula officinalis 1094
Lavandula spica 1766
Leguminosae 1482
Lens esculenta 1105
Lepidium sativum 515
Lepidorhombus whiff 1198
Limanda limanda 551
Linum usitatissimum 1121
Littorina littorea 2061
Lophius piscatoris 1247
Lota lota 330
Lota maculosa 330
Lucio perca lucio perca 1413
Lycopersicon esculentum 1920

Mallotus rillosus 358
Malus 151
Manihot utilissima 384

Melanogrammus aeglefinus 900
Melissa 199
Mentha 1236
Mercenaria mercenaris 449
Merlangus merlangus 2054
Merluccius 904
Mespilus germanica 1197
Metroxylon sago 1596
Micromesistius poutassou 271
Microstomus 1104
Morone labrax 209
Morus 1253
Mugil chelo 880
Mullus surmeletus 1531
Musa 200
Myristica fragrans 1148, 1304
Mytilus edulis 1259

Nasturtium officinale 2030
Neothunnus 1941

Ocimum basilicum 207
Ocimum minimum 207
Octopus 1309
Olea europaea 1323
Origanum marjorana 1179
Oryza sativa 1559
Osmerus 1700
Ostrea 1349

Palinurus 509
Palinurus vulgaris 509
Pandalus 1677
Panicum miliaceum 1232
Papilionacea 385
Paralichthys dentatus 1419
Parellus centrodontus 1635
Passiflora quadrangularis 870
Pastineca sativa 1367
Patella caerulea 1117
Pecten 1626
Pegusa lascaris 1086
Penicillium chrysogenum 1382
Penicillium notatum 1382
Penicillium puberulum 57
Perca 1389
Perseus 181
Petroselinum crispum 1366
Phaseolus coccineus 1583
Phaseolus vulgaris 915
Physalis peruviana 357
Physeter catodon 106
Physeter macrocephalus 106
Pimenta officinalis 98
Pimpinella anisum 135

Piper nigrum 254, 2053
Pistacia lentiscus 1189
Pistacia vera 1416
Pisum sativum 1373
Platichthys flesus 765
Pleuronectes platessa 1419
Pollachius pollachius 1433
Polygonum convolvulus 238
Portulaca oleracea 1485
Prunus 876
Prunus amygdalus 101
Prunus armeniaca 152
Prunus avium 420
Prunus cerasus 420
Prunus domestica 1429
Prunus persica nectarina 1271
Psetta maxima 1945
Psidium guajava 893
Puccinia graminis tritici 256
Punica granatum 1439
Pyrus 1377
Pyrus aucuparia 1746

Quercus suber 496

Raja 1692
Raphanus sativus 1506
Rheinhardtius hippoglossoides 877
Rheum 1556
Ribes 540
Ribes grossularia 857
Ricinus communis 386, 1560
Rosa canina 938
Rosmarinus officinalis 1572
Rubus fructicosus 252
Rubus idaeus 1519
Rubus ursinus loganobaccus 1137

Saccharomycetaceae 2073
Saccharum officinarum 1834
Salmonella 1601
Salmonides 1600
Salmo salvelinus 414
Salvia officinalis 1595
Sardinia pilchardus 1616
Satureia 1623
Satureia hortensis 1623
Satureia montana 1623
Scomber scombrus 1152
Scophthalmus rhombus 315
Secale cereale 1586
Sepia 547
Sepiola 547
Sesamum indicum 1661
Siluroidea 393

Sinapis arvensis 416
Smilax 1617
Solanum melongena 173
Solanum tuberosum 1447
Solea solea 1737
Solen 1521
Sorbus aucuparia 1745
Sorghum vulgare 1748
Sparidae 1635
Spinacia oleracea 1767
Sprattus sprattus 1775, 2051
Squali 1669
Squalus 627
Squalus acanthias 627
Staphylococcus 1788
Sterculia 1036
Streptococcus lactis 1285
Streptococcus thermophilus 2079
Streptomyces orientalis 1983

Taenia echinococcus 954
Taraxacum officinale 1881
Theobroma cacao 460
Thunnus 1941
Thunnus vulgaris 1942
Thymallus thymallus 874
Thymus 1917
Tilletia tritici 1704
Tinca tinca 1892
Tragopogon porrifolius 1602
Trichinella spiralis 1930
Trigla hirundo 897
Trigonella foenumgraecum 727
Trisopterus luscus 1450
Triticum aestivum 2046
Triticum compactum 2046
Triticum durum 1648, 2046
Triticum vulgare 2046
Tsuga canadensis 923
Tuber 1934

Ustilago tritici 1704

Vaccinium 235, 508
Vanilla planifolia 1984
Vicia 1998
Vicia faba 319
Vitis 872

Xiphias gladius 1858

Zea mays 1157
Zeus faber 1028
Zingiber officinale 831